DECEIT
AT
PEARL HARBOR

Ken Landis

DECEIT
AT
PEARL HARBOR

FROM PEARL HARBOR TO MIDWAY

By Lt. Cmdr. Ken Landis, USNR (ret.)
Staff Sgt. Rex Gunn, USAR (ret.)
Msgt. Robert Andrade, (ret.) Technical Advisor

1st Books rev. 6/19/01

"Oh. what a tangled web we weave,
when first we practise to deceive!"

— SIR WALTER SCOTT

About the Book

A vast array of books has been published about Pearl Harbor since World War II. This book is unique, since it was actually written by the last remaining member of Admiral Kimmel's staff as existed on December 7, 1941, plus two other Pearl Harbor survivors; one a crew member of the early warning radar, and another a crew member of the USS Pennsylvania, Admiral Kimmel's flagship.

These three survivors of America's worst military disaster provide an unusual eyewitness report on how this tragic event developed.

Lt. Cmdr. Landis actually served on the USS Isabel, one of the "Tethered Goats" sent out by Roosevelt to intercept the Japanese fleet and be sunk, thereby igniting World War II.

St. Sgt. Rex Gunn tells how his unit actually picked up the incoming air armada by RADAR and their warning was ignored.

Chief Petty Officer Lawrence McNabb, serving on the USS Pennsylvania gives a remarkable, historical background study on how Roosevelt, Churchill, and even Hitler knew of the planned raid on Pearl Harbor, long before it happened.

The events leading up to America's victory at Midway, and how this ambush was orchestrated is revealed as a major intelligence breakthrough in code breaking and interpretation of radio transmission by the Japanese fleet.

Perhaps the most astonishing revelation in this book is the transcript of the telephone conversation between Churchill and Roosevelt, eleven days before Pearl Harbor.

Roosevelt ignored the warning from Churchill that a large Japanese Task Force was on its way to Pearl Harbor, and thus denied thousands of men to make immediate preparations to defend themselves.

This book shows how an American government betrayed their Armed Forces in order to accept the first blow and rally public opinion to allow the United States' entry into World War II. The immediate outcry was "Remember Pearl Harbor" and America prepared itself for its largest and costliest World War.

Much of the contents of the book will shock its readers as the little publicized events are revealed, some for the first time.

About the Author
Ken Landis

Kenneth Landis was born in 1918 in Chicago, Illinois. He attended Evanston Township High School and then went on to college at Northwestern University.

Landis graduated from Northwestern University receiving a Bachelors Degree in Industrial Engineering in 1940, also receiving a commission in the U.S. Navy as Ensign in the Naval Reserve.

At that time war was imminent and Landis shortly received orders to report to the USS Sculpin, a submarine based in Pearl Harbor.

After many months aboard the *USS Sculpin*, Landis received orders to report to CINCPAC at the Sub Base, Pearl Harbor on Admiral Kimmel's staff. This turned out to be indeed lucky for Landis as the *USS Sculpin* was later sunk with all hands lost.

Landis was later transferred to the *USS Isabel* in West Australia and took command of that ship in 1943. The Isabel was a historic ship that seemed to bear a charmed life in two World Wars.

In 1944 Landis was ordered to the DE *750* the *USS McClelland* as Executive Officer and saw extensive duty in Admiral Halsey's Third Fleet at Iwo Jima and Okinawa; winding up the war at Tokyo Bay in 1945; after somehow surviving the waves of kamikaze attacks at Okinawa. Seeing the war from start to finish from Pearl Harbor to Tokyo Bay is remarkable and rare. Few can match this coincidence and actually live to tell the tale.

After discharge in San Diego in 1946 Landis moved to Santa Monica, California where he owned and operated the Beverly Stationers in Beverly Hills, California.

After selling the business Landis was employed as a Systems Engineer for Diebold, and later left to own and operate Hamilton Security, Inc. a bank security company.

Landis retired in 1989 living with his wife, Roslynn, in La Quinta, California. He has two children, son Robert Lawrence, a Purple Heart Vietnam Veteran and reserve Warrant Officer in the US Army, and his daughter Marilynn Kerschner, a graduate of Moorpark College.

Lt. Cmdr. Landis, USNR, (ret.) remains active in The Pearl Harbor

Survivors Association in Palm Springs, California where he is Vice President of Chapter 21. He was present in Honolulu on the fiftieth anniversary of Pearl Harbor along with his family.

About the Author
Rex Gunn

Rex Gunn was born in Little Rock, Arkansas, on September 28, 1920, the youngest of three boys His father, Leo Gunn, died when Rex was six. When he was seventeen, he went on his own to Shreveport, La., where he was graduated from Fair Park High School in 1940. His brother, Hamilton Gunn, had enlisted in the 7th Army Air Corps (At the time called the Hawaiian Air Department) at Hickam Field. Rex joined his brother on Oahu as a member of the Signal Corps, Aircraft Warning Company, Special—first radar outfit in the Pacific. The Japanese attack on December 7, 1941, caught the two brothers about three miles apart: Ham at Hickam Information Center at Fort Shafter. Neither of them was hurt.

Rex was appointed a GI war correspondent for the 7th Army Air Corps picture magazine, Brief, in the autumn of 1943. With Brief, he covered the Tarawa and Abemama Eniwetok; and the Marianas Islands campaigns at Saipan, Tinian and Guam. In the 7th Army Air Corp bombers, he flew over Iwo Jima and Truk, and many other enemy-held islands in the Central Pacific.

After the war, he attended the University of Oregon at Eugene, got a B.A. degree and went to work at the Associated Press in San Francisco on January 1, 1949. Later he earned his master's degree at Stanford University and his doctorate at USC.

In 1949, he received a direct commission as a LtJG in the US Navy Reserve and was placed on the retired list in 1965.

During a 26-year academic career, he taught and worked as an administrator at Stanford, UCLA, San Bernardino Valley College, and the University of California at Davis. In 1995, he returned to live in Hawaii with his Hawaiian sweetheart of World War II days on Kauai. He lived in Hawaii until his death in 1999.

Acknowledgements

TO BOB ANDRADE, Graphic Arts Instructor at the Palm Springs High School — Without his expertise and support this book could not have been published.

TO LAWRENCE McNABB, fellow Pearl Harbor Survivor, War Historian — His contribution was invaluable, proving that even the Germans were aware of the coming attack on Pearl Harbor.

TO LEO PRIEST, fellow Pearl Harbor Survivor. His unfailing help and support contributed greatly to the completion of this book.

TO BILL BYRNE, WW II Navy Combat Aircrewman, historian — His help in getting this book started has been invaluable.

TO MARY HENDRICKSON, Long time friend and associate of Rex Gunn. Her support and encouragement to Rex helped in the completion of his book, which was used as a reference in this publication.

Dedication

To my shipmates on board the submarine
USS Sculpin
still on patrol

Table of Contents

AUTHOR'S NOTE

Author's Note

I began writing this book far too late, even decades after it should have been. However, even if I had started earlier, without the effect of declassifying the massive volume of documents by the passage of The Freedom of Information Act, there would have been little, other than anecdotal facts to reveal.

The coincidence of being a Pearl Harbor survivor on Admiral Kimmel's staff and later Commanding Officer of one of the "Tethered Goats", the USS Isabel, was the main reason that I decided to get together with Rex Gunn, a fellow survivor, and publish this book. Between the two of us, we felt that we had a wealth of facts, photos and other documents that had not been made public and should be.

Credit should be given to Warrant Officer Robert Landis, USAR, my son, and Marilynn Kerschner, my daughter, after years of listening to my stories of war in the Pacific and also to my devoted wife, Roslynn. They encouraged me to put all these stories together in writing. Without my wife's daily encouragement and support, together with the day-to-day writing and editing, this book could never have been written.

My only regret in this venture is that my good friend and fellow Pearl Harbor survivor, Rex Gunn, could not live a few years longer to see the completion and publication of our joint effort.

1

PREFACE

By Lt.CMDR KEN LANDIS

Preface
By Lt Cmdr Ken Landis

Over fifty years have passed, and much of the truth about Pearl Harbor has been covered up. The passage of time and the political correctness of keeping the blame pinned on Admiral Kimmel and General Short makes it all the more important that this narrative be published. I am sure that I am probably the only living survivor of Adm. Kimmel's staff as it existed on Dec. 7, 1941 and probably the last Commanding Officer of the USS Isabel which became the "Tethered Goat" that very nearly ignited World War II.

It is now well known that FDR attempted to justify Americas entry into WW II by accepting the first blow. Sending out the Isabel plus two small schooners as "Pickets" meant they would no doubt be sunk by the Japanese. The United States Press would publish screaming headlines," U.S. Warships sunk by Japanese". The hue and cry would be "Remember the Isabel" and WWII would be in full bloom. Draft boards would be swamped with volunteers. All this could have happened.. .but didn't. Pearl Harbor ended all that and Roosevelt's madcap scheme faded into obscurity.

To this day, no one has been able to explain FDR's elaborate effort to create the impression that he was unaware of the impending attack on Pearl Harbor. The "Tethered Goat" fiasco could very well have been a cover up plan to obfuscate the fact that FDR knew all about the disaster that was about to engulf the sacrificial crews at Pearl Harbor.

The Freedom of Information Act made it possible to release the Top Secret message that was kept from public view. The fact that this suicide mission would doom 75 men and 6 officers seemed to matter little to FDR

Since the Freedom of Information Act, there has been an avalanche of unpublished facts revealing that Washington (FDR) the British, the Dutch, and even the Russians had detailed knowledge of the Japanese attack on Pearl Harbor. The fact that all this intelligence was relayed to Washington is particularly damning because it was ignored.

Gen. George Marshall, who was FDR's closest advisor was particularly responsible. When it became clear to many that on Dec. 6th that the attack on Pearl Harbor was imminent, he made himself unavailable by horseback riding the morning of Dec. 7th. After several hours of delay, he finally sent the final warning to Pearl Harbor, but did not code "urgent".

This was sent by RCA telegram instead of by direct phone, thereby placing it on the same priority as all the "Happy Birthdays" sent to Honolulu that day.

By omitting the "urgent" designation this message was effectively "pigeon holed" for hours. I believe it was seven hours too late when the Japanese boy on a motorcycle delivered the warning. Adm. Kimmel threw it in a wastebasket in frustration.

All these delays made it sure that the warning would be too late. The much publicized "war warning" that Washington sent to CINCPAC on Nov. 27th was extremely misleading. That warning detailed the expected attack to be the Philippines, Kra Peninsula, or Borneo. Nothing was said about Pearl Harbor which was about 5,000 miles away. Some Warning!

And then we come to "Magic". The Purple Machine was busily decoding Japanese messages for over a year before Pearl Harbor. This extremely vital information should have been a godsend to Adm. Kimmel and Gen. Short. The only trouble was that Washington decided to send the Purple Machine to Churchill (2 in fact) , MacArthur in the Philippines, but incredibly, left out Adm. Kimmel.

The other code used by Japan was JN-25 (Japanese Navy) and detailed Naval plans and operations. This too was successfully decoded, but never sent to Adm. Kimmel.

Little has been said about the Dutch and their intelligence capabilities, but they could have been important factor. A little known Dutch outpost in Malaysia, succeeded in cracking the JN-25 code and discovered an attack on Pearl Harbor could come in a few days. This was relayed to an American Colonel Thorpe who rushed the information to Washington, and was again duly ignored.

The British too, had their top spy uncover the details of a Jap attack on Pearl Harbor. When relayed to the FBI they stated the plans looked too detailed, and smelled a trap. Once again.., a warning was ignored.

Three separate aides, Harrison, McCollum and Deane, later testified that Marshall, in fact never did go horseback riding, and perjured himself in a later investigation.

Marshall, in spite of his aides urgent request that he immediately warn Pearl Harbor, made strange delays in reading and re-reading the recently decoded fourteen part "Winds Execute Message" that indicated an imminent attack on Pearl Harbor.

This message was never received in time for it to be of any use to Kimmel, but reached other addressees like the Philippines and Canal Zone in a timely manner.

Obviously, Marshall never sent his warning, watered down as it was, until he was satisfied it was too late.

Marshall, who later testified that he considered loyalty to his Commander in Chief to take priority over his patriotic duty, was obviously as guilty as Roosevelt in the whole cover-up and was a willing co-conspirator.

Author Mark Willey, in his recent book "Pearl Harbor, Mother of All Conspiracies," quotes President Roosevelt provoked the attack, knew about it in advance, and covered up his failure to warn the Hawaiian Commanders.

• FDR denied intelligence to Hawaii

• On November 27, misled the commanders into thinking negotiations were continuing

• Had false information sent to Pearl Harbor about the location of the Japanese carrier fleet.

Many historians have observed that it would be almost impossible to orchestrate a cover-up without the cooperation of many other high ranking officers who were involved. The loyalty of George Catlett Marshall to FDR was never questioned.

The other high ranking officer that had to be entrusted with knowledge of impending attack was Lt. General Douglas MacArthur, a flamboyant publicity seeking Army General with an enormous ego.

MacArthur, who had a Purple Machine, knew that Pearl Harbor was headed for a surprise attack. Instead of warning Kimmel, MacArthur's command sent a series of three messages lying about the locations of the

Jap carrier fleet, saying it was in the South China Sea. This false information was the true reason CINCPAC was caught by surprise.

MacArthur, was given nine hours warning after Pearl Harbor and ordered to use his newly arrived fleet of B-17 bombers to attack Formosa. Upon news of Pearl Harbor he inexplicably locked himself in his quarters and refused to meet with his air commander. Consequently his entire air force was destroyed on the ground, and half the fleet of all heavy bombers in US fleet was lost. This has been called by historians as even more important than the damage at Pearl Harbor, and either the greatest blunder in military history, or he was under orders to allow the planes to be destroyed.

Author Mark Willey writes, "If it were the greatest blunder in history, how did he escape any reprimand, keep his command, and be awarded the Congressional Medal of Honor?"

Gordon Prange, a greatly respected author of "Infamy" writes: "How could the President ensure a successful Japanese attack unless he confided in his commanders and persuaded them to allow the enemy to proceed unhindered?"

Years later, on the bridge of the USS McClelland, I picked up the phone and talked to another ship in the Task Force. This new marvel was called TBS (talk between ships) and utilized ultra high frequencies that only extended a few miles. This made communications possible between ships that could not be picked up by snoopers.

The Japs also had discovered TBS and were using it on their Task Force enroute to Pearl Harbor. They too were unaware of the phenomenon known as skip distance, and transmissions were indeed usually good for only a few miles. However, when the weather was right, transmissions could be picked thousands of miles away.

We know now that the Japanese were using TBS and we were getting a fix from as far away as the Aleutians and even the US West Coast. So Kido Butai (their Task Force) positions were located all the way across the Pacific. These warnings were also ignored.

Washington knew all this but was still determined to accept the first blow. One last thought comes to mind. If FDR and Washington knew the location and intent to raid Pearl Harbor, why didn't they sortie the fleet and engage the Japanese in open sea?

The answer seems clear that in view of the Japanese six carriers to the US two, the fleet would have been destroyed in water thousands of feet deep, instead of the shallow waters of Pearl Harbor. The loss of the entire Pacific Fleet and thousands of irreplaceable men would be a disaster far greater than Pearl Harbor. That explains the sudden disappearance of the two carriers plus all newer cruisers and destroyers, plus submarines from Pearl Harbor. The loss of all the old battleships turned out to be of little consequence. In the words of Adm. Bloch, "In a sense the Japanese did us a favor in getting rid of a lot of old hardware."

In retrospect, Adm. Halsey's fruitless search for Kido Butai on Dec. 7, 1941 was a stroke of luck. His only carrier the Enterprise, would have been overwhelmed by 6 carriers and the only effective fighting force in CINCPAC would have been sent to the bottom in very deep water.

It would have been easy for the Japanese to invade and take over the Hawaiian bastion in the Pacific. Without a forward base with refueling and repair facilities the whole prospect of winning the war would have completely changed and would have to be fought from the West Coast.

Neither side had a crystal ball and mistakes were made on both sides. The United States had an enormous intelligence advantage in decoding enemy codes, but failed to keep its forces in Hawaii advised. It should have been possible to orchestrate an ambush such as we accomplished at Midway, when we wiped out Japan's four carriers with our three, and not only saved Midway and Hawaii, but changed the whole course of the war. The fate of the Japanese was sealed at Midway, mainly due to our intelligence capabilities and the courage and skill of Nimitz Pacific Fleet carrier pilots.

So, the results of Roosevelt's attempt to accept the first blow with only minor casualties turned out to be a disaster. It is quite possible however, that it would have turned out far worse if the Japanese had returned the next day and destroyed the fleets fuel supply and repair facilities. In all wars, luck plays an important part. The unexpected can happen, and often does.

THE SCULPIN STORY

THE RAID ON PEARL HARBOR

THE ISABEL STORY

The Sculpin Story

Historians have probably overlooked the fact that over fifty US Fleet Submarines were lost during World War II. The US Navy has long recognized the fact that submarine duty is extra hazardous, and therefore strictly voluntary. This was the case until the Fall of 1940, when Congress decided that war was probably inevitable and called up the Naval Reserves.

For some inexplicable reason when the Class of 1940 received their Ensign bars at Northwestern University, we were all assigned to Submarine Duty at Pearl Harbor. This applied only to Engineering School graduates, but that list included my name; and my ship was the USS Sculpin (SS191).

This didn't sound to me to be exactly "voluntary", so it was with some foreboding I made my long journey to Hawaii to report for duty; the only reserve officer aboard the Sculpin.

It was soon evident that the Captain of the Sculpin had little or no use for untrained reserve officers, or even any place to put me. Consequently, my bunk was in the Forward Torpedo Room, between two greasy torpedoes. Thus, began my long period of training to learn the complexities of submarine duty.

Of course there were a few good things about sub duty and that was the fact that we lived ashore in Honolulu when in port, and I was no exception. My apartment was in Kahala, the best beach in Honolulu, and was a tropical paradise to anyone raised in the Midwest, or anywhere else, for that matter.

The locals, called "Kamaainas", were quite friendly and I soon become one of them, with the gentle, easy ways of life in Hawaii becoming a reality.

Months passed before I was finally qualified to serve as Officer of the Deck underway and in port. Life ashore was most pleasant, it seemed as though war was only a remote possibility and an air attack on Oahu was not even considered. Everyone seemed to be consumed with the distinct possibilities of sabotage by the huge Japanese civilian population.

That was the situation on October 24, 1941 when the entire Division 22 consisting of twelve Subs, including the Sculpin was ordered to sortie the next day and proceed to Manila to join their increasing buildup of the Asiatic Fleet.

The next day, preparations were made to get underway, the lines were singled up when a messenger ran down the pier waving a white envelope. To my consternation, the envelope held orders for me to be detached and report to the Sub Base for temporary duty. This gave me about five minutes to pack my gear and throw everything on the pier. Sculpin then cast off lines and backed away.. .never to return to Pearl Harbor.

As I watched the Sculpin back away, I never dreamed the fate that awaited her crew. My shipmates were all imprisoned at Truk after a surface battle with Japanese destroyers. Sculpin was sunk 50 miles off Truk and prisoners were taken there and brutally beaten by Japanese guards. The few survivors were shipped on a Japanese Carrier, for transportation to Japan, when the final twist of irony occurred. Sculpin's sister ship, the Sailfish, torpedoed and sank the carrier, killing the remainder of the crew except one. He miraculously survived only to be subjected to the horrors of a Japanese prison camp.

Over fifty years passed before I learned the fate of the Sculpin and how lucky I was. Submarines are known as "The Silent Service" and it is difficult to uncover details of what happened. There is little or no publicity given and information is hard to get.

I did not find out what happened to the Sculpin and it's crew until I read a brief excerpt from the book "Ghost Fleet of the Truk Lagoon", many years later.

If the messenger waving the white envelope had arrived five minutes later, my fate would have been the same as the rest of my shipmates.

For the next few weeks I was Assistant Communications Officer for CINCPAC and was assigned to decoding incoming messages from Washington. What was to transpire the next morning, could never happen, but it did.

The Raid On Pearl Harbor

It was another tranquil morning at my apartment on the beach at Kahala, when a neighbor banged on the door, shouting, "Turn on your radio!" I did.

The next voice was that of Webley Edwards, urging the public to remain calm.... sporadic air raids were occurring over Pearl Harbor: "All personnel return to your ships. This is the real McCoy:" He wasn't kidding.

The resulting mass of cars hurtling toward Pearl Harbor on a narrow, two lane road was exactly what the military did not want. The panic was increased by falling AA shells, low-flying planes making torpedo runs and the constant, quivering voice on the radio; "This is no drill!"

In Kahala, it was not apparent that any attack was underway. The blanket effect of the looming Diamond Head blocked out sight and sound, which quickly changed when I reached Waikiki. There, the smoke and flames and explosions at Pearl Harbor showed that the unthinkable had happened. The traffic was still relatively light but all cars seemed to be travelling at breakneck speed, and so was I.

It quickly became obvious that I should take the School Street route around the city.

At this point, I was convinced that Honolulu was being bombed. Five-inch antiaircraft shells from Pearl Harbor rained on the city. It was months before we knew that our own sailors were wildly firing five inch star shells, armor piercing and AA shells without setting the fuses. The radio voices accused the Japanese of bombing innocent civilians, most of whom were their own countrymen. They didn't. No bombs were dropped on Honolulu, but those AA shells killed more than 50.

Upon concluding the mad race to Pearl Harbor, I reached the Sub Base and ran upstairs to the second floor where I reported to Admiral Kimmel's Communications Officer, Lt. Cmdr. Curts. He promptly assigned me to decoding incoming messages from an obsolete strip cipher.

It didn't take me long to realize that these incoming, innocuous messages were of absolutely no relevance to the disaster unfolding in front of my eyes, right outside a window. In all of the confusion, they simply did not know which messages took priority. Since this was a small office,

I was close enough to see and hear Admiral Kimmel and the rest of the staff. There was no panic, only a sense of helplessness and dismay. I worked on in silence... reserve ensigns do not question admirals.

I do remember that at one point Adm. Kimmel seemed to explode in frustration, when he asked Lt. Cdr. Layton (his fleet intelligence officer) whether the retiring Japanese planes were going to the north or south. Layton did not know.

It seems that Army radar operators who continued to plot, failed to report vital information to CINCPAC. In retrospect, this was indeed fortunate. Adm. Halsey's task force, consisting of one aircraft carrier (the Enterprise) was unable to locate vastly superior Japanese task force, KIDO BUTAI, with their six carriers. For a change, Lady Luck smiled on us.

Eventually, I was told to stop work on decoding by strip cipher and operate the ECM (Electric Coding Machine). This made sense and I again felt a certain relevance. These messages were important, although at times I felt it was some what silly to encode messages. Under such circumstances, wouldn't plain language do and be a lot quicker?

The general atmosphere at CINCPAC that afternoon was a sort of helpless feeling, deciding whether we should stay where we were at the Sub Base, or go to a safer place when the Japanese returned to finish the job. They did not return. Consequently, we survived to fight for almost four years, and win a long and bloody war.

That was their biggest tactical blunder of the war. The vast fuel storage tanks were untouched, so was the shipyard's repair facilities and CINCPAC's office itself.

As that fateful day turned to darkness, the longest night of our lives began. Pearl Harbor became a nightmare of rumor of sabotage, fifth column activities, signal lights on the coast, troop transports landing at Kailua, enemy paratroopers landing at Barbers Point, poisoned water supply in Honolulu.. .the list was endless. All rumors proved false, but seemed very real at the time. No one slept that night.

All enlisted men and low ranking officers at CINCPAC took turns standing watch outside the Headquarters building. Since I already had a 45 caliber Colt, I was assigned duty near the entrance, a job I did not exactly relish. Outside the building sounded like a war with constant gunfire.

Jittery Marines were challenging anything that moved and everyone seemed to be shooting at each other.

At about 2000, word was passed to all ships and stations that the Enterprise planes would be landing shortly at Ford Island. After a few moments, the formation approached with landing lights on.

An unknown, panicky gunner opened up and that brought on a deafening roar of gunfire from every corner of Pearl Harbor. Most of the pilots were shot down. A truly disgraceful lack of discipline caused the death of several of our brave pilots.

For the next few days, Pearl Harbor was in a state of confusion and disbelief that such a disaster could happen. The magnitude of killed and wounded overwhelmed the morgue and hospital facilities.

Another week passed before my orders were received for my reporting to USS Pelias. A permanent Sub Base was to be at Fremantle, West Australia and Pelias was my transportation. Arriving at Fremantle, my orders were to report to USS Isabel. This was to be my home for the next two years.

The Isabel Story

My orders to report for duty aboard the USS Isabel, caused a major wardroom sitcom among some old salts on the Pelias who had seen China service up the Yangtze River in China.

"Its nothing but a big bloody yacht", they guffawed. So it was with some trepidation that I boarded the local train for the overnight trip from Albany to Fremantle.

The old China hands were right. What loomed before me was indeed a very big yacht, almost destroyer size. As a warship she would have been of little use unless modernized by the Australians (that later happened). And then there was something about the crew. Why were there so many Filipinos and Chinese? They understood little English. Was the idea to reduce American casualties in a suicide mission? Isabel's crew then totaled seventy-five men and six officers.

The pitiful remnants of the Asiatic Fleet, including Isabel, got to Fremantle, West Australia. This was it; there was no place to go, the next landfall to the south was the South Pole. The Japanese could easily have continued southward and wiped out the remnants, but again failed to deliver the knockout blow.

The Captain and Executive Officer were U.S. Naval Academy men who couldn't wait to tell me of their indignation about being sent out to act as bait and be sunk as was the Panay.

Day one aboard the Isabel proved to be a historic moment in its long career in two World Wars. Never before had a Naval Officer reported aboard carrying golf clubs. Some consternation was displayed by the two regular Naval Officers, and comments about the qualifications of Reserve Officers echoed around the wardroom for days.

As I was shown this historic little ship, I could not help but notice the comparative luxury both officers and crew enjoyed. Officers and Commanding Officer had panelled mahogany staterooms with showers. The wardroom looked like a tropical cocktail lounge with wicker furniture and thick Chinese carpets. The Chinese stewards waited on the officers with white starched jackets and the food was comparable to a luxury cruise ship. It did not take long to realize that all this apparent luxury was due to the fact that the Isabel had long been the flagship of the Asiatic Fleet and used only by Admirals and their staffs.

For the next two years, Isabel was my home and was used extensively as an escort for submarines and local merchant shipping from this Australian base. Since Isabel was considered expendable, such duties as escorting subs through mine fields were routine.

The two regular Naval Officers eventually left and I was then fortunate enough to take command in 1943. This seldom happens to Reserve Officers. Isabel's officer roster was now six officers.... all Reserves.

Isabel had earlier survived a bombing attack at Cavite, when eight bombs, all duds, rang Isabel's fantail. A similar situation developed in 1943 when Isabel took some near misses during a night bombing raid in Exmouth Gulf, West Australia. The sub tender, Pelias had just arrived there and was promptly bombed at night, but no hits. Pelias and Isabel skedaddled out of there the next day to return to Fremantle. The reason? Too close to Jap bases at Timor.

It was not long before a momentous event in Isabel's history took place. The British troopship Queen Mary arrived in Fremantle with a full Division of troops. Queen Mary's speed of 32 knots had long enabled her to evade enemy submarines; but this time she was anchored in an open roadstead, unable to enter the shelter of Fremantle's harbor. Nightfall came and Isabel (now completely fitted with British Sonar and depth charges), screened the huge ship (the world's largest) from any shadowing sub going after this prize.

About midnight, Isabel picked up a very definite metallic sounding sonar contact, slowly approaching the Queen Mary. Since the water was only 35 feet deep, it was only possible to set the depth charges at the minimum (30 ft.)

So the unthinkable had happened. The mighty Queen Mary was about to be saved by the gallant little Isabel. Thoughts raced through my mind, even at our speed of 26 knots, we only had about 10 seconds before we would be blowing off our own fantail.

However the risk had to be taken, Isabel was expendable, the Queen Mary, with her load of 16,ooo troops had to be saved. The sonar pings were the loudest I had ever heard. At that point my sonarman shouted, "Captain, sink her on the first pass—there won't ever be another". What he was telling me was what I already knew- we were about to blow ourselves up!

Before I could give the order to lay a depth charge pattern, artillery shells and some star shells ringed Isabel. The Aussies from nearby Rottnest Island, not knowing what the hell was going on, were wildly firing on us. To make matters worse a nearby Dutch destroyer challenged us - all this in inky blackness.

Trying to ignore this madness, I gave the order to lay the first pattern of depth charges. There was a wild scramble on the bridge to find and put on life preservers. Huge blasts of water rose in mighty columns and Isabel apparently emerged unscathed. A mighty cheer arose from the crew as we charged around in circles making another run and opened up with our 4" guns firing star shells, hoping to catch the sub on the surface. The extreme elevation of our guns caused the muzzle blasts to seem to be right in our faces on the bridge. The depth charges seemed to be almost blowing the Isabel out of the water. The engine room now reported that asbestos insulation was being blown off the pipes and leaks were everywhere. Pandemonium reigned supreme. Our ears ached!

Suddenly the sonar contact disappeared and an eery silence prevailed. What happened? The sub (which must have been a midget) was nowhere to be found, and at daybreak, the Queen Mary was safely in Fremantle's snug harbor.

The next day was the day of reckoning and I was promptly summoned to Admiral Carpender's office preparing myself for a good chewing out. It never happened. We had saved the Queen Mary and he knew it.

On the way to the Admiral's office my little whaleboat passed several US Submarines in the harbor. We received a rousing cheer from the crew who had evidently heard of last nights battle. Isabel was finally getting the reputation of being a tough little ship, and was getting the respect she deserved.

While waiting in the Admiral's office, my thoughts wandered back to Northwestern University where Admiral Carpender was our Commandant of the Naval ROTC. Would he remember me? He did.

After grumbling about us keeping the whole town awake all night, he shook my hand saying "Well done, Landis, now go out and find that damn sub".

I then left after smartly saluting my former Commandant. "What a small world I thought. I guess he thought he had taught us well".

The next two days were spent aboard a US navy rescue vessel searching the outer reaches of Fremantle roadstead for wreckage, or any other sort of confirmation. Nothing could be found except a fairly large oil slick. However I still had in my possession a paper tape showing the distinct echo of a large metallic object that suddenly disappeared after the first depth charge run. So it was written off as a probable kill, but without wreckage or bodies-no more than that can be claimed. However the main objective was accomplished, the Queen Mary (and 16,000 troops) was saved,

17

All good things must come to an end, and after 30 months overseas, my orders came to be detached and for Lt. Edwin Zacher to assume command. There is no way to describe the feeling of being presented with the commission pennant, and piped over the side for the last time. My new orders called for me to train a new crew as Executive Officer of the USS McClelland (DE 750), and be ready in three months for the invasion of Iwo Jima and later Okinawa.

Two years passed before Isabel was ordered to return to the United States for the first time in over 20 years, and finally be decommissioned in San Francisco.

After two world wars, thus ended the strange history of a "warship" that was never intended to be, and the story of "the tethered goats" faded into the dustbin of history.

A summary of Isabel's achievements included sinking a Japanese submarine, downing an attacking plane, rescuing 187 survivors from a sunken ship, probably saving the Queen Mary and countless other heroic acts that expendable ships performed.

In return, a grateful navy awarded the Isabel the Asiatic-Pacific Medal with one battle star, a medal awarded to everyone else in the Pacific Fleet, no matter what they did.

Considering the fact that Isabel barely escaped being the "Tethered Goat" that started World War II, it hardly seems to be a fitting end for this heroic little ship's deeds to go unnoticed.

INTRODUCTION
BY LEO PRIEST

Introduction
By Leo Priest

A testimonial to a factual drama by two
Pearl Harbor Survivors that will hold
you in suspense from beginning to end.

The pages you are about to unfold contain a compelling story of how the tragedy at Pearl Harbor was actually planned, executed and covered up for decades by Roosevelt and his administration. The Freedom of Information Act actually unleashed an avalanche of information that was believed to have been locked up forever by successive administrations that considered this to be politically damaging.

The co-authors Rex Gunn, a U.S Army non-commissioned officer, and Lt. Commander Ken Landis, were actually there that morning, Dec. 7, 1941. You will see how there is no substitute for being an eye-witness.

Gunn was assigned to the Radar Filter center at Ft. Shafter, where the first reports of enemy planes were plotted at 7:00 am from Opana Radar Station just 28 miles away. These first reports were routinely ignored with catastrophic results.

Landis was Asst. Communications Officer on Admiral Kimmels' staff and was assigned the task of decoding incoming top secret messages. As of this writing , he is the last survivor of CINCPAC staff that was located at the Sub Base at Pearl Harbor. He was an eyewitness to the delivery of a routine priority telegram that was intended to be a warning from Washington, delivered many hours too late, by a Japanese boy on his motorcycle.

Landis' part in constructing the book dealt more in Naval history, the intrigue of interpreting intelligence and inter-service rivalry involved in it's distribution. Since he was later skipper of the USS Isabel, one of the three ships affectionately called "The Tethered Goats", he relates an unbelievable real-life drama in that story alone.

The two authors did not know each other, but both knew that one day they would produce a book with the wealth of information, documents, photos, and facts they possessed. Scores of years later, both became members of the Pearl Harbor Survivors Association Chapter 21, in Palm

Springs, California. It was inevitable that the two would get together in producing a book. Unfortunately, the untimely death of Rex Gunn made it difficult to complete the book, but Lt. Cdr. Landis did so with many additions made possible by the release of formerly classified documents released by the Freedom of Information Act.

This exciting story is all a part of the many battles, deceit by our government, struggles in code breaking, and political unfairness. It is a book that carries a military message of strategic warfare and the brave men that carried it out. But you need not have had to be in or have served to enjoy the suspense of this living drama.

Its documentation, photographs and suspense was blended together making it rapid reading for me, and I truly believe I have a better understanding of the cause of the disaster at Pearl Harbor and the great Pacific War in which, I too, served.

DECEIT AT PEARL HARBOR

BY LAWRENCE MCNABB

Deceit At Pearl Harbor
By Lawrence McNabb

Peace was shattered one Sunday morning nearly sixty years ago, for far more than just one beautiful, tranquil harbor island in the Pacific, it was shattered for an entire nation. The *apparent* sneak attack on Pearl Harbor, by the Japanese Imperial Navy, on December 7, 1941, was to be a world changing event. It is represented in most American History books as a complete and total surprise, not just to the nation, but to the president and his administration as well. This paper will conclude that this was not the case! This catastrophic event did however draw the United States of America into one of its greatest conflicts, WWII.

Every month, Pearl Harbor survivors gather to honor and remember their fallen comrades. The searing horror and human carnage of that hour remains vivid in their memories to this very day. Unable to forget the loss of so many brave fighting men; unwilling to accept the unlikeliness that an event of this magnitude could have been kept a total secret; they, like myself, continue to search for the truth of what really happened in the days and months leading up to the Pearl Harbor attack.

This small treatise is a compilation of as many sources and facts as one sailor could find. It is dedicated to their memory, but even more, to their great sacrifice.

Thousands of military and civilian personnel were killed or wounded that day. We must now pause and consider how this great tragedy may have been avoided. More importantly we must ask, based upon facts, whether our leaders in Washington, both political and military, were completely honest about how it all happened. The final question, will be whether our forces could have or should have been given warning on that fateful day. The evidence I believe, is an unequivocal .. . .YES! These brave men and women were not given a proper chance to prepare and defend themselves. Initial casualties numbered 2,388, later numbers grew to 2,403 killed and 1,272 wounded! Sadly, many more would die later due to serious burns and wounds suffered during the attack!

If there were only one or even two documents or only scattered testimony suggesting President Roosevelt had prior personal knowledge of

Japanese plans to attack Pearl Harbor, perhaps it would be plausible to hold him blameless in this greatest of American Military tragedies. However, this is just not the case. There is a myriad of documents, references and testimonies indicating that he and several other high officials had extensive prior knowledge of the impending attack. For this reason, many careful historians continue to speak and write about the day of "Infamy" and betrayal of our brave fighting men at Pearl Harbor.

Sadly, as the many pieces of information are examined, it becomes evident that our forces were offered like sacrificial lambs on the altar of his firm belief in the necessity of American involvement in World War II! American involvement may have been inevitable, but the question remains, was it necessary to deny the officers and men at Pearl the vast amount of vital information we had been gathering from a variety of intelligence sources for over six months prior to the attack. Had this been done, our forces could have made immediate preparations to defend themselves. Despite their great lack of patrol aircraft, everything available would have been put in the air.

Many students of this event surmise that Roosevelt probably felt he could not risk a successful American defense of Pearl or a Japanese change of plans. He needed an event to justify an America entrance into the war. The proposed Japanese attack, of which he was aware should negotiations fail, was perfect. It easily changed the mood of the American public overnight. The information we discuss in this paper will indicate that our president, following his meetings with Churchill, was committed to finding a way to enter the war. Let us look at some of this information.

Captain Edward Beach USN, Retired, an outstanding naval officer, stated in his book, *Scape Goats,* *"We have an obligation to address the question of truth and justice and our country must not conclude to perpetuate a lie!"* He also stated, *"It's clear today, that among those with responsibility for the Japanese attack, first must be President Roosevelt himself."*

Rear Admiral Robert A. Theobald, USN, Retired, spent years researching this subject as well. In his book, *The Final Secret Of Pearl Harbor,* he gives ample proof that the President worked hard to entice the Japanese into an overt act. Several enticements failed, but Pearl Harbor did not. Admiral Theobald gives many evidences for the fact that Roosevelt knew when and where the attack was coming, and did nothing to prevent it. He even ordered the denial of vital information to our commanders in Hawaii, all the while maintaining his own "plausible deniability!" Among Theobald's strong array of facts are the following:

1) The Japanese Code was broken in early 1941

2) At least six "Magic Machines" were fully operational for the last half of 1941

3) One was sent to the British Isles

4) Two were retained by the Communications Intelligence Unit in the Department of the Navy

5) Two were given to the Signal Intelligence Service in the War Department

6) In April, the last machine was shipped to the 16th" Naval District in the Philippines along with additional personnel for the decrypting unit. This unit was established in the caves of Corregidor Island. Inexplicably, no allocation of a "Magic Machine" was made for the decrypting unit in Hawaii, an act so obviously deliberate as to have no possibility of being an oversight. It is known, he says in his book, that fourteen copies of all intercepted "Japanese Purple Code" transmissions were made daily and delivered by military courier to Roosevelt, Knox, Stark, Noyes, Turner, Wilkinson, but the avenue of negotiations was kept open as Secretary Hull and Ambassador Nomura Kurusu were still exploring all possibilities. Dr. E. Stanley Jones, a widely known missionary of long experience in the Orient, served as an official mediator between Japan and Washington. One of Dr. Jones' own solutions was to give Japan some unexploited area where it could move its growing population and acquire oil (over-population and a need for oil). Japan had earlier encouraged immigration to Manchuria and by the early 1930's 90,000 Japanese had settled there, so his suggestion was to let Japan have New Guinea.

New Guinea was owned at the time by the British and the Dutch, but they had made no real attempt to develop the area. He proposed that the United States pay $60,000,000 to compensate for it, but the leaders in Washington at that time never considered it. They seemed to have no interest in a suggestion that just may have helped prevent a war.

On September 11, 1941, Roosevelt made public an order that American Naval vessels and planes would fire on ships which entered waters vital to American interests. Back in September 28, 1940 Germany,

Italy, and Japan had signed the Tripartite Treaty agreement by which the three nations agreed to make common cause against any nation, not then a participant in the European war or the Sino-Japanese conflict, which attacked one of their signatories.

During September, October and November of 1941 the USS Grear was torpedoed, the USS Salinas torpedoed, the USS Fear was torpedoed and the USS Destroyer Reuben James torpedoed and sunk in the Atlantic by the Germans with a crew of 159 of which 115 were killed. The question arises, why didn't Roosevelt declare war then, knowing that war on one would mean war on all. This would have spared us the great loss and disaster at Pearl Harbor. President Roosevelt's strategy accomplished it's purpose as quoted in the book "OMNIBUS" volume #5 , Page 119, and we continued to hold a weak Pacific Fleet in Hawaii as an invitation to a surprise attack.

Another apparent attempt by the Roosevelt administration occurred in Washington in November of 1941. Admiral Hart, Commander-in-Chief of the Asiatic Fleet, received a dispatch directing him to send out three picket ships to the Indochina Coast, each having one naval officer with a small crew and one mounted machine gun. They were to patrol areas known to be transit locations of the Japanese Navy. The conclusion drawn by Admiral Hart and others was that if the small boats were fired upon or sunk by the Japanese Navy, it would be reasonable for the USA to declare war, but, unfortunately, the attack at Pearl Harbor occurred before these orders could be expedited.

There have been eight congressional "Pearl Harbor Attack" investigations and for some inexplicable reason, the actions of the president and his administration are never called into question, and always vital information deemed inadmissable. Roosevelt sent many messages via Naval Communications channels. The record of these dispatches is designated in the Navy Department as the White House File, and has been classified as an ultra-secret subject. This file has never been submitted to any congressional investigation. One cannot avoid the strong suspicion that little of the Pearl Harbor secret would remain, should the contents of this "White House File" ever become public knowledge.

In Admiral Husband E. Kimmel's book, *Admiral Husband Kimmel's Story,* published in 1955, he tells of an interesting historical note to all of this.

On April 5, 1945, the Democratic-controlled Senate passed a bill, introduced by Senator E. Thomas of Utah, with the purpose of preventing the disclosure of any intelligence information on Pearl Harbor except by permission of the President. This in effect, would have closed the door forever on much vital corroborating evidence. Interestingly enough, Admiral Kimmel himself had not known of this bill until he read of it in a newspaper. He immediately went to work making it known to the public, the press and to various congressmen. So when it did come up before the House of Representatives, it failed to pass.

One of the most compelling indictments of the Roosevelt administration, can be found on page 278 of A. Ralph Epperson's, The Unseen Hand. In his book he recounts the following story as follows. *"The American Ambassador to Tokyo, Joseph C. Grew, was one of the first to officially discover that Pearl Harbor was the intended target of the Japanese attack, as he corresponded with President Roosevelt's State Department on January 27, 1941: 'The Peruvian minister has informed a member of my staff that he had heard from many sources, including a Japanese source, that, in the event of trouble breaking out between the United States and Japan, the Japanese intended to make a surprise attack against Pearl Harbor....'* Apparently, Joseph Grew reported his information to Washington on two separate occasions in 1941, indicating that the Japanese intended to make a surprise attack on Pearl Harbor.

In addition, we now know that a Russian spy, Dr. Richard Sorge, stationed in Japan, informed the Kremlin and Stalin in October 1941 of the Japanese intent and proposed plan to attack Pearl Harbor within 60 days should negotiations with the United States fail. At this point, in time we know that Roosevelt and Stalin were exchanging any and all vital information and it was obviously in Stalin's best interest to have president Roosevelt beholden to him for any information he might have.

During this same general period of time, Congressman Martin Dies, then Chairman of the House Committee on Un-American Activities, provided president Roosevelt with a large amount of information confirming suspicions that the Japanese were studying the possibility of not only an attack but invasion of Pearl Harbor. The Dies committee had evidence that the Japanese were assembling much vital military information about Pearl Harbor. This and much more is available in the congressional record.

The most damning information, however, comes directly from the few "Magic Machine" transcripts that the United States Government has released from among the many thousands they intercepted. The Japanese Purple military code was broken many months before the attack. The final messages, directing all diplomatic and consular posts to destroy codes and ciphers and to burn all confidential and secret material were a dead give away of impending military action on the part of the Japanese, so obvious that even a novice could figure out that all U.S. military installations should be put on high alert.

Amazingly, this important information was never given to the American military command in Hawaii by those in Washington D.C. with the express responsibility to do so. The irony of Admiral Kimmel's predicament was that the very information which the Roosevelt administration was denying its Commander-in-Chief of the American Pacific Fleet was simultaneously being given to the British all through 1941.

From early July until the attack on December 7, 1941, "Magic Machines" in Washington intercepted up to 130 messages a day, which were then rushed in locked briefcases by special messengers to Roosevelt and his chief advisers, who scanned them without taking any notes while the messenger stood by; and then all copies but one were returned and burned. All secret coded intercepts went to only nine (9) persons, according to the testimony of General Miles. Whether it was 9 or 14, he still named President Roosevelt, Secretary of War Stimson, Secretary of Navy Knox, Secretary of State Hull, Chief of Staff Marshall, Chief of Naval Operations Stark, General Gerow, Colonel Bratton and himself.

Despite the obvious conclusion to be drawn from the nature of these secret Japanese communications requesting precise ship locations on a daily basis, not one word was ever given to Hawaiian Army or Navy Field Commanders. The messages from Tokyo to their spies in Hawaii were monitored daily and given to Washington. When they were decoded, such information as to what ships were in Pearl Harbor, whether balloons were

29

flying overhead, and whether anti-mine nets, were provided, was being requested. Even an extremely naive non-military person could guess what was about to happen.

Naval Intelligence officer Arthur H. McCollum had decoded information about Pearl Harbor. He wanted to send a warning, to Hawaii, but his request was denied by Admiral Stark. The Army couldn't reach General Marshall at this vital time, and it was later reported that he was away from his office horseback riding. Admiral Stark was later advised by Secretary of Navy Forrestal, that he could no longer hold a command of importance! At later hearings, Admiral Stark and General Marshall could not recall what they did that day of December 7, 1941!

Secretary of State Cordell Hull, in confidence with his friend Joe Lieb during discussion at a public park in Washington, D.C., explained that Pearl Harbor would be the target of attack December 7, 1941. FBI Director J. Edgar Hoover told Congressman Bender of Ohio that there had been warnings that a Pearl Harbor bombing was a possibility; and he also told Roosevelt about these warnings. Hoover said Roosevelt's reply was that it must not be mentioned and that he would take care of it.

On December 6, 1941, at 6:30 PM, with the Japanese Fleet close to attack position, Japanese spies became so brazen that they actually requested and delivered updated information on open telephone lines; and even more amazingly, all their conversations were monitored and recorded by the FBI. The following three Japanese messages were intercepted and reported; yet, none of this information would ever reach Admiral Kimmel in Hawaii. It can only be concluded that the following messages were deliberately suppressed.

(1) Without any knowledge of the "Magic Machines" and using standard surveillance equipment at the U.S. Naval Intelligence office located at 717 Market street, San Francisco, California, Lieutenant Ellsworth Holsman and his assistant, Robert Ogg, received and plotted the location of Japanese signals from the North Pacific area. They noted signals coming from north of the Hawaiian Islands and plotted them for four (4) days. Each day they were plotted closer to Hawaii until they were only about 500 miles away. This information was consistently reported to the Commander of the 12th Naval District, Captain McCullough. (It is now known that he happened to be a close friend of President Roosevelt.)

It can only be assumed that Holsman and others found it prudent not to concern themselves with why this critical information was not provided to Hawaii. (Details of this odious event were published in the Pearl Harbor Survivors Association publication Gram of July 1987.)

(2) Passenger ship *Lurline* was about 3 days from Honolulu when it's Radioman, a Mr. Hauser, began picking up coded Japanese messages, and he recorded some of them. Upon arrival, the messages were immediately taken to Naval intelligence at the Alexander Young Building. It is sad that they were not taken to either Admiral Kimmel or General Short, alerting them of Japanese naval locations and potential air attack, allowing them to take defensive measures.

(3) In their book, ***Betrayal of Pearl Harbor*** by James Rusbridger and Eric Nave it is reported that, during 1941 alone, over 16,000 Japanese messages were intercepted. Eric Nave was known, as the father of British code-breakers in the far East; and he was one of the British Naval officers who helped to break some of the Japanese naval codes prior to WWII with the *JN-25* decoder, rendering his knowledge and experience beyond reproach when writing on this critical subject. While the attack fleet of Admiral Yamamoto was steaming toward Hawaii between November 20, and December 7, 1941 both British and American code-breakers were busy intercepting and decoding all of the Japanese messages. At least twenty of them are in existence today in the U.S. National Archives, as reported in their book.

We know further that it was the interception of Japanese military Purple Code communications regarding the location of Admiral Yamamoto's personal plane which enabled WWII ace Rex Barber to shoot down Admiral Yamamoto over Rabaul. Yamamoto's death was very convenient for Roosevelt, since public knowledge of Admiral Yamamoto's efforts to avoid conflict with America, his opposition to instituting the very plan he had devised, and Roosevelt administration's rejection of his appeal, would have proven embarrassing to the Roosevelt legacy.

In John T. Flynn's book, *The Roosevelt Myth,* he writes that President Roosevelt knew that in order to drive Hitler out of France it would be necessary to send American armies to France and throw the power of the

31

American navy into the war. Flynn substantiates that the president knew and believed this as early as October of 1940.

The first evidence that FDR intended to go to war was seen when Secretary Knox sent for Admiral J.O. Richardson, then commander-in-chief of the American Fleet in the Pacific. In January of 1941, Knox told Richardson that the President wanted him to establish a patrol of the Pacific, a wall of American Naval vessels stretched across the western Pacific in such a way as to make it impossible for Japan to prevent by force her use of any part of the Pacific Ocean. Richardson protested vigorously. He said such action would be an act of war and that, besides, we could lose our Pacific fleet. This flagrant course of action had to be abandoned; but the President had wanted it in place as early as October 10, 1940. Obviously, the public knew nothing of these plans at the time.

Three weeks after this, FDR gave his famous Boston speech in which he reiterated his promise to the American people that he would not send any of their sons overseas. In fact, earlier that year, May 7, 1940, he had made the decision to keep the Pacific Fleet in Hawaiian waters. Admiral Richardson courageously protested this foolish decision, citing the great potential jeopardy to the Pacific Fleet. Unable to agree on this vital issue, Richardson was fired by Roosevelt early in 1941. Richardson was replaced by the now exonerated Admiral Kimmel. On November 27, 1941, just ten days before the Pearl Harbor attack, the President told Secretary Stimson, who wrote it in his diary, that our course was to maneuver the Japanese into attacking us! On November 26, 1941, and in great secrecy, Roosevelt sent a secret, unconstitutional, inflammatory ultimatum to Japan demanding that she withdraw all troops from Indo-China, and China (Manchuria). (As a historical note They (Japan) had occupied (Manchuria) since September 22, 1931.)

The United States public was not informed that Roosevelt had sent this ultimatum, and most Americans remain ignorant of this fact today.

Roosevelt's eleventh hour message left the Japanese, embarrassingly, with two of their Ambassadors for peace still in Washington, while her warships steamed toward the attack on Pearl Harbor.

Ironically, even Hitler knew when Pearl Harbor would be bombed, as can be learned from the book, *Gestapo Chief. The 1948 Interrogation of Heinrich Muller,* by Gregory Douglas, Volume 3. This book reveals that

32

the Germans had managed to break the supposedly secret AT&T communication phone link between Churchill and Roosevelt. There is a transcript of Churchill's calling Roosevelt, and confirming British knowledge of the coming attack, along with a discussion of how they should respond to the event in public. It confirms, what we already know, namely, the attack was absolutely no surprise to anyone in the upper levels of the Roosevelt administration.

Further incriminating evidence against Roosevelt comes from the unlikely source of Don C. Smith, the Red Cross administrator just prior to the Pearl Harbor attack. Don was privy to several Top Secret operations and was told by the President of a feared pending Japanese attack on Pearl Harbor. The president anticipated many casualties and much loss of life and so instructed Don C. Smith to send workers and supplies in advance to a holding area where they would await further orders to ship them out; no destination was to be revealed. This left no doubt in Mr Smith's mind that none of the naval nor military officials in Hawaii were to be informed.

Ultimately, however, a copy of the Hawaiian Islands' Chapter 5 Annual Report on the fiscal year ending June 30, 1942, confirmed the secret receipt of medical supplies by the Red Cross at Pearl Harbor. Several in the Hawaiian Red Cross Chapter were immediately concerned, but this damaging information has been somewhat effectively suppressed. In any event, it remains a fact that some $50,000 in supplies and drugs mysteriously became available to the Hawaii Red Cross Chapter just before the attack on Pearl Harbor.

Representative Dewey Short of Missouri, put into the congressional record of the house of Representatives on November 28, 1944, the following statement:

"The American people have not been told the truth about Pearl Harbor and when the complete story is told and the whole truth known, the American people will be shocked, angered and grieved!"

Slowly but surely, government admissions are being revealed or are coming to light. On January 4, 1996, the Pentagon admitted its error, and the San Jose Mercury News published parts of the statement which read in part, *"The Commander of the US. Pacific Fleet at the time of the 1941 Japanese attack on Pearl Harbor, was denied information from Washington."* Its fifty-page report states, for the first time, that Navy

Officials and War Department Officials were neither energetic or effective. How is that for an understatement!

Governor Thomas E. Dewey of New York, presidential nominee, learned that U.S. Government had broken the Japanese Purple Code, and he had intended to use this information in the presidential election, informing the public that Roosevelt had prior knowledge of the impending Pearl Harbor attack. When General George Marshall learned of Dewey's intentions, he sent special emissaries to persuade Dewey against such action. He was told that the Japanese were still using these same codes and that his revelation would jeopardize U.S. military operations. Patriot that he was, Dewey agreed not to reveal the terrible truth in order to preserve the greater good.

In Richard Norton Smith's biography of Thomas Dewey, Smith devotes many pages to Pearl Harbor, General Marshall's letter, the actions and statements of Marshall's courier Colonel Carter C. Clarke and Thomas Dewey's knowledge of this whole sordid event. He quotes Dewey on page 241 of his book as saying: . . . *and Franklin Roosevelt knows about it too. He knew what was happening before Pearl Harbor, and instead of being re-elected he ought to be impeached.* Again on page 429, Smith says, *Shaken and angry, Dewey fumed that Roosevelt was a traitor who had willingly or accidentally condemned more than a thousand American men, and most of the Pacfic fleet, to a watery grave. But what could he do? In the end he chose to remain silent He instructed John Burton to collect everything dug up to date, put it away securely and forget it.* Finally, on page 430, Smith concludes that *Dewey went to his grave believing that Roosevelt shared in the culpability of a high command that displayed a fine gift for confusion and self-inflicted disaster in the very hours it should have been taking steps to ward off the worst military defeat in the nation's history.*

On August 9, 1941, Churchill traveled on the battleship *HMS Prince of Wales* and met Roosevelt aboard the cruiser *USS Augusta.* Their rendezvous was Placentea Bay, Newfoundland, and after three historic days they proclaimed the now famous Atlantic Charter. It was during this meeting that Roosevelt said, *I shall never declare war, then bragged, I shall make war!* On the previous October 30, 1940, he had been in Boston campaigning for third term; addressing the nation he had pledged to an audience of parents, *I have said it before but I shall say it again, and again! I am not going to send your sons to foreign wars!* Roosevelt's actions and intent based on private statements are just not consistent with his public pronouncements.

In 1989, a documentary entitled, *"Sacrifice at Pearl Harbor"*, was produced and released by a leading British film company and was aired on the *TV Arts and Entertainment Network,* on December 7, 1989. It gave fully detailed information that indicts President Roosevelt for not warning our fighting men of the impending surprise attack on Pearl Harbor. This British documentary, relied greatly on the recollections of actual participants, and re-examined documents from the American, British, and Dutch Intelligence Agencies. It concludes that these agencies knew what was about to happen in late 1941 and did nothing to warn their comrades.

The inescapable conclusion is that they were prevented from doing so. The documentary concludes that Roosevelt had to know about impending events and potential events all over the Pacific region. It is well known that this was his greatest interest and that he was briefed almost daily on important developments, leading up to the Japanese government's conclusion that an attack on Pearl Harbor was their only option. The documentary was narrated by Edward Herman and is probably the best visual piece ever done.

Secretary of Navy Frank Knox arrived at Pearl Harbor shortly after the Japanese attack, to inspect the damage inflicted upon the U.S. Pacific Fleet. Upon arrival, he first met with Admiral Kimmel and asked, *Didn't you receive the war warnings I sent December* 6th? Kimmel replied, by stating he did not receive any such message. If Knox was telling the truth, the question immediately arises, as to who stopped the warning?

Probably the most damning recent revelations appeared in an article of the May-June 1997 issue of "The Shield", a newsletter of the National Intelligence and Counter-Intelligence Association. Information drawn from an 800-page report of the interrogation of former Nazi Gestapo Chief Heinrich Muller reveals that Muller and his aides were successful in breaking the codes of an AT&T-built scrambling device known as A-3, which was used for supposedly personal, private secure phone transmissions between Churchill and Roosevelt.

According to Muller's testimony given to American intelligence officers after the end of the war, the Nazis decoded and translated a highly secret and explosive conversation between Churchill and Roosevelt concerning information about Japanese actions in the Pacific. Muller dated this particular interception on November 26, 1941. Churchill told Roosevelt that his intelligence sources had learned that the Japanese fleet was headed east and not south as had been previously thought. He further confirmed that her objective was to attack the U.S. Fleet at Pearl Harbor on December 8, Tokyo time. Roosevelt then reportedly replied to Churchill:

"The Japanese are going to do a Port Arthur on us at Pearl Harbor! Do you confirm?," And Churchill's answer was, *"I do indeed!"*

According to Admiral Halsey in his introduction to Theobald's book, it has always seemed strangely suspicious why, out of four Pacific Fleet Carriers, none were at Pearl Harbor at the time of the attack, especially the timing of their removal from Pearl, namely right before the attack. Admiral Halsey's appraisal of the situation in the Pacific, and at Pearl Harbor, in particular, bear examination and again shed incriminating light, implicating the motives behind Washington's ordered movement of all carriers out of the Hawaiian Islands area. He states, *Had we known of Japan's minute and continued interest in the exact location and movement of our ships in Pearl Harbor, as indicated in the 'Magic Messages, "it is only logical that we would have concentrated our thought on meeting the practical certainty of an attack on Pearl Harbor. I am sure I would have protested the movement of my Task Force to Wake Island in late November and early December if Kimmel had possessed this intelligence, he would not have ordered that movement.*

Halsey's flag ships, the carrier *USS Enterprise* and the *USS Lexington* under Rear Admiral Newton, were both suddenly ordered out of Pearl at the last moment. *The USS Saratoga* was already on the West Coast undergoing periodic overhaul. Finally, the *USS Yorktown* was inexplicably transferred to the East Coast, putting great strain on their already slim resources. Finally, he reminds us that we were sadly deficient in long-distance scouting planes. "The only Army planes available were B18's. They were slow, short legged, and unfitted for over seas scouting. There were not sufficient PBY's — Navy scouting planes and good, old, slow and cumbersome workhorses— to run a continuous 360 degree search without wearing out materiel and personnel.

"As recently as June 11, 1999, there was an article by Reverend Thomas J. Edwards, Lt. USN Reserve, who wrote about his grandfather, a Lt. (j.g.) intelligence officer on the staff of Capt. L.H. Mayfield of the 14th Naval District at *Pearl Harbor,* who was fired in December of 1941 for persistence in reporting his unflinching conviction to his Commanding Officer that the Japanese were about to attack Pearl Harbor. On Dec. 5, 1941 he was arrested and placed aboard the SS Lurline and forced to resign his commission for going outside of channels in reporting his convictions to the intelligence officer of the 11th. Naval District at San Diego.

He writes and protests that his grandfather was ordered to keep silent about what he knew, under threat of not only dishonorable discharge but also threat of imprisonment as well. Finally, in exchange for his silence, the Navy arranged a job for him with the San Diego Police Department. His grandfather died an early death some 13 years later, never forgiving himself for accepting the Navy's bribe, or the Navy for nearly compelling him to take it.

In the San Francisco Chronicle of *1975,* an article appeared telling about a man by the name of T. Kevin Mallen, who then was 87 and retired in Menlo Park. Mallen was the IBM representative to the Philippines in the 1940's, and also a close friend of Bishop James B. Walsh, head of the Maryknoll Fathers, a Roman Catholic missionary society with extensive involvement in the Far East.

Bishop Walsh set up Mallen to play golf at Manila's Wack Wack Golf Club. His mystery partner was the missionary order's superior-general and co-founder. He had given Bishop Walsh a 3-part message directly from Admiral Yamamoto and other moderates, including Hirohito. Tojo was determined to have war and they wanted Roosevelt to know that there were many others who wanted to avoid conflict. Amazingly, the message included the exact location of where the Japanese fleet would assemble, Etorofu Jima (in the Kurile Islands) in anticipation of sailing to Hawaii. The dates given for this potential sailing were about the 27th or 28th of November 1941.

Mallen recalls going to Colonel Joseph Evans, Chief of intelligence at MacArthur's Manila Headquarters, where the information was considered lunacy.

Bishop Walsh then flew to Washington on November 15 1941, and passed the same information to then Secretary of State Cordell Hull. The appeal made no apparent impression at all. Actually, the Bishop made two trips to Washington, the first of which was at the request of Japanese Foreign Minister Yosuke Matsuoka. This led to an actual meeting with Roosevelt and members of his administration, but with no result. The second trip by Bishop Walsh was at the request of then Prime Minister Prince Fumimaro Konoye, conveying the message that Tojo can't be controlled much longer. Three days later Tojo replaced Konoye as Prime Minister.

Mr. Mallen states in the article that his reason for waiting so long to speak out on his personal knowledge, is that he decided it was important for the world to know the truth about the ceaseless efforts of these two courageous men, who though on opposite sides, risked a great deal to try and find peace and thus save many lives, than for him to worry about the abuse he would receive for speaking out. In his opinion, these two great men deserve to be recognized for their courage and bravery. Their testimony again brings embarrassing evidence to bear regarding the Administration's many sources for advance knowledge about Japan's specific contingency plans for the Hawaiian Islands.

Note: Unfortunately, Admiral Yamamoto and Bishop Walsh could not know that the very people they were attempting to warn, already had more information than they did. They didn't know it, but they were preaching to the proverbial choir. The administration already knew what was happening, and the efforts of Bishop Walsh were actually, quite inconvenient. Quite simply, the problem was that the president believed that war was necessary and though many questions and alternatives were discussed privately, the president could not be persuaded that any other course of action, other than a Japanese attack, would weigh enough to change the minds of the American voting public. His decision and that of his sometimes wavering staff held the day. That made war inevitable! For those of a philosophical bent, it is the age old question, does the end justify the means? For many it does; but, hopefully, here in America we still believe that if one does what is morally correct in every situation, the end can be left to the Providence of God.

My remarks regarding Japanese Emperor Hirohito

Japanese Emperor Hirohito's death brought many heads of state throughout the world to Japan to show their respect, but over *50* years ago; he was not that deserving of respect.

It was on his approval in 1937 that Japan attacked and raped China, and again on December 1, 1941 in from to Military and Civil leaders of Japan, including the Prime Minister Tojo, he sanctioned War with the United States of America.

The Imperial Navy Headquarters was then told of Emperor's decision, at *5:30* P.M. on December 2, 1941 a radio message was sent to the 32 Ship Strike Force headed toward Hawaii. The message read "Climb Mt. Nitaka", meaning "Begin the War".

At the close of the war when the USA and Allies were holding War Trials of Japanese Officials such as general Tojo, Emperor Hirohito should have been among them. But the Truman Administration and the commander of the U.S. Armed Forces of the Far East, General Douglas MacArthur decided against bringing Emperor Hirohito to trial, but instead leaving him as Emperor without powers. This left him only as a figurehead to his people to help hold Japan together, and to accept a democratic government more in the liking to the U.S.A.

Emperor Hirohito's powers were gone, so he resorted to the study of Botany, whereby exercising his trade in gardens until his death. Emperor Hirohito was born on April 29, 1901 and died of cancer on January 7, 1989.

I am a survivor of the Japanese attack on Pearl Harbor on that fateful day in December 1941, and that combined with the tragic loss of many brave young American fighting men on that day, has caused me to have more than a casual interest in every detail of how and why this tragedy happened and a desire for the unmitigated truth to be revealed! Fate caused me to be stationed aboard the *USS Pennsylvania*, Admiral Kimmel's flag-ship, and I lost several close friends, and many more fighting comrades on that day. As time has passed, I have been haunted and exceedingly concerned with the mounting evidence that the popular understanding of this tragic event, just does not comport with the facts. The massive amount of information received by the British and American intelligence agencies concerning Japanese activities in the Pacific as well as the implications of the breakdown in diplomatic negotiations with the Japanese should have been shared all along and in great detail. My reflections and research have continued right on into my retirement. Now, with more time to read, I have continued my search for every possible clue about the events of that period, regardless of where they may lead. I have come to the inescapable conclusion that, at the least, the attack could have been prevented! And at the most, proper sharing of intelligence and requested equipment, all well within Roosevelt's power to supply, our officers and men would have turned the event into disaster for the Japanese.

That might have delayed America's entrance into the war; but if so, be it. Many U.S. servicemen died needlessly on that "Day of Infamy"; and it is my hope that, someday, the American public will come to have a true understanding of the many old and new facts concerning this most important event in American history. If this has been an ugly cover-up as many believe, let the American people know the facts for themselves. The many professional defenders of Roosevelt and their perpetual obfuscations are wearing thin. Hopefully articles like this one and many others will someday cause the American people to demand the FULL TRUTH!

Never in peace time and in modern history can it be recalled that a Commander-in-Chief who had vital information that his Commanders would be attacked, and did nothing to inform them of this which caused many service men their deaths as well as loss of vital equipment, aircraft and ships.

I am well aware of the many writers and historians, consistently defending Roosevelt and his administration. We know that *"plausible deniability"* was the game then and still is the game today.

The Pearl Harbor history must be corrected, this must be done even if only to honor those who gave, in Lincoln's immortal words, *"...the last full measure of devotion."* Maybe then those brave Americans can rest in peace, knowing the truth is finally being told. It has long been said that, *"History is what happened, not what we wished happened."*

— Lawrence McNabb, Pearl Harbor Survivor

**Lawrence McNabb in
World War II**

Lawrence McNabb today

About the Author

Lawrence McNabb grew up on a farm near Melvern, Kansas. After graduating from Melvern High School, he joined the U.S. Navy and during the entire period of World War II, he served on ships in both the Atlantic and Pacific theaters.

Following the war he participated in two Atom Bomb testings, including the famous test at the Bikini Atoll in the Pacific. During the Korean Conflict, Lawrence served in a variety of overseas assignments.

At the completion of a memorable Naval Career, Lawrence settled down as a realtor in Fresno, California. Now since retired from real estate, he still resides in Fresno where he is active with the Pearl Harbor Survivor's Association, and lives with his wife Loraine. They have been married 49 years.

THE FIRST TALE

THE TETHERED GOATS

The First Tale–The Tethered Goats

The top secret message shown on the next page details a little publicized event just preceding Pearl Harbor. This message shows the President of the United States trying to lure the Japanese in sinking three small ships, thereby igniting World War II.

The sinking of three US "warships " would result in screaming headlines in the US press and a wave of public indignation that would guarantee the entry of the United States in a global conflict that would involve the lives of millions worldwide.

The only ship mentioned in the Top Secret Message was the USS Isabel, the flagship of the US Asiatic Fleet. Since I was ordered to report aboard the USS Isabel a few months later, and took command about a year later, it was inevitable that I would gain inside knowledge of what happened from the officers and crew, who came very close to being the first casualties of World War II.

The first thought that comes to mind, is how could any President create an incident that would surely doom the lives of 75 men and six officers, start a world war, and do all this without the authorization of Congress? Furthermore, how did he cover up the whole story of the Tethered Goats and shift the blame of the disaster at Pearl Harbor to Admiral Kimmel and General Short? The answer is of course "Politics". When a political party is in power, it can and does, cover up, delay, obfuscate and render impossible any real investigation for many years.

All this was done for over fifty years, when the Democratic Party was in power and managed to cover up the blame. After fifty years passed the "Freedom of Information Act" made possible the release of the Top Secret Message, and an avalanche of details never before released was made available.

On Dec. 1, 1941 (six days before the Pearl Harbor attack, Washington time), FDR ordered the office of U.S. Naval Operations in Washington, D.C., to send the top secret message to Admiral Hart's headquarters in Manila.

NAVAL MESSAGE OP-3B-B___   NAVY DEPARTMENT   2U

		MESSAGE PRECEDENCE
PHONE EXTENSION NUMBER 2042	ADDRESSEES	
FROM OPNAV		PRIORITY I
RELEASED BY		ROUTINE
	CINCAF	DEFERRED
DATE 1 December 1941		
TOR CODEROOM		PRIORITY
DECODED BY		ROUTINE
PARAPHRASED BY		DEFERRED

INDICATE BY ASTERISK ADDRESSEES FOR WHICH MAIL DELIVERY IS SATISFACTORY

012356   CR0313

UNLESS OTHERWISE DESIGNATED THIS DISPATCH WILL BE TRANSMITTED WITH DEFERRED PRECEDENCE.
ORIGINATOR FILL IN DATE AND TIME FOR DEFERRED AND MAIL DELIVERY
VKBGX   DATE   TIME   GCT

TEXT

PRESIDENT DIRECTS THAT THE FOLLOWING BE DONE AS SOON AS POSSIBLE AND WITHIN TWO DAYS IF POSSIBLE AFTER RECEIPT THIS DESPATCH X CHARTER THREE SMALL VESSELS

TO FORM A QUOTE DEFENSIVE INFORMATION PATROL UNQUOTE X MINIMUM REQUIREMENTS TO ESTABLISH IDENTITY AS UNITED STATES MEN-OF-WAR ARE COMMAND BY A NAVAL OFFICER

AND TO MOUNT A SMALL GUN AND ONE MACHINE GUN WOULD SUFFICE X FILIPINO CREWS MAY BE EMPLOYED WITH MINIMUM NAVAL RATINGS TO ACCOMPLISH PURPOSE WHICH IS TO OBSERVE

AND REPORT BY RADIO JAPANESE MOVEMENTS IN WEST CHINA SEA AND GULF OF SIAM X ONE VESSEL TO BE STATIONED BETWEEN HAINAN AND HUE ONE VESSEL OFF THE INDO-CHINA COAST

BETWEEN CAMRANH BAY AND CAPE ST.JAQUES AND ONE VESSEL OFF POINTE DE CAMAU X USE OF ISABEL AUTHORIZED BY PRESIDENT AS ONE OF THE THREE BUT NOT OTHER NAVAL VESSELS X

REPORT MEASURES TAKEN TO CARRY OUT PRESIDENTS VIEWS X AT SAME TIME INFORM ME AS TO WHAT RECONNAISSANCE MEASURES ARE BEING REGULARLY PERFORMED AT SEA BY BOTH ARMY

AND NAVY WHETHER BY AIR SURFACE VESSELS OR SUBMARINES AND YOUR OPINION AS TO THE EFFECTIVENESS OF THESE LATTER MEASURES X

1941 DEC 1 23 48

Hart was amazed to have received such a message from the President of the United States, who (not withstanding that he was the commander-in-chief of all U.S. Armed Forces) almost never ordered any field commander to incite any foreign action against U.S. Forces, much less one that obviously was designed to prompt an act of war. The president had even named a ship that he wanted to be used, the *USS ISABEL*.

On Dec. 3, 1941, Admiral Hart summoned the commanding officer of the *ISABEL*, LTJG John Walker Payne, Jr., to his office in Manila. Payne knew nothing about the President's message or his plans for the ISABEL until Admiral Hart briefed him.

"Utmost secrecy was observed," wrote Payne in his report which was recorded in the U.S. Naval Archives in the Washington Navy Yard many years later. "Actual orders were to be given verbally, memorized and recited to the Admiral. No one was to know the actual mission of the ISABEL except the Admiral and myself until we [meaning Payne and the crewmen of the ISABEL] were at sea."

As a fighting ship, the Isabel had always been somewhat of a navy bastard. Built along destroyer lines, 245 feet long with a 28-foot beam, and a respectable speed of 26 knots, she had long served as a relief flagship of the Asiatic Fleet, and had long languished far up the Yangtze River in China, with little to do except provide Admirals with a holiday cruiseship.

In 1941, Admiral Hart used ISABEL as his holiday ship. With her white hull and twin stacks and dimmed running lights, she looked like exactly what she was an aging yacht nearing the end of her service. So, how did FDR know about the ISABEL? Ever since his days as Assistant Secretary of the U.S. Navy, Roosevelt had kept a copy of JANE'S FIGHTING SHIPS within easy reach and he still kept one in the Oval Office when he became president. The ISABEL was listed as one of JANE'S FIGHTING SHIPS

Now, on Dec. 3, 1941, provisioned and fueled to capacity at Cavite, ISABEL left Manila on her first real combat mission, a "reconnaissance station" near Camranh Bay on the Indo-China coast where Admiral Hart's aerial reconnaissance planes had spotted 50 Japanese ships, including cruisers and destroyers, any one of which could have sunk the ISABEL with virtually no risk to itself. But that was exactly what the Japanese were supposed to do—to sink the ISABEL thus pulling the United States into war with Japan and the other Axis powers with the approval of the Philippines government!

On Dec. 5, ISABEL approached the location close to the entrance of Camranh Bay, which had been specified as her "reconnaissance" point by President Roosevelt. At 7:00 am., a Japanese patrol plane approached.

"It circled at an altitude of 1,000 feet, range 2,000 yards, and took pictures," Payne reported. "We took pictures of him, too. This plane continued to appear throughout the day. At 1900 (7:00 p.m.) we sighted the Indo-China coast, 22 miles distant."

But ISABEL had failed to attract gunfire either from the Japanese plane or the cruiser which had launched the plane. She was ordered back home to Manila, and Admiral Hart sent to Washington a secret, priority message:

"Have obtained two vessels, one now en route to China coast. Second one sailing soon as ready . . . ISABEL returning, was spotted and identified well off coast. Hence, utility of the mission problematical."

The second vessel referred to by Admiral Hart as "now en route" was LANIKAI. A third one would have been the MOLLY MALONE—a small vessel, no larger than a fishing boat, half the size of the LANIKAI, but equipped with a three-pound cannon and a pair of machine guns just as the LANIKAI was, to make her a "fighting ship." So, where did the LANIKAI get its Hawaiian name?

Originally christened the HERMES, LANIKAI had been rechristened when she was used in Hawaii in the filming of the motion picture, HURRICANE. She was an 83-foot, two-masted schooner; and as a fighting ship of the U.S. Navy with her 3-pound cannon and two 30-caliber machine guns, the only danger to a Japanese cruiser or a destroyer would have been if the Japanese had laughed themselves to death.

LANIKAI's new skipper, LTJG Kemp Tolley, had assumed command of LANIKAI only as of Dec. 1, 1941. About his new command, Tolley wrote: "She wasn't exactly a ship—she was a windjammer, a two-masted, interisland schooner . . . her entire crew consisted of four or five assorted civilian Filipinos who had come in a package with the ship, which had been chartered for one dollar a year."

47

Meanwhile, the ISABEL returned to Manila on Dec. 7, Manila time (Dec. 6, Honolulu time), where Skipper Payne was greeted by Admiral Hart with these revealing words: "Well, I didn't expect to see you again!"

Now, sailing in the second "tethered goat," it was Skipper Kemp Tolley's turn to approach Camranh Bay on the Indo-China coast in an attempt to provoke an overt act of war from the Japanese. But on Dec. 8 in the Far East, Dec. 7 Honolulu time, the cruise of the LANIKAI was aborted and the cruise of the MOLLY MALONE was never begun—both rendered irrelevant by the massive Japanese attack on Hawaii.

For three decades following World War II, top U.S. Navy brass was questioned long and repeatedly about FDR's secret order of Dec. 1, 1941, to Admiral Hart in Manila.

In 1962, before a Joint Congressional Committee, the Chief of Naval Operations in WWII, Admiral Harold C. Stark, was questioned about the president's motive in having him send the top secret message to Admiral Hart. Due to additional comments from the floor by members of the committee, Stark never had to answer. In another Joint Congressional Committee hearing in 1970, Admiral Hart was asked a similar question about the president's motive in having Admiral Stark send him that top secret message. Due to additional comments from other congressional committee members, Hart was allowed to remain mute.

Hart later explained his silence: "My relationship with him [Admiral Stark] was close and I did expect that he would someday begin to talk about it. He never did. Stark has not given out to anyone, by word or print. I destroyed my record on the subject some time back."

The two men remained silent who knew most about FDR's top secret message of Dec. 1, 1941—Admiral Stark from the transmitting end of the message from his Office of Naval Operations in Washington, D.C., and Admiral Hart from the receiving end in his Asiatic Fleet Headquarters in Manila.

Almost 30 years after he had commanded the LANIKAI as a LTJG, having since ascended to the rank of Rear Admiral, Kemp Tolley shared a luncheon in Washington with Admiral Hart and Admiral Harry Hill. During the luncheon conversation, noted Tolley, Admiral Hart said to Admiral Hill: "I once had the unpleasant requirement to send this young man (Tolley) on what looked like a one-way mission."

Hart then told about LANIKAI's mission of self destruction which was erased by the Japanese attack on Pearl Harbor.

Tolley respectfully then asked Admiral Hart, "Would you tell Admiral Hill if you think we were set up to bait an incident?"

"Yes," Admiral Hart's reply is quoted by Tolley, "I think you were bait. And I can prove it. But I won't. And don't you try it, either."

Essentially, Tolley was being told that a slip of the lip must not sink the reputation of a U.S. president, but Rear Admiral Tolley, with all due respect to his Navy superiors and no political fish to fry one way or the other, is determined to set the record straight. So, he included his proofs of FDR's motives in his book, CRUISE OF THE LANIKAI, 1994.

THE SECOND TALE

THE INTELLIGENCE GAP WITHIN THE U.S. NAVY

The Second Tale–The Intelligence Gap within the U.S. Navy

Generally, among high-ranking military officers who had begun their careers before World War I, aircraft carriers and their planes in 1941 were still thought of in terms of scouting and reconnaissance Prime sea power was calculated in terms of huge guns aboard huge battleships. In the all-male navy at that time, men still rose to high rank through duties related to gunnery in sea duty on destroyers, cruisers and battle wagons and activist visionaries among airmen in the services (such as H.H. Hap Arnold in the U.S. Army) who predicted victory in future warfare through air power were discounted as overly zealous in championing unproven weapons.

But the crucial facts were that aircraft carriers could travel faster than battleships, strike more potently and more quickly and escape without ever sailing within 200 miles of their targets

In Japan, which had been at war in various parts of the Pacific Rim since 1937, the commander-in-chief of the Imperial Japanese Navy, Admiral Isoroku Yamamoto, had quietly built up a fleet of eleven aircraft carriers with highly trained combat pilots who had seen action in China, Manchuria, and Indo-China. He was hampered and occasionally resisted by the thinking of Imperial Japanese Army leaders, but Yamamoto's prestige was great enough to sustain his plans for destruction of the U.S. Pacific Fleet with air power. Accordingly, he had planned the attack on Pearl Harbor for Dec. 8, 1941, (Tokyo Time), providing that the U.S. fleet remained anchored there.

Because U.S. military leaders and diplomats had discounted any such striking power by Japan, when the Japanese Navy created a new, First Air Fleet in April, 1941, with authority over eight aircraft carriers and attached units with an escort force of at least 16 destroyers, U.S. Naval Intelligence remained unaware of it.

U.S. Naval Intelligence officers had been tracking Japanese codes ever since the codes of the Purple machine (a Japanese coding machine used in their embassies) had been broken in Washington, D.C., in September, 1940. They had not been trained to give top priority to the emergence of

52

naval air power in Japan. The U.S. Pacific fleet had only three aircraft carriers, the LEXINGTON, the SARATOGA, and the ENTERPRISE

The forms of thought among high-ranking military officers in Washington and in Hawaii was such that they did not envision an air attack, starting from 4,000 miles away, which would be designed to destroy the U.S. fleet vis-a-vis air power.

But at 2:00 p.m., Tokyo Time, on Dec. 1 in Tokyo, that was the plan that Emperor Hirohito in Room 1, East of the Imperial Palace, heard Prime Minister Tojo Hideki put forth, backed up by service chiefs and senior members of the Japanese Cabinet

The emperor did not speak. Privy Council President Baron Yoshimichi Hara, speaking for the emperor, voiced a reluctant agreement with Tojo, saying:

"The proposal before us cannot be avoided in the light of present circumstances.'

Four-thousand miles away at Admiral Husband E. Kimmel's Headquarters on the Submarine Base at Pearl Harbor, his intelligence officer, LtCdr Edwin T. Layton, was making alterations and additions in pencil on his morning report to the admiral. He had no traffic to report from Japanese aircraft carriers—there's almost a complete lack of information on the carriers today,' Lt. Cdr. Joseph J. Rochefort had told Layton after monitoring Japanese fleet communications from Station HYPO, The U.S. Navy coding station on the East Coast of Oahu, Hawaii. Layton wrote in his morning report about the location of Japanese carriers:

Meanwhile, aboard his flagship AKAGI, Admiral Nagumo was getting up-to-the-minute information on U.S ship movements while Admiral Kimmel was getting no information about the six Japanese aircraft carriers and their escort vessels moving in on him from the northwest. Nagumo received a radio message from Tokyo that repeated the Honolulu Japanese Consulates Friday report on the disposition of the U.S. Fleet at Pearl Harbor:

"Ships at anchor Pearl Harbor p.m. 28 November were 6 battleships (2 Maryland class, 2 California class, 2 Pennsylvania class) I aircraft carrier (Lexington), 9 heavy cruisers (5 San Francisco class, 3 Chicago class, I Salt Lake class), 5 light cruisers (4 Honolulu class, I Omaha class).'

A crucial change in this report did not reach Admiral Nagumo. On Dec. 5, the U.S. Aircraft Carrier, LEXINGTON, steamed out of Pearl Harbor to ferry marine fighter reinforcements to Midway Island. All three of Admiral Kimmel's aircraft carriers were at sea on special missions. All of the heavy cruisers and more than half of the destroyers were at sea protecting the carriers. Only the battleships with light cruisers and destroyers were still at Pearl Harbor.

The Commander-in-Chief of U.S. Naval Operations in Washington, Admiral Richmond K. (Terrible) Turner, was convinced that war with Japan was imminent, but that Japan would strike in the Far East, and perhaps that accounted for his neglect to transfer urgent diplomatic warnings of war in Washington to the military commanders in Hawaii. Turner later maintained that repeated war warnings had been sent to Admiral Kimmel and General Walter C. Short, but Kimmel and Short maintained that they had not received such warnings

Furthermore, any idea of shared intelligence between the navy and the army was hampered by the reluctance of each one to break its own internal security regulations

For example, Admiral Kimmel was briefed on the fact that the Japanese consulates had been instructed from Tokyo to destroy their purple machines (Purple, it needs to be remembered, was the name assigned to a Japanese electrical coding machine used in their consulates). On Dec 3, Layton told Kimmel that Japanese diplomats in Honolulu were burning their codes, but Kimmel didn't tell General Short in their weekly Wednesday meeting about the destruction of the Purple machines or the burning of the codes.

Why not? Security regulations of the navy prohibited repeating that information to anybody outside of the navy.

Layton, a very conscientious man, was particularly frustrated by the lack of information that might have been forwarded to him from the Office of Naval Intelligence and the Office of Naval Operations in Washington. In fact, Admiral Turner had clamped down a tight lid on all intelligence transmissions with the order that they had to be cleared through him. Far from being too loose with secret intelligence information, Turner was hoarding information and keeping it away from those who should have been using it in the field.

In Layton's view, a ton of pre-Pearl Harbor tactical and diplomatic information which should have been forwarded to the military commanders in Hawaii never got there. That included all cryptographic intelligence which was summed up in the general term, "magic."

Layton was well aware that the study of intelligence was irrelevant to rapid advancement in rank in the U.S. Navy. He noted that intelligence never was mentioned in his classes during his four years of study at the Naval Academy in Annapolis, MD. It had no place in the curriculum.

With Admiral Turner as an example, he wrote in his later years, "It is now clear that ranking officers used Magic to further their own authority at the expense of its proper dissemination as the crisis with Japan worsened. The consequences were disastrous.

How did Layton define intelligence? He made that very clear, writing in one of his notebooks:

"Intelligence, as defined by Webster's Third New International Dictionary, is 'evaluated information concerning an enemy or possible enemy or a possible theater of operations and the conclusions drawn there from.' That definition is inadequate because it covers only two of the three essential elements of intelligence. It comprehends acquisition and evaluation, but it omits the vital third element—dissemination. Information can be acquired and evaluated until hell freezes over, but it does not become intelligence until delivered to the commanders who can make proper use of it."

Layton concluded:

"The inability of Naval Communications and Naval Intelligence to adjust their preconceptions to factual information had proved fatal before the Pearl Harbor attack."

Did Naval authorities in Washington, D.C., have intelligence pinpointing Pearl Harbor as the Japanese target before Dec. 7, 1941? Yes, they did! So, did they make sure that such information reached the army and navy commandants or Pacific Fleet intelligence officer Layton in Hawaii? No, they did not!

Here is the incredible truth of what happened:

In October, 1941, Japanese intelligence notified their naval units, which were scattered widely in the Far East, that (without fail, from that time on) they were to monitor Radio Tokyo weather broadcasts.

Why?

Because in the form of wind advisories in the middle of and at the end of weather forecasts, emergency instructions would be given to Japanese navy assault forces to attack within 72 hours any one or more of the following targets:

NORTH WIND CLOUDY

(Kita No Kaze Kumori) execute for: attack Russia

WEST WIND CLEAR

(Nishi No Kaze Hare) execute for: attack British.

SOUTH WIND STORMY

(Minami No Kaze Arashi) execute for: attack Dutch East Indies.

EAST WIND RAIN

(Higashi No Kaze Ame) execute for: attack Pearl Harbor.

The Japanese code had been broken early in 1941 by a Dutch Army wife, Nancy Verkuyl, who was on the staff of the Netherlands East Indies code service at Bandung, Java. By the summer of 1941, that code service was working 24-hours every day intercepting and decoding Japanese messages from everywhere in the Far East. Through one of those intercepts, the wind codes were received at the NET service in Java, causing great excitement and extra alertness.

Then, on Dec. 5 (Java time) which was Dec. 4 (Washington, D.C. time) a vital message was received by the chief military intelligence officer at Bandung, U.S. Army Col. E. R. Thorpe.

The message was: EAST WIND RAIN, meaning that Japanese forces would attack Pearl Harbor within 72 hours.

In his book, EAST WIND RAIN, Col. Thorpe asserts:

"I suppose the most important thing I ever did as an army intelligence officer was to notify Washington of the forthcoming attack on Pearl Harbor."

Col. Thorpe's assertion was testified to by Capt. Laurence Safford of the U.S. Navy and U.S. Army General Albert Wedemeyer, Chief of Army Operations.

There is no doubt that Thorpe's message got to Washington Dec. 4, 1941. Wedemeyer acknowledged that he received it there on that date.

It never reached Kimmel and Short until after the attack—at 1:00 p.m., Honolulu time, Dec. 7, 1941.

Layton did not excuse himself from blame, although he did not know that Washington intelligence sources had received prior information that Pearl Harbor was to be attacked within 72 hours from Dec. 4, and had no way to know that the six carriers in the Japanese task force, Kido Butai, had completed eight days on a straight easterly course across the northern Pacific to a point approximately 1,000 miles north-northwest of Hawaii without being detected. On board the flagship AKAGI a clear reception of Hawaiian commercial radio broadcasting over station KGMB confirmed to the Japanese that the Hawaiian Islands were unaware of the approaching danger. Otherwise, if Hawaii radio stations expected an air attack, they would not have provided a radio beam to guide attackers in. They would have gone off the air.

Kido Butai then swung around to a southeasterly course to begin its approach to Oahu.

Layton recorded in his log book that the focus of his attention on Saturday, Dec. 6, 1941, was on Japanese naval activity in the South China Sea where, he felt, a Japanese invasion of Siam or Malaya or both was imminent.

There was plenty of data to support Layton's conclusion. He had received confirmation early that Saturday that a 25-ship Japanese convoy had been sighted off southernmost Indo-China, followed by ten more ships with two cruisers and four destroyers; and a third convoy of 30 troop transports and a large cruiser in Camranh Bay.

Layton calculated that, if the Japanese convoys maintained their course and speed, the invaders would hit the beaches of Malaya and Siam the next day, and that (possibly) a simultaneous attack would be launched against Manila in the Philippines.

After hearing that briefing, Admiral Kimmel sent Layton to get the opinion of Admiral William Pye, the Battle Force Commander of Pearl Harbor. Pye agreed with Layton that the day's intelligence indicated Japanese action in the far East, but discounted any possibility that the Philippines would be attacked.

"Oh, no, the Japanese won't attack us," Pye told Layton. "We're too strong and powerful."

In Honolulu that Saturday, Radio Station KGMB stayed on the air all night so that its broadcasts would help guide a flight of U.S. B-17s due into Hickam Field from the mainland at around 8:00 the next morning, Dec. 7. Only seven PBY navy patrol planes were scheduled on the dawn anti-submarine patrol off the south coast of Oahu. None was sent to the waters off of the north coast, from which direction the Japanese aircraft carriers would be launching their planes.

At 5:30 Sunday morning, Honolulu Time, a pair of Japanese seaplanes were launched from two heavy cruisers as they steamed ahead of the carriers. They completed a reconnaissance mission over Pearl Harbor, Oahu, and Lahaina, Maui, to confirm that the U.S. fleet was still at anchor in Pearl Harbor. Meanwhile air crews on the Japanese carriers climbed into their cockpits and sat there, waiting for a 6:00 a.m. deadline to take off between 6:00 and 6:15 am., 183 planes vaulted into the air from the six carriers. Only one plane, a Zero, had to be ditched. Flight Commander Mitsuo Fuchida led 49 high-level bombers, 51 dive bombers, 40 torpedo planes, and 43 escorting Zero fighter planes south toward Oahu. Fuchida's navigator estimated they would be over their targets in an hour and a half.

Apparently, the Kido Butai had completed its 4,000 mile trip from home waters to the launching of its attack planes without detection. But actually, it had not.

The last remaining means of U.S. detection and advance warning of the onrushing attack planes was in place on the north shore of Oahu at Opana, Kahuku Point. It was a mobile rig that looked like several sets of bed springs placed end on end, length wise, on the back of a 2-1/2 ton army truck (Radar set SCR 270B), and it was being operated as the Japanese planes approached to within range (approximately 200 miles). by two young Signal Corps, Aircraft Warning Company privates: Joseph L. Lockard and George E. Elliott; and they had a direct telephone connection to the Signal Corps Radar Filter Center (nicknamed "Little Robert") in the Signal Corps Flats area at Fort Shafier, just a few miles from Pearl Harbor

From that Radar Filter Center, an officer on duty could alert navy headquarters at Pearl Harbor, General Short's army headquarters at Fort Shafier, the 7th Army Air Corps Fighter Command at Wheeler Field; Schofield Barracks; and the 7th Army Air Corps Bomber Command at Hickam Field on the east bank of Pearl Harbor.

Although it was only 90 minutes away from its targets, the onrushing Japanese air armada was not home free just yet.

THE THIRD TALE

RADAR: AMERICA'S BEST KEPT SECRET

The Third Tale–Radar: America's Best Kept Secret

Radar is a device that uses radio echoes from a solid object in the sky or on or under the sea and sends back signals which can be read and plotted for distance, time and bearing.

We had it and used it and it worked, but only a couple of army privates acknowledged what it meant.

Officially, Army Privates Lockard and Elliott, whose shift in the darkness at Opana radar station had started at 4:00 am., were off duty at 7:00 am., and had the chow truck been on time to take them to breakfast, they would have shut down the radar set. But the chow truck was late, and the two men decided to use the time for one last look around.

They already had been scouring the horizon north of Oahu for three hours without seeing anything unusual except for small radar blips on the grass line to the left of their scanning range at *6:45* a.m. These echoes from two slow-moving planes figured to be PBYs on dawn patrol. Actually, the sightings were from the two float planes which had been launched by cruisers in advance of the Japanese aircraft carriers, but the two radar operators had no way to discern that.

Then, at 7:00 am., 136 miles away, the green grass line suddenly came alive with electronic blips. Elliott and Lockard were amazed at the radar activity. They checked the equipment to make sure that it wasn't malfunctioning, but the equipment was okay. The lively echoes persisted on the radar screen.

The two men had just looked at the first sighting at 136 miles, but at 7:02 am., they plotted a sighting 132 miles to the north. In other words, they transferred the distance and heading from the etched lucite over the radar screen to their plotting board. What they saw was not an image of planes or of any signals from the planes, but a constant jumble of multitudinous blips, indicating a mass flight approaching Oahu from almost due north, azimuth three degrees.

Lockard and Elliott had sighted the radar echoes of the 183 Japanese carrier planes launched in the first wave and being led by Commander Fuchida. It indicated the largest flight that Lockard ever had seen on the radar screen and he decided to call it in to the Radar Filter Center in the Signal Corps Flats Area of Fort Shafter, "Little Robert." "Little Robert" was located in a very unimposing structure built on top of a warehouse down by the Fort Shafter dump, 28 miles from Opana.

Normally, when the Radar Filter Center was fully manned, plotters would have been pushing van-colored arrows about on a large map of Oahu, marked with grids on which they could indicate flight paths of any planes within the radar scans of six radar stations located on the circumference of Oahu. On a platform above the plotters, supervisors and officers on duty identified flights which had been reported that day from the various services—Army, Navy, Marine Corps, Coast Guard and also civilian. But the plotters were gone and the only officer on duty that Sunday, (14 shopping days before Christmas) was Kermit Tyler, a 7th Army Air Corps fighter pilot from Wheeler Field. The only large flight he had been informed about was that of B-17's, due at Hickam Field from the West Coast at between 8:00 and 9:00 am.

Lockard placed his call into the switchboard manned by Pvt. Joseph McDonald at the Radar Filter Center at Fort Shafter, 28 miles away from Opana.

Lockard sought to impress Tyler, saying that these were "the biggest sightings he had ever seen." Any of 42 fighter planes could have been dispatched from Wheeler Field to identify the incoming bogeys (unidentified planes) within 30 minutes. There were 49 combat planes at the Marine base at Ewa, 33 Navy combat planes at Kaneohe, 35 bombers at Hickam Field and 70 Navy planes of various kinds at Ford Island in the center of Pearl Harbor.

All told, the US. operational military planes on Oahu totaled more than 200, and the U.S. Aircraft Carrier, ENTERPRISE, was just 200 miles to the west of Oahu, returning from its voyage to Midway

Tyler wasn't really prepared about whom to notify if he took Lockards report as a cause to sound a general alarm for all services on Oahu. He would be on duty only until 8:00 a.m. and there were no liaison officers present to direct calls to Navy Headquarters at Pearl Harbor or to Pacific Fleet Headquarters at Hunters Point. He hadn't been informed that war with Japan was considered to be imminent and he knew that there were frequent false alarms about unidentified flights in the Hawaiian Islands, all of which had turned out to be unreported, friendly planes.

What about IFF equipment (Identification Friend or Foe), which could be switched on in the cockpit to identify friendly planes with a radio signal? IFF wouldn't be installed on friendly aircraft in the Hawaiian Department until March, 1942.

No high rankers could be reached directly by Tyler.

General Short and his wife had been to a dinner-dance at Schofield Barracks on Saturday night and Admiral Kimmel had gone to a small dinner parry at the Halekulani Hotel at Waikiki. They could be reached only by their staff officers and a duty officer would have to be convinced that there was cause for general alarm before anyone could get through to the high rankers. Men not of high rank, but in key positions, like Layton, the Fleet Intelligence Officer, had no direct linkage to the Radar Filter Center. He and his wife had dined and danced at the Royal Hawaiian Hotel at Waikiki until midnight.

In listening to Lockard's news of the massive echoes coming in from *132* miles north of Oahu, Tyler had no definite plan to convey the information to higher authority. As a matter of fact, there wasn't any direct linkage from Tyler to higher authority except at Wheeler Field where pursuit planes could have been ordered into the air by a duty officer, but not readily at 7:00 am Sunday morning, unless the duty officer was persuaded that he should wake up bird colonels and generals and sound the alarm at that time.

Tyler felt that the massive sighting must have something to do with the 12 four-engined B-17s which were due in from the mainland within an hour or two. Actually, the B-17s approaching Oahu from. the east were less than 200 miles behind the Japanese, and just like Fuchida's flight, they were being guided in by Radio Station KGMB, but at 7:00 am. they had not appeared on any Signal Corps, Aircraft Warning radar screens.

Tyler shrugged and told Lockard, "Well, don't worry about it." But Lockard and Elliott did worry about it and plotted the sightings all of the way into Oahu at 7:02, 7:05, 7:08, 7:11, 7:13, 7:15, 7:16, 7:18, 7:20, 7:23, 7:25, 7:27, 7:30, 7:31, 7:33, 7:35, 7:37, and 7:39 am.

It was the most crucial 37 minutes recorded in the history of aerial warfare. Had sightings been heeded and the alert sounded, all crews on board 92 U.S. Navy ships at Pearl Harbor could have been at general quarters, and since it took the Pearl Harbor duty destroyer, MONAGHAN, only *45* minutes to raise steam and get under way, every ship in the harbor could have been on the move before Fuchida's flight would have arrived above them. The possibilities of what might have happened in that case boggle the mind.

Certainly, it would have been a very different scene at Pearl Harbor than the one which ensued. Unspotted by anyone in the first beams of the morning sunrise, the scout plane from the Japanese cruiser CHIKUNA (headed back to the north after viewing Pearl Harbor), radioed to the Kido Butai at 7:35 am.:

"ENEMY FORMATION AT ANCHOR.
NINE BATTLESHIPS, ONE HEAVY CRUISER, SIX LIGHT
CRUISERS IN HARBOR."

Simultaneously, the other scout plane from the Cruiser, TONE, radioed Fuchida that there were no American warships in Maui's Lahaina harbor. Lockard and Elliott's warning hadn't been the only one ignored by higher authority that morning.

In the dark waters off of Pearl Harbor at 3:42 am., Honolulu time, the U.S. minesweeper CONDOR signalled by blinker lamp to the destroyer WARD:

"Sighted submerged submarine on westerly course one and 3/4 miles south of the entrance buoys, speed nine knots."

The WARD skipper, Lt. William Outerbridge, zeroed in on the bearing, ordered general quarters, and conducted an hour-long sonar sweep. When no contact was made, the duty officer at the Bishop's Point naval radio station did not notify the Naval Control Center at Ford Island of the sighting. The net boom at the Pearl Harbor Channel entrance was opened and CONDOR and a second minesweeper entered the harbor, unaware that they were followed in by at least two midget Japanese submarines.

At 6:30 am., Honolulu time, the skipper of the supply vessel ANTARES, spotted a conning tower of a small submarine. The same object was spotted by the helmsman on the destroyer WARD. Lt. Outerbridge once again ordered general quarters and sought to ram the sub

63

at full speed while hurling depth charges overboard. Then, he radioed to the commandant of the 14th Naval District:

"We have attacked, fired upon. and dropped depth charges upon sub operating in defensive area."

The naval radio station at Bishop's Point acknowledged WARD's report, but no alarm sounded at 14th Naval District Headquarters or at Pacific Fleet Headquarters.

At 7:00 a.m., Honolulu time, only a couple of minutes before Lockard and Elliott made their crucial telephone call to the Fort Shafier Radar Filter Center at "Little Robert," a pilot of one of the PBY patrol planes radioed that he had sunk a submerged submarine one mile off the entrance to Pearl Harbor.

Still, no alarm bells were rung at 14th Naval District or Pacific Fleet Headquarters.

Finally, at 7:45 a.m., Admiral Claude C. Bloch was informed of the sighting by the CONDOR, the ANTARES, and attack by the WARD, but he shared the opinion of his staff officers that WARD's report was just another false alarm. Admiral Kimmel, when informed of the submarine alerts off the entrance to Pearl Harbor, agreed with his duty officer that the situation wasn't serious enough to rouse the rest of his headquarters staff

So, the warnings from both the Army and the Navy sources went unheeded.

As Fuchida's plane roared over Kahuku Point at the northern tip of Oahu, he ordered his radio operator, "Notify all planes to attack"

The radio operator tapped out, "To, To, To," short for "Totsugeki" (Charge). Seconds later, he tapped out "To ra, To ra, To ra," ("Tiger, Tiger, Tiger") and the attack was on.

THE FOURTH TALE

THE ED SHEEHAN STORY

The Fourth Tale–The Ed Sheehan Story

At 7:40 a.m., the first attack wave of 183 planes, led by Lt. Commander Fuchida, roared along the western shore of Oahu from Kahuku Point and split into two flights of 88 and 95 planes.

At 7:49, offshore from Haleiwa, the 95-plane flight went in and attacked Wheeler Field at Schofield Barracks.

At Wheeler Field, they destroyed 42 combat planes on the ground.

At Kaneohe Naval Air Station, they destroyed 27 planes on the ground and damaged six others

At the Marine Corps Air Base at Ewa, the 88-plane flight destroyed 33 combat planes parked wing-tip to wingtip (so grouped to guard against sabotage).

At Ford Island in the center of Pearl Harbor, they destroyed 33 of 70 navy combat planes.

Then, over Pearl Harbor, the two flights reconverged. The sky was full of low-flying planes with red circles on their wings. Massive explosions sounded along battleship row, but the most spectcular blow hit the ARIZONA

When you are caught in 2,000 degrees of heat, you can't breath, but the brain doesn't stop functioning immediately. You have a few seconds to realize that you are being cremated alive, providing that shock doesnt blot out everything. That's what happened to the men caught below decks in the forward part of the ARIZONA.

Everything depended upon where you were on Oahu that morning.

Quartermaster Lou Conter was standing on the quarterdeck with Captain Franklin Van Valkenberg and Rear Admiral Isaac C. Kidd. As the first explosions sounded, Conter was ordered to sound general quarters and secure the quarterdeck. Captain Van Valkenberg and Rear Admiral Kidd headed for the bridge. A 3/4-ton bomb crashed through the forward deck and into the ships magazine. More than 100 tons of TNT exploded. Everything forward of the mainmast caught fire. Captain Van Valkenberg and Admiral Kidd were among those killed instantly. Conter was saved by the ship's superstructure. The ship sank to the harbor's bottom, with about two feet of water covering the main deck. A torpedo hit close to the quarterdeck and Conter found himself in the oil-covered water. Then, the water seemed to catch fire as oil leaking from the ARIZONA ignited. Lou Conter survived. How? He wasn't quite sure.

Eleven-hundred and 77 men died on the ARIZONA or in the oil-covered waters around her. Most of them remained on the ship. Officially, they are buried at sea.

Marine Master Sergeant Don Jones was hospitalized at Hospital Point entrance to Pearl Harbor. When the shooting started, he dived into a ditch alongside the hospital. A sailor dived in beside him. A Japanese Zero crashed over the ditch, killing the pilot and causing Jones to crouch down in the ditch to avoid being hit by the plane. The sailor, clinging to rosary beads, dropped them, grabbed one leg of the dead pilot, and started beating on the leg, yelling:

"I'll kill you! I'll kill you!" Then, realizing how ridiculous his actions were, he put down the leg and picked up the rosary beads again.

Jones went back into the hospital and started carrying water to the burn victims there.

THE ED SHEEHAN STORY

One of the civilian dock workers at Pearl Harbor on Dec. 7, 1941, was Ed Sheehan, a good writer who recorded his vivid memories of that day from the door of the shop where he was working, which fronted on the long pier, facing Ford Island. In his book, DAYS OF '41 (Pearl Harbor Remembered), he wrote:

"It was like looking into Hell on a sunshiny day.

"Each of the great battleships, so strong, clean and powerful yesterday, was in agony, tortured in an inferno of orange flame and vile smoke. Only the cage-like top sections of the masts on the WEST VIRGINIA and TENNESSEE were visible through the roiling filth. The CALIFORNIA looked half-sunk, listing on one side in snapping fires. The ARIZONA was almost completely hidden. Her superstructure tilted at a crazy angle amid oily clouds rising like thick black cauliflowers. The OKLAHOMA had rolled completely over. with her long bottom showing above water, she looked like an immense floating sausage. Tiny figures clustered on the higher places. Others were sliding down the rounded sides into the water.

"Small boats moved back and forth, going in where tiny heads bobbed in the oily water or doll-likefigures spilled over sides of broken ships. Muffled explosions belched and more flames lashed up as fires ignited fuel and ammunition stowages. The bursts were ghastly, vomiting pieces of the ships, and God knows what else.

"To me, the strangest thing of all was the awful clarity with which I was viewing the scene, this incredible carnage in a tropic morning. I had to tell myself that I was truly alive and awake and that this horror was real, not a bad dream—the water afire, the jarring, sickening explosions, and the small boats stark against the churning smoke and tongues of flame. All these abominations were utterly, terribly close to my eyes, but my mind could not believe that this catastrophe was actually happening.

"Close by, at dockside, the cruiser HELENA had been hit and was listing. The minelayer OGLALA, moored outboard, was being pulled away by tugs. Somehow I knew the OGLALA was slowly sinking. I could feel as much as see it happening. Aboard the HELENA, men darted about on the decks. Others were on the pier, waving arms and shouting. Suddenly I found myself in a line of men passing shells aboard. I remember a feeling of relief at doing something. But soon the chore was over, the line broke up, the others disappeared, and I was left alone. I felt useless, weak, insignificant. I looked for familiar faces to share a few words with, but none was near. For a chilling moment I had the thought that someone might shoot me, for loafing about so stupidly at such a devastating time. I started down Ten-Ten dock thinking: There must be something I can do. Or perhaps someone will tell me what to do . . . I half ran, as if on some important errand, then saw a boat coming across from the battleships. They might need help, I thought. No one's on the dock to take their lines. I was waiting when she came in, a launch filled with dark figures. The coxwain brought her bumping against the piling and someone threw me a line. I lashed it around a chock as best I could, tying knot upon knot, until a voice cried, 'Hurry up for Christ's sake!' That was the coxwain, holding a stern line. I had forgotten there were two. He threw it, slithery with oil and hard to manage. But I hung on and secured that one too, knowing my technique was amateurish and wrong, but that the rope would hold.

"The men started climbing ashore. Some were in mucky fouled denims, others wore whites soaked and shining with oil. All reeked of oil and smoke. *A few talked and cursed, making little sense. Others were quiet, many had bloodless faces, their eyes in a glaze of shock. Five or six had to be helped ashore very carefully. One man screamed with every movement; his legs were rubbery and dangling uselessly. It took a long time to ease him up and I remember thinking how awful it would be if we dropped him in the harbor. He was covered with oil and difficult to hold.*

"The hardest job was lifting those wounded who were lying on the launch's deck. Two or three were quite still. A few others made weak movements, or clutching motions. They were dead weights when lifted, and the launch's sides dipped low in our struggles to raise them to the dock. I helped carry two over to an open area in front of the machine shop. I knew that one was dead. He was utterly limp, and his head rolled from side to side against my chest. I shall never forget the feel of that man. And I could tell from the eyes of the sailor helping me that he too, knew his shipmate was gone. We put the boy down gently among the wounded lying by the side of the road.

"Now a few other boats were coming in from the chaos along Ford Island. The battleships were still being eaten by fires and and enshrouded in billowing, coal-black smoke. Sometimes breezes cleared air spaces for a few seconds, and we could see.

"Soon, the boat I had helped was heading out, straight into that Hell. The coxswain looked small, his legs apart on the stern as he held the tiller under his arm. He also looked very brave. The launch tossed up a grayish wake. Beyond it, brutal flowers of flame and smoke rose from the buckling ships.

"Far away and high above, the Waianae Mountains slept on in their massive beauty, unmoved, untouched, as if nothing had happened.

"I found a bucket and a faucet and I brought water. It seemed to be a useful thing to do. Soon, a row of men lay in the area between the crane tracks and the machine shop. Some were dead, their faces covered with caps or bits of clothing. Others stirred, and their friends crouched close, talking and urging them over and over again to take it easy. I offered my cigarettes and the pack disappeared in a minute. One young sailor was sitting by himself sobbing beyond control. He kept pointing across the channel, trying to get his words out, but only choking sounds came.

"Planes were still visible, high up, moving well above the shrapnel puffs. We could hear big and little guns thudding and rattling from Ford Island and Middle Loch ahead of us, and from the drydock near by and the repair basin behind. Trucks and cars began arriving and we who were unhurt helped the wounded men into the vehicles. Again, after that, I had nothing to do for awhile. I had time then to consider how frightened I was, how drenched in fear, as I stood thinking. Those bastards are coming back and next time I will be killed. How can men do this to one another? I felt sickened, helpless, useless. A foreign part of me was moving and walking through all this misery and horror. The part I was aware of was staring, wondering and tense. I started for Drydock One with the thought: That's where my job is, that's where I should be.

"One big ship was in the stream of East Loch—the battleship NEVADA, obviously trying to get out of the harbor. She too had been badly hit. Her bow was down, fire flickered and smoke trailed her decks. But she was underway, a fine and gallant sight. I remember saying to myself: Thank God there's at least one left."

Dr. Russell Jensen was the only medical doctor on duty at Hospital Point that morning. He had not been trained to treat burns and virtually all of the casualties which quickly filled the 30 beds of the hospital had terrible burns. Many had shrapnel and bullet wounds, too. Jensen did what he could for each of them, but he was so traumatized that he has never again seen even pictures of burns victims without experiencing the horror of that morning.

I was in the supply room beneath 'Little Robert" at Fort Shafter, one story down from the plotting room where Lockard's warning had been ignored. One lone Japanese bomber came over, but did not recognize the Radar Filter Center, and disappeared to the north without dropping a bomb. I took an oscilloscope tube up to our radar station at Fort Shafter. Looking down from there, the attack was in full force at Pearl Harbor and Hickam Field. Huge columns of smoke and flame were rising from battleship row and broken bombers littered the ramps at Hickam Field.

My brother, William Hamilton (Ham) Gunn was eating breakfast when the attacking planes began spitting fire through the massive windows in the new mess hall at Hickam. He dived for cover and escaped, but 121 men died at Hickam Field, 60 of them in that mess hail.

Kimmel was still in his bathrobe when he got the first news of the attack from a yeoman. He was still buttoning his white jacket as he stood in a neighbor's yard where he could see planes circling over the harbor.

"I knew right away that something terrible was going on," he later recalled, "that this was not a casual raid by a few stray planes."

Fuchida's flight sprayed bombs, torpedos and bullets for 25 minutes; then there was a 15-minute lull before 140 Japanese dive bombers and high-level bombers continued the attack on Pearl Harbor. While the first attack was still going on. the first of the B-17s from the U.S mainland came in for a landing at Hickam Field. The pilot had no idea he was flying into a war.

A flight of zeroes from the AKAGI attacked. The B-17 pilot gunned his engines and headed away from Hickam toward Bellows Field, but more zeroes from the SHOKAKU were waiting for him there. He came in high, wrecked his landing gear and slammed into a ditch at the end of the runway. The crew escaped with three wounded.

When a second B-17 attempted to land at Hickam, the AKAGI zeroes struck again, wounding several crewmen, one mortally. Eight of the big planes landed at Hickam, two at Haleiwa, one on a golf course at Kahuku, and one among the wrecked plane runways at Wheeler Field.

Astonishment was almost the universal reaction among U.S.. military forces during that first 25 minutes of attack from 7:55 to 8:20 —almost, but not quite. One navy Lieutenant was not all surprised to see the rising sun emblems on the attacking planes. He was John A. Williams, the only radio traffic code analyst who had argued that the prolonged radio silence of the Japanese carriers meant that they were at sea, not in their home bases. When the first explosions rocked the underground headquarters of intelligence station Hypo, he went upstairs to identify the attackers and came down to tell his co-workers flatly:

"They're Japanese aircraft and they're attacking Pearl Harbor."

The fleet intelligence officer, LtCdr Edwin T. Layton, acknowledged that he was astonished. Initially, most of the fury at Pearl Harbor was out of his sight and hearing. He lived east of Diamond Head. As he sped toward Pearl Harbor in his neighbor's, Lt. Paul Crosley's Cadillac roadster, the terrible explosions at Pearl Harbor sounded in their ears.

"I remember feeling that this was just a bad dream, that it could not be true," he later said.

All of the battleships were damaged. At the head of battleship row, OKLAHOMA's port side had been ripped open by torpedoes. When she capsized, more than 400 crew members were entombed.

Forward of ARIZONA, prompt flooding of the magazines had saved the WEST VIRGINIA from a monstrous explosion like that which destroyed the ARIZONA.

The MARYLAND and the TENNESSEE were least damaged of all the battleships. CALIFORNIA took two torpedoes and sank by the bow. NEVADA got up steam and made a run for the harbor entrance, but fear of blocking the harbor entrance caused her skipper to beach her at Waipio Pt. However, the NEVADA had drawn Japanese bombers away from the PENNSYLVANIA, the fleets flagship, which was a sitting duck in Dry Dock Number one.

Layton and Crosley arrived at the sub base, across the loch from the dry dock, just as a terrific explosion rocked the southern end of the harbor. A bomb had blown the bow off of the destroyer SHAW, which was sharing Dry Dock #1 with the PENNSYLVANIA and the destroyer CASSIN. When the dry dock was flooded, the burning oil on the water's surface ignited the magazines of the SHAW and the CASSIN. The explosion of the SHAW sent fingers of fire into the sky in all directions.

Looking out the window of his office, Layton could see the OKLAHOMA lying upside down and the ARIZONA engulfed in flames. It was just after 9:00 am. when the SHAW blew up with an explosive force second only to the explosion of the magazine on the ARIZONA.

When Layton went down to the operations room, he still did not know whether the Japanese carriers were launching their planes from north or south of Oahu. It never had occured to him to call the Army's Radar Filter Center at Fort Shafter. He was depending only upon Navy equiptment, mainly the 75–foot antenna of the top secret CKK–X direction finder concealed on a jungle peak to the north of Pearl Harbor. It later turned out that the Navy's telephone lines to it were army circuits, and the army had pulled the plugs when the attack began.

Informed that Layton didn't know whether the aircraft carriers were north or south of Oahu, Kimmel exploded:

True enough, no one had foreseen the breakdown in military foresight which accounted for the neglect of the radar reading from 7:02 to 7:39 a.m., tracking the 183 Japanese carrier planes being lead by Commander Fuchida in the first wave of attackers from 132 miles to within 30 miles north of Oahu. But due to the disregard of their record data, the very clear flight patterns from the north to south had remained at Opana, and never made it to the Radar Filter Center, "Little Robert" at Fort Shafter.

The attacking planes regrouped and flew back to their six carriers a few minutes before 10:00 am. It was all over in two hours, but no one on the stricken island of Oahu knew that that they would not be back. On the contrary, everyone assumed that the raiders would be back.

Fuchida's plane had been damaged, but after the other Japanese bombers had flown back northward toward their carriers, he circled high above Pearl Harbor photographing the scene below him. He reported:

"I counted four battleships definitely sunk and three severely damaged and extensive damage had been inflicted upon other types of ships. The seaplane base at Ford Island was all in flames, as were the airfields, especially Wheeler Field."

From Layton's count, Fuchida's tally of the destruction wrought was conservative. Four battleships and the UTAH had been sunk; four more severely damaged and only two were repairable locally. Three light cruisers, three destroyers, and three auxiliary craft had been put out of action, sunk or were a total loss. Further, the navy had lost 13 fighter planes, 21 scout bombers, 46 patrol bombers, and four dive bombers.

On the Japanese aircraft carrier AKAGI, as the time neared 12 o'clock noon, Admiral Nagumo feared that he had lost his flight commander, Fuchida. But eventually, Fuchida's bomber showed up, the last plane to be recovered by the AKAGI. The bomber had been damaged by Amrican anti–aircraft fire. One cable had been severed, but the plane could still land under the pilot's control. After Fuchida's estimate of damage to the U.S. fleet, Nagumo wanted to know two things:

1. Had the U.S. fleet been damaged enough to keep it out of action for six months?

2. Where were the American carriers?

Fuchida's answer to question number one was, "yes;" his answer to question number two was, "I don't know." He proposed launching another strike as soon as possible with the main targets to be Pearl Harbor oil storage farms and dockyard installations, particularly repair installations. Commander Minoru Genda, tactician on the staff of Admiral Nagurno, agreed with Fuchida that they should strike Pearl Harbor again as soon as possible. While the planes were being refueled and re-armed, Nagumo thought about it.

Like Admiral Nimitz, Nagumo was worried about the location of enemy carriers. The Japanese had lost only nine planes Out of the first *183* attackers, but 20 planes had failed to return out of the 167 planes in the second flight. Nagumo could expect even heavier losses from antiaircraft and fighter defenses which would be thoroughiy alerted for an afternoon raid.

Nagumo decided against further raids and ordered the Kido Butai to head for home.

Astonished when he saw what was happening, Fuchida dashed up to the bridge to protest. He was met by Nagumo's Chief of Staff, Rear Admiral Ryunosuke Kusaka, who confronted Fuchida, saying:

"The objective of the Pearl Harbor operation has been achieved."

So, at 4:30 p.m. (1630 hours), the massive fleet headed for home. Nagumo carried with him more than 400 Japanese pilots who were sure that they could have "finished the job." Fuchida was speechless with annoyance and frustration. "We could, at least, have blown up their fuel tanks," he thought.

If the attackers had destroyed the fuel reserves of the U.S. fleet, it would have forced our ships back to the West Coast. There was no place closer where we could have refueled. The fuel tanks were uncamouflaged and stood out clearly near the submarine base at Pearl Harbor.

THE FIFTH TALE
WHEN ARE THEY COMING BACK?

The Fifth Tale–When Are They Coming Back?

By shortly after 10:00 a.m., the Japanese planes had departed, leaving behind them the greatest destruction ever suffered by the U.S. Navy, including 2,403 American fatalities at a cost of 29 Japanese planes, 55 fatalities and one midget-submariner taken prisoner.

It was inconceivable to us, the American survivors (military and civilian), that after such a stunning blow, the Japanese would not press their advantage and make sure that the surviving ships in the U.S. fleet could not be repaired and refueled in Hawaii, that those ships which could make the trip would have to go to the West Coast, thus delaying any recovery of the U. S. fleet for operations against Japan by at least six months and maybe longer.

The unanimous question among Americans on Oahu by mid-morning of Dec. 7, 1941, was not, are they coming back, but when are they coming back?

It was not a question being asked just among stunned military forces as we buried our dead and began the incredible job of caring for the wounded and getting ready as fast as we could for the next attack with whatever armaments we had left. After all, everyone who lived in the Territory of Hawaii, regardless of occupation or ethnic background, had a stake in whether the Japanese would return and attempt to occupy Hawaii. Feeling against the Japanese military had run strongly among Chinese and Korean groups in Hawaii ever since the infamous "rape of Nanking" in 1937. Among the Korean-Hawaiians there had been repeated rumors of Comfort Women!! taken from Korea as unwilling prostitutes for Japanese troops in combat areas. (Those rumors, whether or not they were true at the time, later turned out to be all too evident in the Gilbert and Marshall Islands campaigns). Among Filipinos, the Japanese military was hated. And Hawaiians of Japanese ancestry felt caught in a trap by the Japanese attack.

Dan Inouye, who later would become a famous U.S. Senator from Hawaii, was a teenage senior at McKinley High School, who remembered his outrage as he rode his bicycle to the first-aid station at Lunalilo School during the Japanese air raid:

"They had worked so hard. They had wanted so desperately to be accepted, to be good Americans. And now, in a few cataclysmic minutes, it was all undone And then, pedaling along, it came to me at last that I would face that trouble, too, For my eyes were shaped just like those of the attackers and my people were only a generation removed from the land that had spawned these bombers, the land that had sent them to rain destruction on America, death on Americans. And choking with emotion, I looked up at the sky and called out, You dirty Japs!"

At least 57 Oahu civilians died and 280 were injured, some mortally. Records on civilian casualties were not well kept. Most of them occurred in Honolulu, and were due to faulty anti-aircraft fire. The attacking Japanese did not target civilians or any civilian landmarks, such as Honolulu Harbor or the Iolani Palace.

At 11:41 am., the army ordered the Honolulu commercial broadcasting stations off the air so that enemy planes could not use the radio signals for guidance. That sent virtually everyone in Honolulu who had short wave radio to spinning their dials in search of police and fire calls. At 7:14 that evening, it seemed that the long awaited resumption of hostilities had begun. A police broadcast sounded through the night air: 'Pearl Harbor is being bombed again."

Everyone in the vicinity rushed to a vantage point, looking toward Pearl Harbor. Surely enough, massive firing began. Tracer bullets lit up the sky and some planes caught fire and crashed, but the awful truth was that they were our planes. No Japanese planes were attacking. U.S. Navy pilots with empty fuel tanks from the carrier, ENTERPRISE, were trying to land at Ford Island in Pearl Harbor.

One of the pilots, Jim Daniels, remembered all too well what happened. Daniels was second-in-command of a flight of six F4F fighter planes and six scout planes which were sent off in the wrong direction (south of Oahu) to find the Japanese fleet. When they turned back toward the ENTERPRISE, they were refused permission to land and told to go on to Pearl Harbor:

"We turned on the heading toward Pearl," said Daniels. Everything was blacked out except burning ships, which we thought were burning cane fields. As we passed Diamond Head we turned toward Ford Island in

a loose formation and were given permission to land. Most of our gauges had indicated we were running out of fuel for the last 20 minutes.

"When we broke formation in preparation for landing, everything in Pearl Harbor opened up on us with their anti-aircraft batteries. The sky was ablaze with gun tracers.

"Ltjg. Fritz Hebel, the squadron commander, took off toward Wheeler Field, but was shot down and killed when he tried to land. Ens. Herb Menges crashed and was killed at Pearl City. Ens. Gale Hermann's plane took a 5-inch shell through his engine and spun in right on the Ford Island golf course. He survived. Ens. David Flynn bailed out over Barber's Point and we found him 10 days later at Tripler Army Hospital with a broken leg. Ens. Eric Allen was killed by a .50 caliber machine gun bullet after parachuting from his crippled plane.

"I called the Ford Island tower and told them I was coming in. I put my wheels down and headed back right over the harbor about 50 feet above the water.

"I roared past the foretop of the NEVADA. They turned all their guns on me, but nothing connected.

"Moments later I touched the runway. I overshot. There were two crash trucks in front of me at the end of the runway. I slammed on the brakes and spun around in a full circle on the first green of a golf course just beyond the field.

"I taxied back up the field. A marine gunner sprayed the plane with bullets. He just missed my head.

"Of the six planes and pilots, I was the only one to land intact; three others were killed."

Hardly anyone on Oahu slept that night. Two-and-a-half-ton trucks, loaded with punctured helmets, blood-stained uniforms and blankets rumbled into the armory all night at Kapalama and School Streets at Fort Shafter. Blackout was enforced. People weren't used to driving with blue cellophane over their headlights, and every few minutes, someone would crash over the street island on Kapalama.

Tripler General Hospital, Queens Hospital in Honolulu, and all other medical facilities were overloaded with the injured.

Nervous guards triggered machine-gun blasts aimed at wind-blown litter, dogs, cats—anything that moved. Soldiers sent out to relieve other soldiers on guard duty started singing God Bless America to keep from getting shot.

Everyone feared there would be another dawn raid, perhaps backed up this time by enemy landing troops.

An extra issued by the HONOLULU ADVERTISER contained a few scores of rumors which were being repeated 'round the island of Oahu. Readers were warned to be "on the watch for parachutists reported in Kalihi for a party of saboteurs that had been landed on Northern Oahu, distinguished by red discs on their shoulders for parachute troops sighted off Barber's Point," and for a man of "unannounced nationality" apprehended in the Punchbowl, "carrying a basket of pigeons."

It was hard to separate rumor from fact. Rumors spread like the wind.

There was the rumor that arrows had been cut in sugar cane fields to guide the attacking pilots to Pearl Harbor. Plantation managers near Pearl Harbor conducted a thorough search of their fields for such arrows. No arrows.

Another rumor was that Japanese drivers had deliberately blocked traffic on the roads to Pearl Harbor. Traffic jams froze cars, all right, when service personnel and civilian workers of all ethnic groups rushed to answer the first radio calls to get to their duty and employment stations. No sabotage was needed to explain those traffic jams.

Another rumor had Japanese plantation workers firing on soldiers from ambush on the big island of Hawaii. The commanding officer of army forces there found that "several engagements were fought by sentries at lonely outposts during the darkness against wandering porkers and stray mongrels."

The scariest rumor for GIs was that enemy paratroopers had landed and were calling on Japanese-Americans to join them.

What was so scary about that?

Well, one-third of Hawaii's population was of Japanese ancestry, approximately 120,000 Japanese-American citizens plus another 40,000 lsei or first-generation Japanese. Had the Japanese-Americans really been organized for sabotage, they would have been very hard to control. But there was a verified case of only one Japanese-American who was persuaded by a downed Japanese pilot to take over a piece of Hawaiian real estate.

That occurred on the island of Niihau, a small, isolated island, where sailing ships used to land for a supply of yams, located just three miles off the west coast of Kauai. In those days of the sailing ships, sailors called it "Yam Island." The pilot was Imperial Japanese Navy airman first class Shigenori Nishikaichi, Zero fighter pilot from the carrier, KIRYU. News of the attack on Oahu had not reached Niihau at the time that Nishikaichi crash-landed at 2:00 p.m.

Niihau was absentee-owned by the Robinson family who lived on Kauai. Its only connection with the outside world was by sampan to and from Kauai once a week (on Mondays). Niihau had no airport, no newspaper, and no radio station. Nearly everyone in the islands only town, Puuwai, was Hawaiian. One of the Hawaiians, Hawila Kaleohano, took away the pilot's identification papers and pistol, and placed him under arrest, intending to hold him and send him to Kauai when the weekly sampan arrived the next day.

However, the sampan failed to make its run on that Monday, Dec. 8, and Nishikaichi decided to re-arm himself and take over the island of Niihau. That was when he persuaded a young Japanese-American Nisei named Yoshio Harada to join him in taking the machine guns off of the wrecked Zero and to kill everyone in the village of Puuwai if they did not follow his orders.

A huge Hawaiian, Benehakka Kanahele, and his wife resisted the takeover, and the Japanese pilot shot the Hawaiian three times, wounding him in the left chest, left hip, and penis. That made Kanahele mad, "real mad," as he expressed it later, and he picked up Nishikaichi by the neck and leg and dashed him against a stone wall. Benehakka's wife, Ella, broke loose from Harada's grasp and beat the pilot with a rock. Kanahele drew a hunting knife and cut the airman's throat. The Japanese-American, Harada, then shot and killed himself

An American navy investigator reviewed the case and found cause to suspect that Japanese-American residents of Hawaii might switch allegiance if Japan should invade the islands, but his view was discredited by the fact that the U.S. army lieutenant who led 13 soldiers from Kauai across the channel to Niihau aboard a lighthouse tender to put down the brief threat (Lt. Jack Mizuha, Executive Officer, Burns Field, Kauai) was also a Japanese-American Nisei. Lt. Mizuha was amazed to find that

Kanahele and his wife put down the "Invasion of Niihau" all by themselves before he got there.

Another scary rumor was that the water supply on Oahu had been poisoned by Japanese parachutists. Unrelated facts seemed to verify that rumor. It was absolutely true that when the USS ARIZONA blew up, the ship settled on the 12-inch main water supply line from Oahu to Ford Island and crushed it. A six-inch water supply pipe from Ford Island to the navy yard side also was cut off due to other damage in the harbor. Emergency water supplies were pumped in from an artesian well on Ford Island and from a water tank, but water was in short supply and had to be rationed.

The idea that sabotage had something to do with it was understandable, but no poisoned water ever was involved.

Meanwhile, world news made it clear that Japan's raid on Pearl Harbor had been synchronized with bombing raids on Guam, Wake Island, Singapore, Hong Kong, Malaya, and two bombing raids on the Philippine Islands.

It never has been explained by anyone why General Douglas MacArthur lost three-fourths of the fighter aircraft under his command in a 30-minute bombing and strafing raid at Clark Field and on other air strips north of Manila, fully nine hours after he was informed of the attack on Pearl Harbor. Part of that was due to the fact that MacArthur knew nothing about radar. He was depending on coast watchers for air raid alerts. The raiding planes flew in from Formosa and caught U.S. planes on the ground. All were destroyed all except 17 of the B- 17 bombers (those 17 B-17s had been sent to Mindanao the day before the raid)..

Said one of MacArthur's B-17 pilots, "Our general and leaders committed one of the greatest errors possible to military men, that of letting themselves be taken by surprise.' How MacArthur escaped any charge of accountability for the loss of the U.S. air force in the Philippines, while Kimmel and Short were immediately judged guilty of negligence for the surprise attack at Pearl Harbor is a question that never has been answered.

Equally ignorant of radar and contemptuous of the chances of an aircraft attack against a powerful battleship was the British Commander of one of the Royal Navy's newest and biggest battleships, the PRINCE OF

WALES, Vice Admiral Tom Phillips. With no air cover at all and ineffectual air reconnaissance, the PRINCE OF WALES and REPULSE accompanied by four destroyers sailed from Singapore to take the new Pacific war to the Japanese on Dec. 8, Pearl Harbor attack day in the Far East. Two days later, on Dec. 10, both battleships were sent to the bottom in less than an hour with the loss of over 800 officers and men in an attack by 34 Japanese high level and 51 torpedo bombers.

In his own personal tragedy, as the result of fighting the first big Pacific Naval battle of World War II with World War I ideas, Vice Admiral Phillips went down with his flag ship, the PRINCE OF WALES. With the Vice Admiral went down any hopes of putting together immediately any sizable Allied naval force to thwart the Japanese advances in the Pacific. Not one aircraft carrier was available to Admiral Hart in the Asiatic fleet.

THE SIXTH TALE

NEVER MIND THE WAR–WHOM DO WE BLAME?

The Sixth Tale—Never Mind The War–Whom Do We Blame?

On the day after, Dec 8, Admiral Kimmel assembled his staff in his blacked-out submarine base headquarters, amid the stifling fumes and the odor of burning oil off of battleship row, and announced plans to begin offensive operations against Japan.

Pearl Harbor, he acknowledged was a disaster, but it was not the knockout of U.S. Naval forces that Admiral Yamamoto had designed it to be.

With the three undamaged aircraft carriers as nuclei, Kimmel could send two task forces into battle immediately, and could build up a third task force as soon as the SARATOGA (which was on its way to Pearl Harbor) arrived. Nine heavy cruisers and all but two light cruisers had survived the Dec. 7 attack, and so had all US. submarines.

As it turned out, that Monday was the only day that Kimmel would have to plan an attack with his staff, free of interference from higher authority in Washington. A panicky dispatch from Admiral Stark on Dec. 9 called for a pullback of all except patrol craft, naval aircraft and subs to the US Pacific Coast. Stark's dispatch wasn't advisory. It was a command. As one officer put it, Stark's dispatch seemed to envision the U.S. Navy as the defensive line for the Rocky Mountains.

That was on Tuesday. Then, on Wednesday, Dec. 10, Kimmel received the news that the PRINCE OF WALES and the REPULSE had been sunk off of Malaya, and the U.S. Asiatic Fleet and Air Force had been mostly destroyed at Cavite in the Philippines. Kimmel recognized immediately the tactical import of that news for the U.S. Pacific fleet. Without air cover, Allied forces in the Philippines would be lost and the Japanese would be free to rampage with their troop ships landing in Malaya, Indo-China, Wake Island, Guam, Hong Kong, Singapore, and Midway. There was no way that he could get the Pacific fleet to Manila in time to thwart the Japanese there, but he could get a task force to Wake Island and save the Americans and their base there. No, better than that, the offensive-minded Kimmel could use Wake as a trap for the Japanese. He started planning how to do that.

84

On the Allied political front in London, an eager Churchill had declared war on Japan on Dec. 8, two hours before FDR did in Washington. Then, the American president, unwilling to risk the unified outrage of the American people against Japan to be distracted by a U.S. declaration of war on Germany, waited for an arrogant Hitler to fulfill his tripartite pact with Japan and Italy and declare war on the U.S., which Hitler obligingly did on Dec. 11. Hitler's move made Roosevelt's Declaration of War against Nazi Germany just a reciprocal action. Meanwhile, Secretary of the U.S. Navy Frank Knox boldly advocated the evacuation of Hawaiian-Americans of Japanese ancestry as well as alien Japanese in Hawaii to the island of Molokai (never pausing to reflect, providing he was aware of it at all, that he was talking about one-third of Hawaii's population and many of its outstanding citizens) and asked and got FDR's approval for a personal visit to Oahu "to avert the prospect of a nasty congressional investigation."

Of course, Knox's investigation of Pearl Harbor would do nothing to avert a congressional investigation, and not to be outdone by the navy, the army planned its investigation of Pearl Harbor. So, in icy cold weather, the parallel army and navy investigations were launched within a few hours of each other from the east coast, with the army plane carrying Col. Charles W. Bundy as its chief investigator and the navy Lockheed carrying Knox as its chief investigator.

Only one of the planes made it to the West Coast. Bundy's plane crashed into the High Sierras and killed all aboard. A shaken Frank Knox made it to San Diego and switched to a four-engine PB2Y Coronado flying boat. The base archeological officer assured Knox that he would have smooth flying weather from the West Coast to Hawaii, but Knox insisted that the weather forecaster make the flight with him. The flying boat was packed with blood plasma and serum for burn victims on Oahu, and the takeoff had to be attempted a second time before the plane got clear of the water. The San Diego archeological officer had to stand up for the entire flight, due to the presense of three Knox staff members. What the archeological officer thought of the Navy Secretary would not bear repeating.

It was Admiral Kimmel's idea to get Knox's approval for the Pacific fleet to take the offensive. Kimmel's preparations for the relief of Wake

Island were occupying him and his staff when Knox landed at Kaneohe Bay early on Thursday am., Dec. 11. It had been a red-eye flight with all aboard huddled in flying gear and blankets. The only military experience that Knox, a former newspaper publisher, could boast of was that he was one of the "rough riders" who had charged up San Juan Hill with Teddy Roosevelt. To preserve his impartial posture as an investigator, Knox had ordered that he "would not be the guest of any senior officer." Instead, he was driven to the Royal Hawaiian Hotel, where he was met by Admiral Kimmel for their trip to Kimmel's submarine base headquarters at Pearl Harbor.

Tired, disgruntled, horrified, frightened, angry and outraged would sum up the state of the Navy Secretary as he rode the ferry across to Ford Island through burned, oil-soaked bodies which were being fished from the ruins of ships in Pearl Harbor. Equally horrible were the sights of burns victims at Hospital Point, where Knox toured the wards. Some of the men still breathing were charred beyond recognition.

At Kimmel's headquarters, Knox mostly listened, but he did ask Kimmel if the admiral had received the Saturday alert from Washington that Japan planned to attack Pearl Harbor within 72 hours.

Kimmel's response was: "What alert?"

Incredulous, Knox asserted:

"Well, we sent one."

Kimmel concentrated on a strong plea for sending a relief expedition to Wake Island, and got the Navy Secretary's approval for that.

Afterward, Knox went to the intelligence office of LCdr. Layton, where he saw all of the photographs of the attack which had been taken by navy photographers. All were restricted. None had been released for publication. It was hard for Knox to remain objective about that. After all, he had been publisher of the Chicago Daily News and with just one of those spectacular photographs, he could have provided his old newspaper with the scoop of the century. But he resisted the temptation.

Instead, he asked Layton the same question which he had asked Kimmel:

"Did you get our message?"

"What message?" Layton asked.

"We sent a message to tell you to be alert for an attack," Knox replied.

Layton shook his head, "Sir, as far as I know, we never got one; at least, I never saw it."

General Short came to Pearl Harbor and met briefly with Knox, then had a longer meeting with the navy secretary at Fort Shafter the next morning. Short received no immediate impression that he was being adjudged by Knox as responsible for the surprise attack.

Just 32 hours after he arrived in Hawaii, Knox collected the navy photographs of the attack, took along some hachimaki bandanas which the Japanese pilots had worn about their temples, and a few spent Japanese machine gun bullets, and left Kaneohe for the return to the mainland with his three aides. As the plane took off, he said to one of the aides, Capt. Frank Reilly:

"Frank, you will be glad to hear. . that the relief force for Wake Island soon will be on its way.

Meanwhile, U.S. Marine Major James P. Devereaux and his 500-man garrison at Wake Island repelled a Japanese invasion fleet consisting of two light cruisers, four destroyers, and four troop ships by sinking two of the destroyers and a troop ship.

It was the first cheering news Kimmel had received since the Pearl Harbor attack. He directed his staff to bring every U.S. ship the Pacific fleet could muster into the relief operation for Wake Island. He would use Wake Island as the bait to lure the Japanese navy into a trap.

The LEXINGTON would make a diversionary move in the Marshall Islands to pin down enemy air and surface forces there. Admiral William F. Halsey's Task Force 8 with the aircraft carrier ENTEPRISE would operate west of Johnston Island as cover for Oahu and a support force for Wake. The SARATOGA would be the strike force to make sure that the seaplane tender, TANGIER, would land ammunition and supplies to the Wake garrison.

It would all get started as soon as the SARATOGA (which was on its way from the West Coast) arrived at Pearl Harbor.

But for Kimmel, that's as far as he would be involved before the axe fell on him from Washington. FDR announced that a formal investigation would be made by a presidential commission to be headed by Supreme

Court Justice Owen J. Roberts. But before other members of the commission were named on Dec. 17, Knox announced the removal of Kimmel and Short from their commands on Dec. 16, and the appointment of Rear Admiral Chester W. Nimitz as Commander in Chief, Pacific.

The abrupt removal of Kimmel and Short assisted final responsibility for the attack before any official investigation was announced, much less carried out. That certainly took the heat off of anybody in Washington for not having sent to the Pearl Harbor commanders a pre-attack alert that Pearl Harbor was the next target and completed the cover-up for the Department of Naval Operations, the Department of Naval intelligence and the Roosevelt Administration. Absolute secrecy was imposed in the name of national security which successfully gagged the two scapegoats, Kimmel amd Short, until years after the fact of their dismissal.

Until Nimitz would arrive at Pearl Harbor, Admiral Pye was to be temporary Pacific fleet commander. That dumbfounded Layton. Pye was the man who had discounted Layton's predicition of any Japanese action against the U.S. Pye really had not recovered from the shock of being so categorically wrong in his pre-raid smugness that Japan would not attack the U.S anywhere in the Pacific. He surely was not the man to seize the initiative in the bold manner which Kimmel had outlined for the Pacific fleet at Wake Island. He liked to wait for enemy action and then react to it.

Pye entered his own staff into the funereal Kimmel headquarters at Pearl Harbor, but he had to rely on Layton for intelligence and to depend upon Kimmel's war plans section for the Wake operation.

On the rainy Christmas morning, 1941, when Admiral Nimitz flew in to the east loch of Pearl Harbor, his first question was:

"What news of the relief of Wake?"

He was told that the island had surrendered and the relief expedition had been recalled.

Nimitz became silent and remained so during the trip in a whaleboat past the upturned hulks of the OKLAHOMA and UTAH. The harbor still reeked of oil fumes and bloated corpses were still surfaceing from submerged ships.

When he saw Kimmel at the submarine base wharf Nimitz said simply, "You have my sympathy," and invited him to sit down for a working breakfast.

High rankers, army and navy, generally are not good listeners. They usually give commands and listen only to very few subordinates, if any. Nimitz was an exception. He really listened. He showed the same consideration to Kimmel's staff that he had to Kimmel, and he won them over with his determination to lift their morale and restore the reputation of the fleet under his command.

Layton assumed that because he had failed to read the silence of the Japanese carrier forces correctly, he would 'go down with the ship" as Kimmel had. He, in effect, offered his resignation as Fleet Intelligence Officer, saying he wanted to go to sea, preferably in command of a destroyer. Similar offers were made by other members of Kimmel's staff.

Everyone on the staff knew that the American military situation in the Pacific was desperate when Nimitz, acting as a submariner, broke out his four-star flag on the deck of the submarine, Grayling, at Pearl Harbor, Throughout the long Pacific war, his flagship would be a submarine.

Thanks to Kimmel's planning, Nimitz had before him within three days of his installation as CINCPAC, detailed proposals for a series of carrier strikes against the Gilbert and Marshall Islands. Added to the Pacific fleet on orders from Admiral King was the carrier YORKTOWN, recalled from duty in the Atlantic. YORKTOWN was to operate with troop convoys to reinforce Samoa.

Nimitz drew fire from other flag officers at Pearl Harbor, but he had a firm backer in Admiral Halsey, his old friend, and Halsey immediately sailed with the ENTERPRISE and Task Force 8 with orders to join up with YORKTOWN. However, before those two carriers got into action, disaster struck Nimitz's fleet again.

Five-hundred miles south of Oahu, the carrier SARATOGA was torpedoed, limped into Pearl Harbor, and had to go to the West Coast for major repairs.

The new damage fell heavily on Layton as Nimitz's fleet intelligence officer. It was vital to Nimitz to know what the Japanese fleet was doing and just as vital to prevent the enemy from learning of his plans.

On Jan. 3, 1942, all allied commands were alerted not to use any U.S. codes and ciphers which might have been captured on Wake Island by the Japanese. Nimitz made it clear that he understood and appreciated the role of intelligence. He assured Layton that he considered him well qualified and competent for his job, told him to come to his office at any time with any bits of information on a priority basis. Layton and Nimitz's flag secretary were the only two members of his staff so privileged. Then, Nimitz added:

"I want you to be the Admiral Nagumo of my staff. I want your every thought, every instinct as you believe Admiral Nagumo might have them. You are to see the war, their operations, their aims from the Japanese viewpoint and keep me advised what you are thinking about, what you are doing, and what purpose, what strategy, motivates your operations. If you can do this, you will give me the kind of information needed to win this war."

Layton was inspired and resolved that the mistakes which had led to Pearl Harbor would not be repeated, and he knew where the acid test for his intelligence operaton in the Pacific would probably center. It would be when the Japanese fleet made its move on Midway. Through hell and high water, he would not tolerate intelligence blockage from Washington or anywhere else this time.

THE SEVENTH TALE

WHERE IS THE ASIATIC FLEET?

The Seventh Tale–Where Is The Asiatic Fleet?

What happened on that first day of World War II in the Pacific to eliminate the U.S. Far East Air Force as an effective weapon?

Back in Washington, D.C., that's what Major General Henry (Hap) Arnold, Chief of the U.S. Army Air Corps, wanted to know. Immediately upon receiving news of the Pearl Harbor attack, Arnold had telephoned the Air Force Commander under MacArthur, Major General L. H. Brereton in the Philippine Islands, to warn him that the war with Japan had started and not to get caught with his planes on the ground. That call was completed about 4:00 am., Dec. 8, Manila time, 2:00 p.m. or 1400, Dec. 7, Washington time; 9:00 am., Dec. 7, Honolulu time.

An hour later, at about 5:00 am., Manila time, Brereton tried to see MacArthur to get his permission to bomb Japanese air bases on Formosa as soon as his bombers could get armed and air borne. Brereton got as far as MacArthur's chief of staff, Brig. General Richard K. Sutherland, but could not get through to MacArthur. After some delay, Brereton was told by Sutherland to prepare his bombers for the attack on Formosa, but to await word from MacArthur before launching the attack.

Meanwhile, Japanese bombers struck Luzon at dawn. Mindful of Arnold's warning not to get caught with his planes grounded, Brereton, ordered all U.S. planes at Clark Field air borne, but also mindful of Sutherland's admonition not to attack the Japanese without MacArthur's approval, the bombers flew without bombs.

Shortly before noon, the all clear sirens sounded without any Japanese bombers having appeared over Clark Field. The 35 B-17s landed, and their crews went to eat lunch. All of the U.S. fighter planes were low on gas and circling to land.

Bear in mind that neither MacArthur's army nor Harts Asiatic fleet had any radar guarding the Philippines bases

Why?

Well, because MacArthur and his staff had not done their homework about the uses of radar. In other words, they were ignorant and untrained about it, even though it was available to them through the U.S. Signal Corps. MacArthur had made no attempt to get it shipped and installed or to learn how to use it. As for Admiral Hart, he had been given so little information by MacArthur that he didn't know what the man was or was not doing. MacArthur acted as if his plans for U.S. Army Air Forces in the Philippines had nothing to do with Hart's plans for the Asiatic fleet.

After learning from Sutherland and MacArthur that his Asiatic fleet was completely unprotected by coastal radar in the Philippines, Admiral Hart received assurance from Admiral Harold R. Stark in Washington that a fine new radar installation was in operation off the coast of Chile on the Galapagos Islands. Hart replied that it made him very happy to learn that the Admiral Yamamoto had given the U.S. fleet time to recover any offensive power, what a difference that would make.

Meanwhile, 78,000 American GIs and untold thousands of Filipino soldiers would pay a terrible price in Japanese war prisons for the negligence of their commanders. Twenty-nine thousand of the American POWs would die in those prisons. That number was small compared with the fatalities which would be suffered by the Filipinos.

The Philippines were lost when MacArthur's air force was lost and the Asiatic fleet, what was left of it, fled south to Australia.

Admiral Hart's navy "air force," Patrol Wing 10, consisted of 28 seaplanes (very slow and no match for Japanese Zeroes or dive bombers) which escaped destruction by being shipped to Davao or concealed in high grass behind Manila or at Olongapo or at Sangley Point. Seaplane tenders CHILDS, WILLIAM B. PRESTON, and HERON were scattered to escape destruction by bombing.

Five days before the war started, Hart had set up Task Force I with himself as commander, based on Manila Bay. Task Force I consisted of 29 submarines, tenders OTUS, CANOPUS, and HOLLAND, with rescue ship PIGEON, Patrol Wing 10, six motor torpedo boats, five destroyers; and two tankers, PECOS and TRINITY.

At war's outbreak, Task Force 5 was already steaming away from Manila, headed south. It included cruisers HOUSTON and MARBLEHEAD, eight destroyers and their tender, BLACKHAWK, under command of Rear Admiral William Glassford. At the last minute, the cruiser BOISE was added to Task Force 5. BOISE's primitive radar gave some help to Admiral Glassford in directing his little force southward. In his log, Glassford noted:

"Not once during the ensuing days were our feeble efforts at sea, either on the offensive or the defensive, supported in the air. While lacking many things, we felt the lack of air support more than anything else."

Task Force 5 crawled south at the speed of its slowest ship, TRINITY (top speed, 10 knots). In Makassar, capital of the Celebes, the rumor was that a large, unidentified naval force was headed toward Task Force 5. Was it Japanese?

Commander Albert de Bats, a Dutch naval officer, climbed into the only aircraft available adjusted his goggles (it was an open two-seater) and shouted to the ground crew above the roar of his single engine, "If I don't come back, they are Japanese." He came back to Task Force 5 and survived, temporarily.

When the Japanese bombers raided Cavite on Dec. 10, the crew of LANIKAI did not wait for orders or for their captain. They headed out of harm's way and hid along the bay shore. From their safe vantage point, they could see fiery destruction at Cavite, and they agreed among themselves regretfully that their skipper must lie slain somewhere in that catastrophic funeral pyre. But the next morning, they dutifully returned to Cavite and found Skipper Tolley alive.

Tolley had orders from Lt Commander D. L. Smith, skipper of the OAHU, to "search for and report all approaching vessels and aircraft."

For the next week, enemy planes would attack Corregidor, then drop at low level to strafe whatever was still floating in the harbor. LANIKAI sailed slowly back and forth outside of the Harbor entrance, drawing occasional machine gun fire from a strafing aircraft, which the LANIKAI crewmen answered with their two .30 caliber Lewis machine guns. Unfortunately, LANIKAI's guns could be elevated only about 20 degrees skyward, and Tolley noted ruefully that they never hit any of the attacking planes. On the other hand, the strafing planes didn't hit the LANIKAI either.

LANIKAI had been picking her way through minefields every day for the first week of the war, but on Dec. 17, tragedy struck a much trimmer and faster vessel, loaded with 700 refugees from Manila (the 1,900 ton, 318 feet long CORREGIDOR—top speed 22 knots).

For some reason unknown, the CORREGIDOR, whose skipper had just received clear instructions on how to maneuver a dog-leg past the

94

minefield, veered sharply and picked up speed as she headed directily into the minefield. Lt. Commander George E. Pollak described what happened then:

"A few moments later she struck a mine. Within a few minutes only debris, floating on the swift and deep-running currents of the channel, remained as indications of the short-lived tragedy. The small boats that ventured into the area managed to pick up some survivors .

MacArthur's dramatic promise to "fight to destruction at the beaches" faded into a retreat of the regular U.S. Army, the Philippine Army and Reserves, and the Philippine Scouts into Bataan Peninsula. That followed shortly after Japanese troops first came ashore at Lingayen.

The increasing desperation of all American forces in the Philippines brought no meeting of the minds between MacArthur and Hart. MacArthur continued to issue unilateral orders without any consultation with Admiral's Hart, Rockwell, or any other Navy men. When Hart offered to discuss with MacArthur navy plans, MacArthur made no response, asked no questions and generally acted if the navy's plans had nothing to do with him and vice versa.

The climax of this non-communication with any other service came on Dec. 24 with MacArthur's announcement that he was declaring Manila an Open City, which left naval vessels at Cavite even more vulnerable to air and ground attack. Belligerents are not supposed to bomb places which their enemies have declared "open cities," but the Japanese paid no attention to that.

Two days later, Admiral Hart, having cleared his remaining ships out of Manila, sailed for Java on the U.S. Submarine SHARK.

LANIKAI and everything else left afloat by the U.S. Navy was relieved of any scouting duty and left to fend for itself. Of the surface warships which threaded their way out of Manila Bay past the mined and heavily-bombed Corregidor Channel, the only one that was still afloat in April was the LANIKAI, from then on dubbed "the lucky LANIKAI."

She sailed at night and tried to reach a safe hiding place by daylight. To chart their moves the crewmen had a journal which gave descriptions of places where they might anchor. On Dec. 27, 1941, they anchored in a semi-enclosed bay on the west coast of Mindoro, which was described in their journal as, "Well protected from wind and sea, an admirable sand beach, and high escarpments surrounding three sides that make an effective place of concealment."

Five Japanese bombers roared over them at 11:00 am., apparently didn't see the LANIKAI or didn't consider it worth bothering with, and flew on. But in the area that the LANIKAI had just left, 18 heavy Japanese bombers hit Corregidor at lunchtime; 18 more hit defenseless Manila; and a few minutes later, 18 more bombers hit Mariveles; followed by ten more bombers over Corregidor; nine over Manila at 12:45 a.m.; and another 18 at 1:30 p.m. over Corregidor.

In response, six American PBYs attacked Japanese-occupied Job, south of where LANIKAI's skipper, Kemp Tolley and his small crew of Filipinos and Americans tried to get some sleep amid all of the enemy air activity.

Four of the six PBYs were shot down. Five survivors were captured. Two were tortured and burned to death for refusal to give information.

LANIKAI's only link with civilization was an "Echophone" radio receiver, a little grey metal box. When five minutes of news was announced by the sounds of London's Big Ben, all pumps, generators, the Coca-cola cooler, and anything else that could cause electrical interference was cut off, and the crew listened intently to the clipped British accents of the announcers for news of the war. Very little about the Far East came across, but through heavy static, the LANIKAI listeners heard the announcment that Hong Kong had fallen and that 11,000 British prisoners had been captured .by the Japanese.

Tolley reflected that perhaps it was just as well they didn't receive much news. In late December, there was nothing but disasters for the Allies to report, and in their small ship, without money or orders and no home port, making their way blindly in search of safe anchorages, hunted by day and in strange waters by night, morale could not stand much more bad news. Not only was their eventual destination unknown. Their day-by-day destinations were unknown.

LANIKAI's situation was a little worse than typical, but the entire allied naval situation was chaotic, and from his beleagured "rock" (Corregidor) MacArthur wasted no time in placing the blame for his disastrous situation on the navy. He radioed Washington:

"I suggest Washington employ counter propaganda especially with reference to activity our navy to offset crescendo of enemy propaganda which has appeared in all elements of society, claiming U.S. inactivity in support of Filipino effort, with especial reference to apparent inactivity of U.S. Naval Forces. This theme is now being used with deadly effectiveness and I am not in a position here to combat it."

That was the beginning of verbal warfare between MacArthur and the Navy, extending from Washington to Australia. Admiral Hart had not yet arrived in Java aboard the submarine SHARK. When he did and learned of MacArthur's charges against the navy, the fireworks started.

On Christmas Eve, Wake Island fell to the Japanese.

That New Year's eve among American forces in the Pacific was the gloomiest any American armies had spent since Valley Forge. In blacked-out Honolulu, martial law prevailed and the Roberts Commission from Washington, D.C., had been in town for nine days, investigating Pearl Harbor.

THE EIGHTH TALE

VICTORY DISEASE

The Eighth Tale–Victory Disease

It had all been too easy and the Japanese, even in their central Pacific bastion (the Marshall Islands, where they should have been most alert) were suffering from victory disease. Relaxing comfortably over banquet toasts of warm sake with the victories at Pearl Harbor, Wake Island, Hong Kong, and in the Philippines; the Imperial Japanese Naval Intelligence was further cheered by the report from Submarine I-6 that it had torpedoed and sunk the American aircraft carrier, LEXINGTON.

Actually, they had torpedoed the SARATOGA, which looked so much like the LEXINGTON that it could be considered a reasonable mistake, but neither carrier was sunk. The SARATOGA limped into Pearl Harbor for repairs that made her seaworthy again, and then went on to the West Coast for extensive repairs. The LEXINGTON steamed ahead undamaged, getting ready for its next assault on Japanese territory in the central Pacific.

But at Naval intelligence headquarters in Tokyo, they didn't realize that the SARATOGA had joined the U.S. fleet in the Pacific, and they took the first report of the submarine I-6 at face value and counted the LEXINGTON as sunk, which by their reckoning reduced the U.S. carrier force in the Pacific to just one—the ENTERPRISE. Therefore, they concluded that Nimitz had been forced to cancel all ideas of launching an offensive operation for at least six months.

How could they make such a crucial mistake?

It was because our two remaining task forces, based around the LEXINGTON and the ENTERPRISE, maintained radio silence. So the Japanese auditing of radio signals gave them no clue of the carrier which was actually headed for Kwajalein in the Marshall Islands, the ENTERPRISE.

Furthermore, Yamamoto had no intelligence officer on his staff to double check his commanders in the field. In fact, the very evening before the American attack, Rear Admiral Sukeyoshi Yatsushiro threw a victory banquet celebrating the supposed sinking of the USS LEXINGTON. The Japanese superbattleship YAMATO was anchored at Hashirajima with direct cable, radio and telephone connections to Tokyo.

100

Just as in the case of Lockard's and Elliott's radar warning at Oahu on Dec. 7, 1941, the Japanese ignored an advance warning. Their 6th Communications Unit at Kwajalein. transmitted a warning to Tokyo Intelligence Headquarters that recently there had been an increase of a dozen or so new American radio call signals—a sure sign that the Americans were up to some kind of offensive action. But the Tokyo Intelligence Hq. did not issue any general alert to the field commander at Kwajalein, Admiral Yatsushiro.

After all, they reasoned, the Americans could not possibly mount any threat to the Marshall Islands for at least six months. That had been Admiral Nagumo's conclusion after he headed back home from Pearl Harbor, and who was qualified to second-guess him? Admiral Yatsushiro went ahead with his banquet and did not call an alert at Kwajalein.

Yatsushiro suffered a fate worse than Admiral Kimmel had. It cost Kimmel his career, but it cost Yatsushiro his life. Yatsushiro became the first Japanese flag officer killed in the Pacific war. He was promoted posthumously from rear admiral to admiral. [Of course, Yatsushiro was not the first flag officer killed a few hours before the Pacific war began. That was American Rear Admiral Kidd, killed aboard the USS ARIZONA at Pearl Harbor].

At the same time that the Japanese were becoming complacent and negligent in their Intelligence operations, the Americans were learning fast not to take anything for granted and to expand their intelligence activities.

For example, Admiral Halsey had borrowed a radio intelligence unit from Oahu's Station Hypo to accompany him on his flagship ENTERPRISE as it sped toward Kwajalein. The four-man unit consisted of a marine captain who spoke Japanese, Bankson T. Holcomb, Jr., and three radio operators. Halsey hoped to intercept some clue as to whether or not he had been detected by the Japanese.

Late in the afternoon before the attack, Holcomb intercepted a radio message from a Japanese pilot in a patrol plane, saying he had reached the limit of his patrol area, was returning to his base, and had "nothing to report." The date was January 31, 1942, less than two months had elapsed of the minimal six months which the Japanese supposed it would take for the Americans to make an offensive move in the Pacific.

A gleeful Halsey, confident that his ships had not been detected, dictated a "Thank you for not spotting us" note, and addressed it to "the commanding officer of Marshall Islands forces." Captain Holcomb translated it into Japanese and mimeographed leaflets which were dropped along with the bombs from the attacking planes on Kwajalein and the other Marshall Islands bases the next day.

Ruefully, Yamamoto's Chief of Staff Matome Ugaki, Etajima classmate and close friend of Admiral Yatsushiro, wrote in his diary:

"We were asleep at the switch. To be so completely suprised, long after the start of a war, is incredible."

For nine hours, starting at dawn, American pilots from the ENTERPRISE strafed and bombed Japanese ships and shore installations at Kwajalein. Not only Japanese complacency, but the weather also was with the Americans. Halsey retired with good cloud cover under a northeast weather front. American pilots claimed that they had sunk a submarine, auxiliary vessels, and a small carrier. It was not so. The ENTERPRISE planes had not sunk a single Japanese ship, and had lost 13 of their own planes, but they had killed Yatsushiro and done extensive damage both to warships and supply vessels in the harbor and to shore installations at Kwajalein.

Frantic attempts by every Japanese radio intelligence station from Tokyo to Jaluit in the Marshall Islands tried to track Halsey's ships, but the American task force got away without being detected.

Back at Pearl Harbor, Nimitz's fleet intelligence officer Layton had made another valuable discovery as a result of Halsey's raid. The Japanese had no radar installed in their Marshall Islands fortresses. They apparently did not realize that the radar installed at Oahu had done its job and that it was human error at the Oahu filter center which had failed to sound the alert at Pearl Harbor. Were they unfamiliar with the potential of radar for advance warning of air raids in their homeland as well as in their advance bases in the Pacific or, as had been the case with us in Hawaii, just neglectful in their uses of it?

In a prophetic statement from Tokyo, Captain Yashitake Miwa, Yamamoto's Chief of Naval Operations, was quoted as saying:

"Whatever happens, we must absolutely prevent any air attack on Tokyo"

Layton realized that the Japanese capability to decipher our radio traffic was improving just as our ability to read their radio traffic was. Decoding Station Hypo on Oahu had worked out that the letter "M" clearly stood for locations in the Philippines, that "MINI' represented Manila, "MD" appeared to be Davao; "R" was Rabaul; "PT" was Truk in the Caroline Islands (a huge Japanese naval base); and "PY" was Jaluit.

But our ace-in-the-hole was radar, both land-based and aboard U.S. warships.

In a move which made a lot more sense than had been used in nailing Admiral Kimmel and General Short as responsible for the Pearl Harbor disaster (while leaving Chief of Naval Operations Turner, Admiral Stark, General George C.Marshall, and members of the Roosevelt Administration in Washington blameless) the Roberts Commission recommended that the Distinguished Service Cross be awarded to Private Joe Lockard and sent him to Officer Candidate School as a full-fledged hero back in the states. (Why they didn't do the same for Private Elliott who had worked with Lockard on every radar reading that fateful morning of Dec. 7, 1941, I don't know and they never said).

In the Signal Corps, Aircraft Warning Company on Oahu we knew that Elliott had been the trainee who prompted Lockard to continue scanning the area north of Kahuku Point when their chow truck was late to carry them to breakfast, but little facts like that seemed to escape the Roberts Commission along with some very crucial facts, i.e. in Washington, witnesses from the war and navy departments had been permitted to hear each other's testimony and were even told "to cooperate in their answers." But neither Short nor Kimmel were so privileged, which gave the impression of a lack of cooperation between the commandants of the army and navy forces in Hawaii.

The biggest mistake that the Roberts Commission encouraged for press coverage was that Kimmel knew as much about war warnings as Washington did. After a month of hearings, the commission carefully omitted any mention of "Magic," the vital intelligence source in Washington, from its report. That must be kept secret, the commission maintained. The effect was to omit Washington's failure to inform Kimmel and Short of Radio Tokyo's East Wind Rain directive to their task force, Kido Butai.

When Roosevelt released the Roberts' Commission report to the press in Washington (on a Saturday, in time for full coverage in Sunday's papers) newsmen and editors concluded that Kimmel and Short were entirely to blame for lack of preparedness for the attack, and that the secretaries of state, war, and the navy had "fulfilled their obligations," along with the chief of naval operations.

Short resigned immediately. Kimmel held out till Jan. 28, 1942, then resigned. FDR directed that retirement had been granted to both officers "without condonation of any offense or prejudice to future disciplinary actions." Both officers were essentially gagged and prevented from examining the secret intelligence files in Washington by the need for wartime secrecy and national unity.

Hate mail to Kimmel and Short poured in, containing death threats and charges of treason. They had to remain silent for fear of violating national security.

Meanwhile, less than two months after the disaster at Pearl Harbor, Admiral "Bull" Halsey returned to Pearl Harbor, the nation's first triumphant combat hero. Sirens, horns and whistles cut loose in a gala welcome as sailors lined the rails of every ship in Pearl Harbor to cheer the ENTERPRISE.

Admiral Nimitz didn't wait for a gangplank. He was hoisted to the deck of the ENTERPRISE in a bosun's chair to greet and congratulate his old friend, Bill Halsey, personally.

Japanese troops were pushing MacArthur's army down the Bataan Peninsula. American and Dutch naval forces were being driven out of the Dutch East Indies. The Japanese were invading Singapore. But Halsey's victory in the Marshalls claimed the headlines in the states. It was the only good news for the Allies in the Pacific since the war had started.

The Japanese civilians were told nothing about the Kwajalein raid. Radio Tokyo reported only Japanese victories throughout the Pacific. But Admirals Yamamoto and Nagumo suffered no longer from victory disease. They needed better intelligence about the number and whereabouts of the American aircraft carriers, and Yamamoto made plans to draw the American carriers into a trap at Midway.

Figure 1
Honolulu 1941. The last days of peace.

Figure 2
Lt. Comdr. Ken Landis, USNR

Figure 3
Staff Sgt. Rex Gunn, USAR

Figure 4
**Called the Pink Palace of Waikiki or the Pink Lady of Waikiki, The
Royal Hawaiian Hotel, catered to very wealthy and prominent
tourists. An evening of dining and dancing at the Royal was
considered the height of elegance. After Marital Law was declared,
the Navy, in particular, Submariners, took over the Royal.**
Photo by Ken Landis

Figure 5
Young U.S. Navy Ensign Ken Landis sits outside his Kahala Beach apartment, little dreaming that the beach soon would be strung with barbed wire and manned by U.S. Infantry troops.
Photo by Ken Landis

Figure 6
A peacetime outrigger crew prepares to launch from the
Moana Hotel Beach.
Photo by Ken Landis

Figure 7
The familiar and popular Banyan Tree court at the Moana Hotel in the middle of Waikiki beach. The scene is virtually the same in 1999. Extensive remodeling has preserved the 1920's decor of the hotel and Banyan Court.
Photo by Ken Landis

Figure 8
November 1941. On the beach at Kahala, Honolulu's finest beach.
Koko Head looms in the distance.
Photo by Ken Landis

Figure 9
**Japanese boy in front of sampans, long suspected as being used for
espionage on US. Fleet. November 1941.**
Photo by Ken Landis

Figure 10
June 1943. Hula dancers on the grounds of the
Royal Hawaiian Hotel.
Photo by Ken Landis

Figure 11
Diamond Head as viewed from the Halekulani Hotel.
November 1941.
Photo by Ken Landis

Figure 12
Battleship row consisting of the sunken West Virginia and Tennessee
burn furiously as small craft try to save survivors in the water.
U.S. Navy Photo

Figure 13
First official notification of Pearl Harbor attack.
December 7, 1941.

Figure 14
The wreckage of the destroyers Cassin and Downes in Drydock #1.
The battleship Pennsylvania in the background was not as severely
damaged and was repaired quickly.
U.S. Navy Photo

Figure 15
**Admiral Husband E. Kimmel (center), Commander in Chief of the
U.S. Pacific Fleet in 1941, conferring with his chief of staff, Captain
William Smith (right), and his operations officer,
Captain W.S. DeLany.**
U.S. Navy Photo

Figure 16
USS Arizona burns furiously after being destroyed by a direct hit on forward ammunition magazine.
U.S. Navy Photo

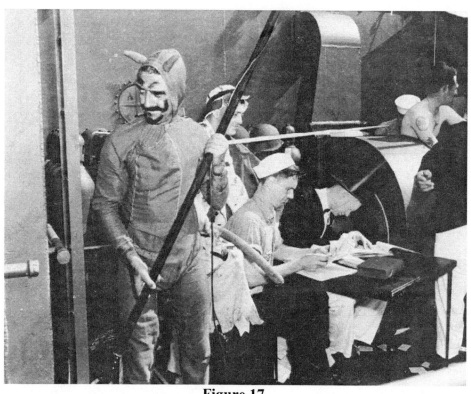
Figure 17
"Crossing the Line" ceremony, Spring 1942. First convoy to
Australia, USS Pelias.

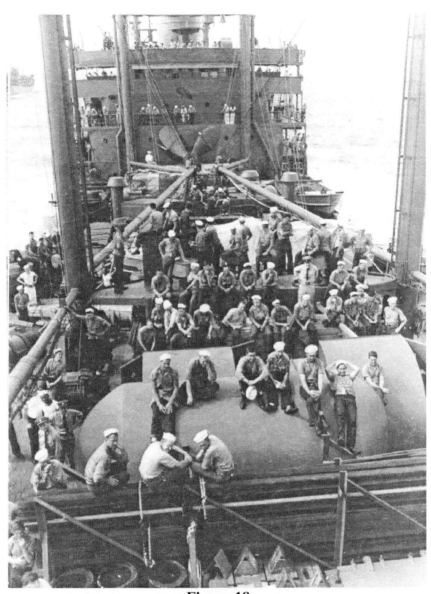

Figure 18
First convoy to Australia, USS Pelias.
Photo by Ken Landis

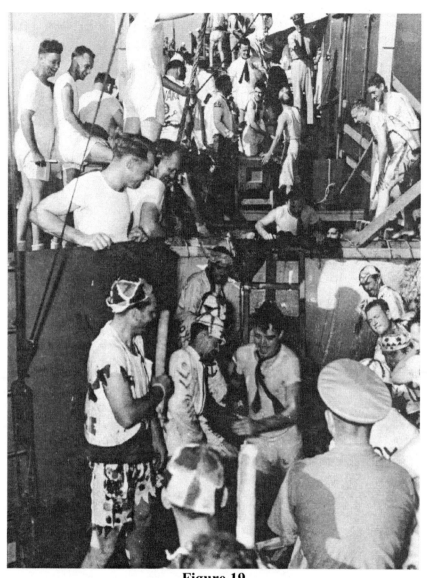

Figure 19
Shellbacks punishing lowly Pollywogs, USS Pelias.
Spring 1942.
Photo by Ken Landis

Figure 20
More Shellbacks punishing lowly Pollywogs, USS Pelias.
Spring 1942.
Photo by Ken Landis

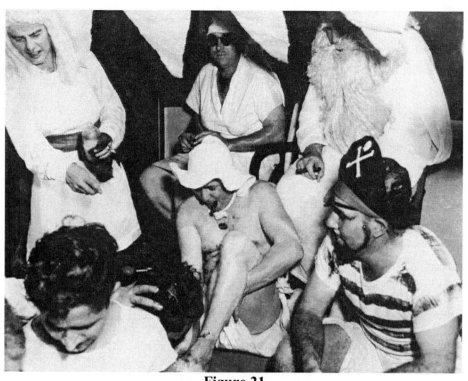
Figure 21
Hapless Pollywog kisses Royal Baby's feet as Neptunus Rex and Court observes.
Photo by Ken Landis

Figure 22
The Shellbacks of Neptunus Rex.
Part of "Crossing the Line" ceremony.
Spring 1942.
Photo by Ken Landis

Figure 23
USS Isabel, Shark Bay, West Australia, 1942.
Photo by Ken Landis

Figure 24
Depth charge attack, USS Isabel, Exmouth Gulf, West Australia.
Photo by Ken Landis

Figure 25
Bag-pipe band of Australian soldiers, Perth, West Australia, 1943.
Photo by Ken Landis

Figure 26
Street scene in Perth, Australia. Notice lack of auto traffic due to
acute gasoline shortage. December 1943.
Photo by Ken Landis

Figure 27
Perth, West Australia, showing lack of civilians after years of war.
Spring 1943.
Photo by Ken Landis

Figure 28
St. George's Terrace, Perth's Main Street.
Photo by Ken Landis

Figure 29
USS McClelland (DE-750). Taken at Iwo Jima, 1945.
Photo by Ken Landis

Figure 30
Torpedo firing, Okinawa, 1945.
Photo by Ken Landis

Figure 31
Survivors of the fire bomb raids wait in line for food stamps, Tokyo,
September, 1945.
Photo by Ken Landis

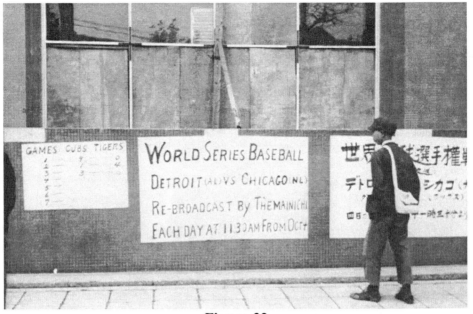

Figure 32
This amazing photo shows the Japanese were still following the World Series. Tokyo, October, 1945.
Photo by Ken Landis

Figure 33
American GIs in the ruins of Tokyo, October 1945. After the
devastating fire raids of May, 1945.
Photo by Ken Landis

Figure 34
The ruins of Tokyo, October 1945. After the devastating fire raids of May, 1945.
Photo by Ken Landis

Figure 35
Homeless civilians wandering in the ruins. Tokyo, October 1945.
Photo by Ken Landis

Figure 36
Americans and civilians wandering in the ruins. Tokyo, October 1945.
Photo by Ken Landis

Figure 37
**HIMJS Haruna, Tokyo Bay, October, 1945. The last remaining
Japanese battleship. An American crew was attempting to get the
ship underway and out of Tokyo Bay to be sunk in battle practice.**
Photo by Ken Landis

Figure 38
HIMJS Haruna
Photo by Ken Landis

Figure 39
The final surrender ceremony aboard USS Missouri, Tokyo Bay,
September 2, 1945.
U.S. Navy Photo

THE NINTH TALE

THE HAZARDS OF VICTORY

The Ninth Tale–The Hazards Of Victory

"I can't help but shudder at the thought of enemy aircraft attacking masses of our rejoicing people celebrating a great victory."

Entry on March 12, 1942, in his diary by

Matome Ugaki, Yamamoto's Chief of Staff

Because Admiral Nagumo had not ordered his carrier planes to return and destroy the fuel tanks, repair facilities, and dry docks at Pearl Harbor when he had the Americans stunned and on the defensive, the U.S. had snapped back in only two months, even though outnumbered by the Japanese carriers 3 to 1, and taken the offensive.

The American raids were hit-and-run raids. All of the land bases captured by the Japanese in December and January were still in Japanese hands, but the momentum in the naval forays was shifting back and forth across 6,500 miles of water from the U.S. West Coast to Tokyo, and in both capitals, Tokyo and Washington intelligence sources were jittery about what might happen on the big national holiday in Japan, Empire Day, Feb. 11, 1942.

Both intelligence headquarters issued alerts. False estimates of enemy fleet movements abounded. But Admiral Nimitz had become increasingly aware that his own HYPO decoding station on Oahu was issuing more accurate predictions of enemy fleet movements than the power-grubbing operations and naval intelligence departments in Washington, which now were spending much of their time and effort in feuding with each other for bureaucratic control.

Admiral Ernest J. King, chief of all navy fleets in the Atlantic and the Pacific (COMINCH) wanted his own intelligence organization and, although Admiral Stark would remain until the end of March, 1942, as Chief of Naval Operations, King felt that he had been authorized by FDR and Secretary of the Navy Knox to shape up Washington's intelligence center and send the old chiefs down with the ships at Pearl Harbor, so to speak. The first to be reassigned to sea duty were the directors of Naval Intelligence and Naval Communications.

In their places, politically adept navy high rankers ingratiated themselves with Admiral King and gained the helms of the intelligence and communications organizations.

Nimitz and his fleet intelligence officer, Layton, were enjoying a unified effort for combat intelligence, headed by Joe Rochefort at Station Hypo. Rochefort at Station Hypo didn't have to wrestle with command diplomacy in his communications with Layton, and through Layton, to Nimitz.

Meanwhile, without radar to verify on-the-spot advance warning of carrier plane raids, the Japanese commanders were sounding alerts all across the Pacific. In early February, Emperor Hirohito was advised by a nervous Imperial Navy chief of staff that two American task forces were operating west of Midway and might attack the Marshall Islands by Feb. 20, or be off the coast of Japan by Feb. *23.*

Part of the causes of these jitters was strictly technical. In Task Force 8, Halsey was using voice radio from ship to air under the mistaken belief that such high frequency circuits were limited to the horizon. Neither we nor the Japanese realized that those transmissions could skip clear across the Pacific by bouncing off of high/heavy cloud cover.

However, the Japanese commanders had real cause for concern about the hit-and-run tactics of American carriers. Halsey's Task Force Eight had sailed from Pearl Harbor on Feb. 14 to raid Wake Island and, possibly, Marcus Island, 650 miles from Wake and only 1,000 miles from Tokyo.

False alerts by the Japanese in the mandated island (the Marshalls) caused them to use huge amounts of fuel and give up tactical position to protect their moves into New Guinea and north of Australia at Rabaul.

Wherever the U.S. ships could venture with even temporary air control for a few hours and make a quick escape, they were doing well. On Feb. 24, Halsey's planes from the ENTERPRISE raided the Japanese garrison at Wake Island, reinforced by Admiral Raymond A. Spruance's heavy cruisers. The half-hour raid knocked out patrol vessels, flying boats and coastal gun emplacements.

Three days later, Japanese Third Fleet heavy cruisers caught the joint ABDA (American, British, Dutch, Australian) naval force without air cover and sent five cruisers to the bottom of the Java Sea—one American, one British, two Dutch, and one Australian.

The Allied Asiatic fleet was virtually helpless without air cover. Admiral Nimitz congratulated Halsey on his success at Wake, and added: "Desirable to hit Marcus if you think it possible."

Again, in the absence of Japanese radar installations on Marcus, Halsey struck without warning on March 4, and knocked out Marcus Island's transmitters and power supply.

Frantically trying to intercept Halsey, Yamamoto ordered Carrier Division 5 to pursue him, but got sidetracked by a false sighting report that enemy ships were heading for the Japanese coast.

Just one day later, on March Fifth, 15 minutes after midnight, bogeys (unidentified planes) were spotted heading for Pearl Harbor. It was a moonless, rainy night, and the wind was blowing palm trees almost to a right angle. Radar operators at Kokee on the coast of Kauai had caught three blips coming in from the west (from the open sea). Then, Opana Radar Station at Kahuku Point on Oahu (the same one that Joe Lockard and George Elliott had manned on Dec. 7, 1941) tracked the same three bogeys from 20 miles east of Kauai until they neared Oahu.

This time, the Radar Filter Center at Fort Shafter, "Little Robert," was completely alerted with a full complement of plotters or "shuffleboard pilots," tracing enemy planes on the grid which was superimposed on the giant map of Oahu.

The public—in fact, even their friends and neighbors—knew nothing about the women's organization or the work that they were doing. The women had been trained in secret, long before women's organizations in the Army (WACs), Navy (WAVEs), Marine Corps and Coast Guard ever came into existence.

It had all begun about 4:00 am. on a mid-December day, about one week after the Pearl Harbor devastation when Brig. Gen. Howard C. Davidson, Commander of the 14th Pursuit Wing, 7th Army Air Corps, at Wheeler Field, called a Red Cross leader in Honolulu, Mrs. Una Walker, and requested a list of 20 young Honolulu women between the ages of 20 and 32. Mrs. Walker, awakened without a clue at four in the morning with a request for 20 young women's names naturally asked, "What for?"

The general quickly explained that they would be replacing soldiers for combat duty, would be tested, had to pass physical tests, an army IQ test, and be willing to work shifts around the clock at the Fort Shafter Radar Information Center, "Little Robert." as a Civil Service detachment of the Army Signal Corps, Aircraft Warning Service. More than that, he would not say except to emphasize that their work would be vital and essential to the defense of the Hawaiian Islands. She could have the list ready in an hour, said Mrs. Walker. What should she say to the women? Tell them, said General Davidson, that an organizational meeting will be held early on the morning of the day after Christmas, Dec. 26, 1941, at the Royal Hawaiian Hotel; and incidentally, he added, the women must be childless, but it's okay if they are married. The military had taken over the Royal Hawaiian Hotel and barbed wire was strung along Waikiki Beach. After an orientation meeting there, the women recruits gathered in the room of Iolani Palace, where the entire senate chamber had been barricaded and draped with blackout materials. Under martial law, Iolani Palace had been taken over by the military. Officially, the women became a detachment of Company A, Signal Corps Aircraft Warning Regiment, Special, appointed as Civil Servants by Executive Order #9063. They rejected the name of WADs (Women's Air Defense) and approved of calling themselves WARDs (Women's Air Raid Defense). Their number was expanded from the original 20 to 104.

After intensive training on a plotting board in Iolani Palace, they were issued gas masks, helmets, and non-combatant arm bands; and put into quarters at Fort Shafter, where they ate at the Officers' Club, and pulled shifts around the clock at "Little Robert."

It was a rainy winter in Honolulu. Nancy Oakley Hedemann described the scene that her shift went through on the way to the plotting room at "Little Robert."

"At the entrance to the muddy wasteland the road was rutted and scarcely paved . . . To approach the entrance of the Command Center we had to walk through very slushy terrain. We'd emerge from the rear of a, truck and move as a group past the initial sentry station near a small building by the turn-around area... We'd move in a single file along a boardwalk that was roughly laid down to support the pedestrian from contact with puddles of water and deep mud . . . Winifred "Bam" Sperry was noted for a belly flop in the mud and once she had the audacity to sound out 'foe?' when the guard outside Little Robert uttered a classic challenge, 'Halt, who goes there, friend or foe'.

All joking ended in Little Robert on the night that WARD Jean Fraser tracked three Japanese planes with a string of arrows as they headed for Oahu. Suddenly, every officer on the balcony above the plotters was very

149

interested. Although it was past midnight, as if by magic, bird colonels and generals appeared out of the night and raced to the filter center. The WARDs on duty put on their helmets and plotted the enemy planes with their gas masks beside their chairs.

It was the first real test of the WARDs and they were doing fine, but there was confusion in the Air Defense Command. First, they sent up interceptors to find the bogeys and next, sent patrol planes out looking for enemy carriers. Then, about 2:00 am., the public air-raid alarm was sounded and anti-aircraft batteries were alerted, but with our own planes darting through the rainy skies in a futile search for the bogeys, the generals ordered no further action for fear the ack-ack would hit our own planes.

The Japanese pilots were having their troubles, too. They were flying "Emilies," our code name for the 24-ton, four-engine Kawanishi H8K, long range flying boats which had been designed to make the round trip to Pearl Harbor from its base in the Marshalls. But Emily could not make the range she was designed for without refueling. So, these three Emilies had dropped down at French Frigate Shoals and refueled vis-a-vis submarines. Now, as they approached Oahu, Pearl Harbor was covered with clouds and blacked out on this moonless, rainy night.

So, the Emily pilots could not see what they were bombing when they dropped their light load of 550-pound bombs. One jettisoned its bombs into the ocean just outside of Pearl Harbor. The other two dropped their bombs about a mile from Roosevelt High School in Honolulu's Makiki District and did only minor damage to a cluster of algaroba trees on the slope of Mount Tantalus.

The Japanese planes escaped and headed back to their Marshall Islands base at Wotje.

Fragments of bomb fins and fuses were later recovered from the Tantalus bomb site and proved to be identical to those dropped on Dec. 7 at Pearl Harbor. They were delivered to Fleet Intelligence Officer Layton's office at the submarine base at Pearl, and Admiral Nimitz examined them there, then asked if Layton had any idea how this long-range bombing foray had been accomplished.

Layton hit the nail on the head by guessing that the Japanese flying boats had taken off from Wotje in the Marshall Islands and refueled from submarines at French Frigate Shoals. Nimitz promptly ordered the seaplane tender, BALLARD, a converted destroyer, to patrol French Frigate Shoals under radio silence and deny any future raiders a refueling stop there. Later, he had a defensive minefield laid to discourage any future visits by Japanese submarines.

The WARDs had performed well at Little Robert filter center on Oahu, and their organization was expanded to filter centers at Lihue, Kauai; Wailuku, Maui; and Hilo, Hawaii.

Each of the Outer islands was staffed by women from that island, and the base pay for WARDs was $120.00 per month.

Japanese submarine action was not subject to radar detection, and Admiral Nimitz was concerned that enemy subs might duplicate the pattern of their attack on the Ellwood oil fields at Goleta, California, on Feb. 23, 1942. At Goleta (which is only a few miles from Santa Barbara, California) Japanese subs had surfaced and lobbed shells from their deck guns into the oil fields.

Intelligence Officer Layton had warned Nimitz that Pearl Harbor had been reconnoitered three times in moonlight by small float planes from Japanese submarines. Such raids were used more for propaganda than for any actual damage they might cause. The float planes could carry only a small bomb load, but notwithstanding the light physical damage which they could do, they could mount attacks far away from their home ports and add to wartime jitters for Americans at home in the U.S. mainland as well as in Hawaii.

Out of the second Japanese raid on Pearl Harbor by the ineffectual Emilies came coding information at Station HYPO on Oahu that would prove vital in the next three months. A garbled intercept from Tokyo naval intelligence was readable enough to recognize that the initials "AH," used in the March 5 raid, stood for islands in the Hawaiian group. But also used in the March 5 raid were the initials, "AFH and AF areas." AF had appeared in Japanese messages before, but this was the first time that Layton or Rochefort had seen "AFH."

It was not immediately apparent to the decoders at Station Hypo what the Japanese meant by the letters "AF", but in a Tokyo message addressed to air group commanders in the Marshalls on March 9, Tokyo included a two—day forecast of wind force and direction "AF."

Rochefort interpreted that the Japanese were referring to U.S. Island bases within range of the Japanese bases in the Marshalls. AFH meant the Hawaiian Islands, and Rochefort couldn't be sure yet, but it was his first inkling that "AF" could mean Midway, whereas the addition of the "H" meant the Hawaiian Islands. Midway is, after all, the westernmost island, the one closest to Japan, in the Hawaiian Archipelago—closer to Japan than the Hawaiian Islands are to the American mainland.

THE TENTH TALE

WHY AND HOW DID MacARTHUR FLEE THE PHILIPPINES?

The Tenth Tale–Why And How Did MacArthur Flee The Philippines?

The people who most urgently needed to be removed from Corregidor to avoid capture by the Japanese during the final stages of the battle for the Philippines were those in radio intelligence networks, particularly Station Cast.

If those linguists, cryptanalysts, radiomen and their coding and decoding equipment fell into the hands of the Japanese, torture and terror (which our enemies had proven already at Wake Island, in Malaya, and at Shanghai that they had no qualms about using on their captives; and which they would prove ready to use again at Bataan and Corregidor) might make them reveal details of code breaking which would erase the U.S. advantage in that vital area of operations and jeopardize all of our plans for future operations in the Pacific.

Admiral King thought it "of such importance to the successful prosecution of the war in the Far East" that the intelligence team, right down to the last man who had been working without relief in the Malinta Tunnel of Corregidor, had to be removed to Australia by any means available.

The U.S. submarine SEADRAGON removed the first 17 men and equipment on Feb. 5th, bound for Australia.

On March 11, thirty more intelligence personnel left Corregidor for Australia aboard the U.S. submarine PERMIT.

The last 21 men worked until the early hours of April 8 under continual bombardment (which led to surrender of American forces on Bataan later that day), then were ferried out to SEADRAGON, survived a depth charge attack and made it to Fremantle on the west coast of Australia.

It's noteworthy that, although MacArthur blamed his defeat on the navy, it was the navy that got him out of Corregidor and safely to Mindanao. Otherwise, he would have become a war prisoner along with Brig. Gen Johnathon M. Wainwright and 78,000 GIs he left behind.

What MacArthur would have done if left to his own decision (whether he would have gone down with his army or opted to escape), he never had to decide because, on Feb. 22nd, President Roosevelt ordered him out of Corregidor.

He initially planned to go from Corregidor to Mindanao by submarine, to stay in Mindanao a few days, and then go by B-17 to Australia; but the last week of February went by and found him still at Corregidor.

On March 1, a PT boat commander, USN Lt. John Bulkely, received a mysterious directive to take MacArthur aboard for some sort of ceremony. Bulkely was an authentic, swashbuckling hero, a heavily-bearded marauder against Japanese surface craft, tireless, always red-eyed from lack of sleep, girded at the waist by two pistols (Patton style). He had been awarded the Distinguished Service Cross by MacArthur a few weeks before. Now, when he got down to his last load of torpedoes, he was planning a quick run for China.

What did MacArthur's visit mean?

As MacArthur came aboard and auspiciously pinned a DSC medal on Bulkely, the intrepid skipper discerned what was really going on.

MacArthur didn't want to go in a submarine. He wanted to go in Bulkely's PT boat (the PT-41), along with the three other PT boats still afloat in the Philippines. Bulkely was commanding a flotilla of four PT boats all of the way to Mindanao

According to Admiral Rockwell, MacArthur wanted "a deck to pace, and fresh air, which he thought he would get more of in a PT-boat." Strict secrecy was maintained. The PT skippers told their crews that they were moving to Cebu. Their decks were strengthened with plywood to support fuel enough for the trip and supplied with twenty 50-gallon oil drums each on the topside.

Quite a few people went along with the general. With Bulkely in PT-41 were the general and his wife, his young son and a nurse, one naval and four army officers. In PT-34 with Lt. R.G. Kelly went Admiral Rockwell and three army staff officers. Four more generals and a Lt. Col. rode in PT-32 with Navy Lt. VS. Schumacker; and an additional four army officers loaded onto PT-35 with the skipper, Ensign A.B. Akers.

Not mentioned among all of those high rankers was Associated Press Correspondent Clark Lee, but Lee made generous mention of it in his book, THEY CALLED IT PACIFIC. Why he was chosen to go along with all of the top brass was never clarified.

155

Not that it was a pleasure trip. It was anything but a pleasure trip. On an inky black night with no moon, and a rough sea, the torpedo boats took a fierce beating. In fact, they were tossed about like corks in a washing machine, and became separated. PT-32 suspected it was being attacked by a Japanese submarine when PT-41 loomed astern of her, pitching and bucking in the darkness. PT-32 dumped her deck load of fuel and sped away. PT-35 broke down and had to search for shore.

By this time, MacArthur had all he wanted of torpedo boat travel. He and most of the passengers were too seasick to be overly concerned about getting killed. When on the afternoon of the first day at sea, Skipper Bulkely pulled into an island of the Cuyo group, MacArthur was anxious to await the submarine that was scheduled to rendezvous with them there. Instead, they were joined by PT-34 with Admiral Rockwell, who in spite of the danger they were in, was amused to see landlubber MacArthur so eager to leave his PT-boat for the smoother riding submarine.

"He (MacArthur) was very anxious to wait for the submarine to pick us up rather than continue on the PT boat. He finally agreed to continue in the PT, but he turned to General Sutherland, his chief of staff and said, 'Dick, I can't do anything to Rockwell, but if this is another bad night, so help me, I'll boil you in oil!'"

With 21 passengers aboard, the two remaining PT boats headed into weather that was even worse than the night before. They must have presented quite a picture of misery to Brig. Gen. W. F. Sharp, commander of the three divisions of the Visayas-Mindanao Force who met them at Del Monte, Mindanao.

Bulkely, undoubtedly with a seaman's glint in his eye, recounted later in describing their Cuyo Islands anchorage: "Palm trees waved lazily over a snowy white beach. The cove had a coral bottom and the water was emerald clear."

MacArthur's super-secret journey had been revealed to no one on the operational level. No B-17 was there in Mindanao to take him on to Australia. Four B-17s eventually were dispatched, but one cracked up on takeoff, two others aborted their mission in the Australian desert, and MacArthur took one look at the one which finally lumbered into Del Monte and sent off a joint message to General Marshall in Washington and Australian General Brett that, "the three best planes in the United

States should be made available . . . with completely adequate and experienced crews."

On March 16, two specially dispatched B-17s flew MacArthur and his retinue to Darwin, Australia.

MacArthur was lavish in his praise for the navy and recommended the Congressional Medal of Honor for Bulkely. With his usual dramatic flair, MacArthur reported to Marshall that the trip had been unique in military annals . . "due entirely to their [the PT boat personnel's] invincible resolution and determination."

Congress awarded Bulkely the Medal of Honor. The navy gave lesser awards to the other PT boat people. Never in history did any military commander abandon his post with more heroic posturing. (that is, once he got over being seasick). From then on, in every newspaper in the United States, MacArthur was pictured as the Phoenix who rose from the ashes of defeat to reclaim the Philippines, striding up the surf with jaw out-thrust, firmly gripping the stem of a corn-cob pipe and the picture inevitably captioned: "I SHALL RETURN"

He never could have left and he never could have returned if it hadn't been for the U.S. Navy.

The men he left behind came up with two embittered works which expressed their feelings about the situation they were left in:

(Sung to the tune of THE BATTLE HYMN OF THE REPUBLIC).
We're the battling bastards of Bataan;
No mama, no papa, no Uncle Sam;
No aunts, no uncles, no nephews, no nieces;
No pills, no planes, no artillery pieces;
And nobody gives a damn.
Dugout Doug MacArthur lies ashaking on the Rock safe from all the bombers and from any sudden shock dugout Doug is eating of the best food on Bataan and his troops go starving on.
Dugout Doug's not timid, he's just cautious, not afraid he's protecting carefully the stars that Franklin made four-star generals are rare as good food on Bataan.
And his troops go starving on.

(MacArthur wrote nothing about the Prisoners of War which he left behind him to face prison-camp horror and Japanese military brutality in the Philippines, U.S. Army version of the Philippines campaign doesn't mention POWs either; and there is no memorial to those 78,000 war prisoners in Washington, D.C., 29,000 of whom did not survive their imprisonment).

In Washington, retired Admiral Tom Hart could only shake his head at the ignorance and gullibility of the U.S.Congress and President Franklin D. Roosevelt when it came to their adulation of the man who Hart considered chiefly responsible for the U.S. disaster in the Philippines.

Before Hart left Java aboard the HMS DURBAN, headed for India and from there, to the United States, he sent this message to the first "tethered goat," his former flagship ISABEL:

"May God bless you and keep you during the difficult days to come."

No one knew better than Hart how difficult those days were going to be for the U.S. navy. ISABEL's crew lined up topside to wave goodbye. Rear Admiral W. A. Glassford, Jr., inherited what was left of the U.S. Asiatic Fleet.

In March, the Joint Chiefs of Staff reorganized the command structure in the Pacific, complicating Nimitz's job considerably by appointing MacArthur in Australia Commander-in-Chief of the Southwest Pacific Area. Although he was really a refugee from his own captured army, that put MacArthur on a par with Admiral Nimitz, who was Commander-in-Chief Pacific Ocean Areas (Cincpoa) as well as Commander-in-Chief Pacific (Cincpac). The official dividing line between them was the 160th meridian. Nimitz was assigned the Allied Naval Forces in the Eastern approaches to Australia, including the Coral Sea, and that (the Coral Sea) was where the Japanese fleet was headed.

One thing was for sure. One of the unquestioned masters of the rhetoric of self righteousness in Washington D.C., where rhetorical self-righteousness abounds and is most competitive for power and influence in the United States, was Douglas MacArthur. It wasn't until the 1950s that Douglas MacArthur ran into a U.S. president whom he could not fool. That was another kind of man entirely—Harry S. Truman.

THE ELEVENTH TALE

ENEMY BOMBERS OVER TOKYO

The Eleventh Tale–Enemy Bombers Over Tokyo

Chief of Staff Ugaki's nightmare of enemy bombers flying over Tokyo came true on April 18, 1942.

How could that happen? That was only four months and a few days after the Japanese attack on Pearl Harbor, which was supposed to have knocked out the U. S. fleet in a place more than 4,000 miles from the Japanese homeland and to have kept it on the defensive for at least six months.

This is how it happened.

Admiral King's Navy Department in Washington. D.C., hatched the scheme early in 1942. It was really conceived of as an attack on Japanese morale and an attempt to bolster U.S. morale. We could accomplish that, King believed, with an attack on Japan's homeland, which was sacred soil to the Japanese.

The idea of the U.S. fleet raiding Tokyo was quite a shock when it was transmitted to Admiral Nimitz on March 19. Nimitz was being asked to assign two of our four aircraft carriers in the Pacific to America's biggest gamble of the war—to bomb Tokyo.

The U.S. Navy Dauntless dive bombers which we used on carriers didn't have the range to do it. Our carriers would have to steam too close to Japan and risk coming under bombardment from land-based Japanese planes to launch the dive bombers.

But King and other members of his staff took the problem to General Henry (Hap) Arnold and discussed with him whether any of our planes, not necessarily the ones being used on our carriers, had the range and could be launched from a flight deck.

Within a week, Arnold reported back to King that the army's B-25 two-engined medium bomber had the necessary range and could be launched from a carrier at a distance of 500 miles from the Japanese coast.

The training for the raid began under Lt. Col. James H. Doolittle at Eglin Field, Florida. He chose U.S. Army Air Force pilots from the 17th Bombardment Group, who were trained for short takeoffs by a navy pilot, Lt.Henry F. Miller. The outline of a carrier flight deck was painted on an airstrip.

The plan was to fly across the East China Sea after striking targets in Japan and land at airfields in eastern China. That plan required negotiations with the man who then headed China's government, Chiang Kai-shek. Everything was handled as top secret and no part of the plan was ever put in writing. Even the Chinese were not given specific details of the plan, but China had been at war with Japan since 1937, and welcomed any chance to strike back at the Japanese because all of the bombs in that war had fallen on China up to that time.

After he had been briefed on the plan (while the army pilots were still in training in Florida), Nimitz realized that with Army B-25 medium bombers filling the flight deck of the aircraft carrier, HORNET, the carrier's own planes could not be used for air patrol; so, Nimitz would have to assign that job to another carrier. Nimitz chose the ENTERPRISE, commanded by Admiral William (Bull) Halsey.

Task Force 8 sailed from Pearl Harbor on April 8 to rendezvous with the HORNET (which had left San Francisco six days earlier) Lashed to the deck of the HORNET were 16 of the two-engined B-25s. Just as the Japanese had chosen to send the Kido Butai task force to attack Pearl Harbor vis-a-vis the northern Pacific route, the combined HORNET and ENTERRISE, code-named Task Force MIKE, did the same thing going from east to west, steaming along the stormy, isolated northern Pacific route under radio silence.

It was a daring raid, putting at risk two U.S. carriers. The LEXINGTON was in dry dock for overhaul at Pearl Harbor, and our only other carrier task force was in the Coral Sea to prevent further Japanese advances into the south Pacific. But Nimitz was reassured by Rochefort's radio intelligence briefs that the Japanese were concentrating their carrier activity in the south Pacific and not off the eastern coast of Japan where Task Force MIKE would attack. The Japanese already were in total control of the Indian Ocean and the American army had suffered its biggest defeat in history when Bataan fell on April 9.

Here was the disposition of the four American carriers in the Pacific on the eve of the raid on Tokyo: YORKTOWN was on duty in the Coral Sea. LEXINGTON was two days out of Pearl Harbor, steaming south. HORNET and ENTERPRISE were 700 miles from Tokyo, set to launch the B-25s when they reached a point 400 miles from Tokyo.

161

What were the Japanese doing?

They had a three-phase plan. The first phase was rapidly drawing to a close. It included the surprise attack on Pearl Harbor, the capture of the Philippines, Malaya and the Dutch East Indies.

Yamamoto wanted the second phase to include an attack on Midway with the strategy that this attack with a landing force would lure the American carriers out of Pearl Harbor to their destruction. The war plans section of the Imperial staff in Tokyo felt that the Midway operation would be too dangerous, but Yamamoto prevailed with arguments that included an implicit threat to resign if the Imperial staff didn't include the attack on Midway along with seizing the islands of Fiji, Samoa and New Caledonia. In other words, he wanted not only to sever the lines of communication between Australia and the United States. In the process, he wanted to destroy the U.S. fleet.

Yamamoto prevailed. He got his Midway operation and his army opponents got the occupation of Fiji and New Caledonia, but only with the plan to destroy the facilities of Samoa, not to occupy Samoa. That would be phase two.

The third and final phase of Japan's master plan called for the capture of Hawaii, attack on the United States, Canada, the Panama Canal and Central America "until the United States loses its fighting spirit and the war can be brought to a conclusion."

Imperial general headquarters gave its final approval April 15, after the Emperor gave a nod to the second phase of the plan, which was scheduled to begin on May 7 with the capture of Port Moresby. Assaults on Midway and the Aleutian Islands in Alaska were scheduled to start in April. By the third week in July, phase two was to be completed.

But something happened on the way to phase two. It was the bombing of Tokyo.

HORNET's plan to launch the B-25s 400 miles from the Japanese coast had to be scrapped when Halsey's radar detected two vessels on the Japanese picket line. Scout planes were launched at dawn on April 18 and their pilots sighted another enemy picket ship. The planes sank that vessel, but not until she had radioed Tokyo that she had spotted the enemy planes.

With the knowledge that complete surprise probably was lost, Halsey and Doolittle decided to launch the B-25s as quickly as possible, even

162

though they were considerably more than 600 miles away from the Japanese east coast. The first B-25, piloted by Doolittle, cleared the HORNET's flight deck at 0725.

Halsey flashed to the HORNET, "Good luck and God bless you," altered the ENTERPRISE's course 90 degrees, and maintained radio silence as he raced northeastward at 25 knots.

It was four hours later when Doolittle's bombers roared over Tokyo, stirring up a flurry of alerts to Japanese warships with sirens wailing throughout the capital city. Once again, Halsey got away without being intercepted by enemy planes or ships, in spite of Yamamoto's urgent signal to his forces:

"ENEMY TASK FORCE CONTAINING THREE AIRCRAFT CARRIERS AS MAIN STRENGTH SIGHTED 0630 THIS MORNING 730 miles EAST OF TOKYO . . . OPERATE AGAINST AMERICAN FLEET."

Only two American carriers were involved but Yamamoto had received a report that there were three.

Battleships, cruisers, and destroyers raised steam and headed out though the inland sea to give chase. A submarine squadron en route to Truk made a sweep north of the Bonin Islands. Admiral Nobutake Kondo ordered his cruisers out of Yokosuka. None of them made contact with the enemy. Land-based Japanese planes, scoured the seas hundreds of miles offshore, but were hampered by poor visibility.

On the next day, every warship from the homeland to the Marshalls and the Marianas joined in the hunt. Soviet freighters north of Japan were stopped and boarded in case they had picked up any American flyers who had ditched. The widespread search went on for two days at the end of which time, Yamamoto issued the order:

"CEASE OPERATIONS AGAINST AMERICAN FLEET.

What had the raiders done?

Thirteen of the B-25s had attacked Tokyo, each carrying four 500-pound bombs. The other three planes, each carrying only incendiary bombs, had raided Nagoya. Kobe, and Osaka.

There was no significant military damage. The bow of one warship in dry dock was damaged. Fifty houses and shops were demolished. A school had been struck by bombs and 12 people were killed. Three B-25 fliers were captured, tried as war criminals and beheaded. Four of our fliers were killed when they crash landed in China.

Yamamoto wrote: "Even though there wasn't much damage, it's a disgrace that the skies over the Imperial capital should have been defiled without a single enemy plane shot down. It provides a regrettably graphic illustration of the saying that a bungling attack is better than the most skilled defense."

U.S. newspaper headlines blared: JAPAN BOMBED and DOOLITTLE DOOED IT. Radio Tokyo punned that the Doolittle raid had, indeed, "done little."

But the Japanese military, both the navy and the army, had suffered great psychological damage in the homeland because their top leaders had said repeatedly that Tokyo would never be bombed. That had proved to be a lie. How many other lies were they being told? More subtly, but perhaps more significantly too, it swelled an undertow in public opinion in Japan that the Japanese people were not going to prosper in spite of all of these highly touted victories—now, in addition to prolonged rationing and other sacrifices, they were in danger of being bombed in their own homes.

The raid had a brutalizing effect on Allied fliers who were shot down and taken prisoners by the Japanese in all subsequent campaigns of the war. The fliers were considered war criminals and in many cases were bayonetted or beheaded by their captors. Three of the Doolittle fliers were beheaded in a public display of legalized execution. The inadvertent bombing of a school with the loss of 12 lives in Tokyo was widely cited in Japan in support of the idea that the fliers were war criminals.

The commanding general of the 7th Army Air Corps, which would be leap-frogging from the Hawaiian Islands to the Gilberts, then to the Marshalls, the Marianas, Iwo Jima and Tokyo, had this to say about the conditions under which Allied airmen were flying: (The 7th AAC was flying the longest missions in the Pacific with the four-engine B-24s).

"Any understanding of the war in the Pacific must be based on an appreciation of distance. The mission of the 7th Air Force involves land-based air operations in a theater which extends over some 16-million square miles, or more than five times the size of the United States . . . The usual check points, such as rivers, mountains, and railroads are nonexistent . . If they are shot down or disabled over the target they face what to them is the stark horror of capture. If they go down in the ocean their chances of rescue, despite the vigilant navy rescue service, are problematical." (The quotation is from the commanding general of the 7th Army Air Corps, Major General Willis Hale.)

On top of morale problems caused by the bombing of Tokyo, the stringent rationing in Japanese civilian life now would have to be stretched to take care of 140,000 war prisoners from the Philippines, Malaya, the Dutch East Indies and Singapore—something which the Japanese militarists were not prepared to do. From camp to camp, they vacillated between killing prisoners outright, starving them, or giving the able-bodied ones enough food to keep them working in labor battalions.

Instead of prosperity through conquest as promised by the militarists, Japanese in the homeland were experiencing burgeoning problems, no matter how many conquests the militarists celebrated.

THE TWELFTH TALE

STAND-OFF IN THE CORAL SEA

The Twelfth Tale–Stand-Off In The Coral Sea

The analysis of intelligence data is not for singular-minded people. Just when you think that you have a pile of data figured out another decrypt redirects the meaning of the whole thing. Once the code-breaking is solved and analyzed, the matter of relevance and dissemination is at issue, In other words, who gets this data, who interprets it, when do they get it, and what do they do with it? In the military, all of this is further complicated by the chain of command and security regulations.

If the man at the top of that chain, such as Admiral Nimitz, is knowledgable enough about intelligence to know what he can use it for in combat, that's fortunate. If the man at the top of that chain in a vital tactical situation, such as Frank Jack Fletcher aboard his flagship, YORKTOWN in the Coral Sea at the beginning of May, 1942, has a personal agenda based on indifference or contempt or hostility toward his intelligence officer, then he becomes his own worst enemy.

Admiral Nimitz was favorably impressed by Admiral William (Bull) Halsey's use of his four-man radio intelligence crew on the ENTERPRISE in the Marshall Islands, Wake and Marcus Island campaigns. Nimitz placed four-man intelligence crews on all of the Pacific fleet flat-tops. Intelligence units never had been so valued by any admiral before.

In the World War II Navy, young officers like Edwin T. Layton had pursued naval intelligence at their own risk. They weren't likely ever to reach flag rank or get the credibility that went with flag rank. Although no one was likely to know any more about the tactical plans of an enemy than intelligence officers did, old-school admirals of all nations were reluctant to take the advice of junior officers on tactical information.

All of those considerations are what made the working relationship of Admiral Nimitz and LtCdr. Edwin Layton so extraordinary. Nimitz knew what kind of intelligence expertise he had inherited by retaining Layton on his staff when the young officer was ready to resign because of the disaster at Pearl Harbor, where he had been fleet intelligence officer under Admiral Kimmel.

Layton knew the Japanese language and Japanese social customs and their systems of military communication and intelligence. As a young U.S. naval officer, he had studied in Japan from 1929 to 1932, and had been sent back there in the spring of 1937 to observe and get what information he could about their military build-up, particularly in the mandated islands.

In July of 1937, he worked closely with Yamamoto's office during the search for the missing American aviatrix, Amelia Earhart, in the vast ocean area around tiny Howland Island, and since that search included the recently fortified Marshall Islands, the Japanese were wary of what Earhart's intentions had been in flying close to the Marshalls and about the intentions of U.S. naval commanders in steering their ships around the Marshalls, the Carolines and the Marianas Islands in their search for her.

All sorts of rumors stemmed from Earhart's disappearance with her navigator, Fred Noonan; that they had been captured by the Japanese and taken to Saipan; that they had been executed as spies by the Japanese; that they had been sent back to Tokyo and were being held captive by Japanese intelligence officers, ad infinitum. [These rumors persisted throughout the war and even led to auditing by Amelia Earhart's husband, U.S. Army Major Howard Putnam Palmer, from listening outposts on the coast of China to determine if Amelia was being used as a propagandist for the Japanese. Palmer heard broadcasts by various female announcers from Radio Tokyo, but concluded that Amelia's voice was not one of them].

Back in 1937, Layton had termed replies to his queries in Yamamoto's office about the missing fliers "polite but not whole hearted."

Yamamoto, who had served as a Japanese naval attache in the U.S. in 1926, felt a kinship with Layton, and Layton had been Yamamoto's guest at Kabuki Theatre performances in Tokyo, at a duck-hunting party (done with nets and ending with duck sukiyaki), and in a bridge game (all three rubbers played were won by the admiral even though, Layton affirmed, he was doing his best).

However, Yamamoto's invitations never extended to military operations, such as air reviews or troop maneuvers, and Layton never got to within a thousand miles of the mandated islands (mandated by the League of Nations to Japan after World War I), and Layton suspected that submarine and amphibious airplane bases were being constructed there, especially in the Marshals and at Truk in the Carolines.

Only one steamship line had offered passage to those areas, and after Layton pointedly refused to accept the oft-repeated excuse that every sailing on the schedule had been booked for a year, the senior passenger agent finally acknowledged that he had been instructed "not to sell any foreigner passage to the mandated islands."

More than a decade earlier murder and intrigue had resulted when a U.S. Marine Corps undercover agent, Major Earle Ellis, posing as an expert in nature studies who wanted to examine plant life in the Carolines, had gained passage to those islands in 1923. Word was sent back to U.S. naval attaches that Ellis had died of unknown causes on the island of Palau in the Western Carolines. Ellis appparently had gotten close enough to observe the massive buildup in the Japanese naval base at Truk before his life was snuffed out.

The intrigue deepened when an American pharmacist, Lawrence Zembsch, went to Palau to investigate and returned to Tokyo with Major Ellis' ashes. However, Zembsch himself was in a stupefied condition, apparently drug induced, suffering from amnesia. He was hospitalized in the American Naval hospital at Yokohama. but never left there alive. The official word was that Lawrence Zembsch died there in the hospital in the great earthquake of Sept 1, 1923.

Yamamoto never talked of military matters with his American friend. He liked to speak to Layton in Japanese and conversed informally with him in his office. On one occasion, Layton asked the Admiral about a news item which had appeared in the Tokyo newspapers about the unusually long time which the construction of two cruisers was taking in shipyards which were closed off from public view by construction barriers. Yamamoto brushed the question aside, but Layton learned later that two cruisers were taking too long to be constructed because they were being converted to the aircraft carriers, SHOHO and ZUIHO.

Yamamoto knew the United States better than any other Japanese admiral and thought highly of Americans, causing antagonism with his warlord superiors in Sombo Hombu (the Japanese Army and Navy headquarters in Tokyo). As vice minister of the navy in the late 1930's, Yamamoto had risked both life and career by trying to steer successive Japanese governments away from confrontation with the United States. He also opposed the tri-partite pact which Japan entered into with Germany and Italy.

When Prime Minister Fumimaro Konoye appointed Yamamoto Commander-in-Chief of the combined Japanese Fleet on Aug. 30, 1939, Yamamoto did not change his beliefs. He still urged avoidance of war with the U.S. at all costs, and advised Konoye:

"If we are ordered to do it, then I can guarantee to put up a tough fight for the first six months, but I have absolutely no confidence as to what would happen if it went on for two or three years."

No more prophetic words were ever spoken in the Pacific war setting.

The result of all that was that Layton needed no history or Japanese language lessons to understand the background of what he was reading in the messages from his counterpart at Oahu's Station Hypo, LT. Joseph Rochefort, who also had studied as a young U.S. navy officer in Japan, and spoke and read Japanese fluently.

Nimitz, who neither spoke nor wrote Japanese, found that he could depend on his fleet intelligence and Station HYPO officers to track the Japanese fleet. He found their work in the Pacific to be superior for practical purposes to the decoding work and analysis that was being carried out in Washington, D.C., by Station Negat, the OP-20-G for the office of Naval Intelligence, which had to operate with constant, overbearing interference from the Office of Naval Operations Commander-in-Chief Admiral Richmond Kelly Turner.

Admiral Turner was characterized by Layton as "the navy's Patton."

Both Turner and Patton, Layton wrote, "possessed that amalgam of military brilliance, opinionated paranoia, and instinctive courage that leads men into enemy gunfire, but immoderate self assertion soured cooperation down the ladder of command."

As soon as he moved in as Chief of Naval Operations in Washington in 1941, Turner had undercut the authority of the Office of Naval Intelligence and maintained that he should be the sole authority for evaluation and dissemination of intelligence and "the major strategic overall picture."

Turner took the attitude that all valid analysis of intelligence data came from his office in Washington. That led to the attitude that the best intelligence research was being done there and to the frequent issuance of presumptive messages like the one which Nimitz received on the evening of April 20, telling Nimitz that "a joint army-navy committee is studying Pacific logistics."

To that, Nimitz noted laconically in his daily log:

"So are we."

Nimitz's immediate superior in Washington was not Turner, but Admiral King, and Nimitz persuaded Admiral King of the superior intelligence being amassed and analyzed for his benefit by Joe Rochefort at Station Hypo on Oahu to such an extent that Admiral King asked Joe Rochefort directly for Hypo's analysis of enemy carrier movements on the eve of the Doolittle Raid on Tokyo.

Joe Rochefort recalled, "we were a little surprised that he would ask us what our views were. I personally felt that he was not even aware of our existence." Within six hours after King had requested it, Rochefort sent his analysis to King, and future events were to bear out what Rochefort predicted.

Now, on the eve of the battle of the Coral Sea, Nimitz had dispatched two task forces based around the carriers LEXINGTON and YORKTOWN to prevent Japanese carriers from carrying out a successful launching of Phase Two in their Pacific battle plans, starting with the landing of troops at Port Moresby. Task Force 11 had support vessels clustered around LEXINGTON and Task Force 17 around YORKTOWN.

That was when the Task Force 17 commander, Admiral Frank Jack Fletcher, pulled a command blunder which cast a long shadow on the eventual loss of one U.S. aircraft carrier in the Battle of the Coral Sea and severe damage to the other. Actually, it wasn' t the YORKTOWN, Fletcher's flagship, which was lost. It was the LEXINGTON, the carrier in Task Force 11.

At a luncheon meeting in the board room of his flagship, Fletcher, flanked by his entire staff, met with Ltjg Forrest R. Biard and ordered the lieutenant, who headed the four-man Intelligence unit on the ship, to tell him and his staff "all about your communications intelligence organization and the code breaking it does."

Biard knew that he was being instructed to break security regulations which he had been sworn to uphold because Fletcher's staff officers had not been cleared for intelligence security. He respectfully refused to do that.

172

It was the admirals blunder because all that Fletcher had to do was to command Biard in private, out of the presence of staff officers who were not cleared to receive such information about his intelligence operation. As a flag officer, Fletcher was cleared for all security purposes to receive any information or explanation which he might require from anyone on his ship.

Fletcher compounded the blunder by becoming so hostile toward Biard that the junior officer was not allowed to communicate to the admiral the vital data that he received on a continuing basis as to the whereabouts of the enemy carriers in the crucial days from May 1 to May 8, 1942.

Never since the Japanese task force, Kido Butai, had been heading undetected for Pearl Harbor from Nov. 27 to Dec. 7, 1941, had the question: "where are the enemy carriers?' been more crucial. But Admiral Fletcher was so miffed at Biard that he would not listen to him.

Due to a false report by a YORKTOWN scout plane that the pilot had sighted two Japanese carriers and two cruisers heading off Misima, south in the Coral Sea~ Fletcher, without reference to his intelligence unit, took it for granted that was the main force of the Japanese. He immediately sent 93 planes from YORKTOWN and LEXINGTON roaring off at 10:15 am. on May 7. The scout pilot then came rushing back to Admiral Fletcher to report that he had made a coding error. What he actually had seen and reported as two carriers, were two cruisers, escorted by two destroyers.

Biard came in to inform Fletcher that a Japanese carrier had been spotted nearby, but not where the YORKTOWN pilot had reported seeing Japanese carriers.

Too late, Fletcher realized that he was caught between enemy carriers, fore and aft, boxed in between enemy carriers with his combined force of 93 strike planes roaring off in the wrong direction to the northwest.

Fletcher bellowed at the errant pilot:

"Young man, do you know what you have done? You have just cost the United States two carriers!"

According to Biard, "Here was the commander of a vital naval task force shouting in the presence of officers and several enlisted men that we had already lost a battle we were yet to fight."

Then, came a chilling call from the U.S. oiler, NEOSHO, which was out of range of land-based Japanese bombers. The oiler and an escort destroyer, the SIMS, were being bombed by a 76-plane strike force from the ZUIKAKU. The SIMS was sunk and NEOSHO was left helpless in the water. But Admiral Yoshimichi Hara realized too late that what his scout planes had mistaken for two American carriers were really the oiler and the destroyer.

Similar errors were being made aboard their flagships by the opposing task force commanders in the Coral Sea.

When Admiral Hara recalled the 76 planes and they turned 180 degrees to go back to the ZUIKAKU, Lt. Biard picked up the enemy carrier's repeated homing signal on course "280 degrees, 20 knots."

Biard immediately informed Fletcher that the Japanese carrier force was closing distance astern. In other words, instead of being 400 miles away in another direction, they were about 250 miles astern of the YORKTOWN—just 50 miles out of their 200-mile strike range! Fletcher ignored Biard's information and credited Admiral Aubrey Fitch's interpretation on LEXINGTON of the same message that Biard had heard. Fitch's radio intelligence unit had misinterpreted the message, giving the location and speed of the ZUIKAKU, thinking that the Japanese were referring to the location and speed of the YORKTOWN.

Biard pointed out to Fletcher that the message in question could not possibly refer to the YORKTOWN because, "we had not recently been on any course approximating 280 degrees and our steaming speed was nothing like 20 knots."

Fletcher would acknowledge that Biard knew what he was talking about and that Fitch did not.

To compound matters, LEXINGTON pilots sank a Japanese ship and radioed triumphantly, "Scratch one flat-top'" That turned out to be the one-time submarine tender, converted in 1940 to the light carrier, SHOHO. She went down after 13 bomb and seven torpedo hits by planes from the LEXINGTON and YORKTOWN, 80 miles south of Woodlark Island, with 500 casualties.

But the big carriers, SHOKAKU and ZUIKAKU were still in a deadly game of hide and seek with the LEXINGTON and YORKTOWN.

Now, at 1400 (2:00 p.m.) on May 7, Fletcher's hostility toward Biard continued to act on his tactical judgment like a boomerang. Biard explained that the two enemy carriers were vulnerable to a search and strike mission, because Biard knew from the Japanese radio messages they had decoded that two Japanese carriers were "within fighting distance and looking for us."

Fletcher turned a deaf ear. He ruled out a search and destroy mission, even though his planes were fueled and armed and lined up on the flight deck, ready to take off with more than four hours of daylight left.

A couple of hours later, about 1600 (4:00 p.m.), Admiral Hara got the word from one of his scout planes that he could be within strike distance of the American carriers before nightfall. SHOKAKU launched 12 bombers and 15 torpedo planes about 1630 and went on a search and destroy mission in heavy weather. They found the YORKTOWN at 1830 (6:30 p.m.) and attacked.

It was the first good look that Japanese pilots had ever gotten at an American carrier.

Fitch had fighter cover, but the fighters were outnumbered by the attacking planes. He sent up 23 remaining dive bombers to reinforce his fighters, but two torpedoes slammed into LEXINGTON's port side below the waterline.

With her maneuverability virtually destroyed, LEXINGTON became an easy target, took bomb hits which set fires below decks. The YORKTOWN also was hit near her island, and she lost way with her boilers temporarily shut down. Then, LEXINGTON's returning fighter planes came back low on fuel, tried to land on her battered deck, and several planes were lost when they skidded overboard.

The Japanese pilots flew back to their carriers, convinced they had sunk both enemy carriers, and Admiral Hara believed them.

Fletcher had plans to take LEXINGTON'S planes aboard the YORKTOWN and send the LEXINGTON back to Pearl Harbor for repairs. His preliminary report to Nimitz was:

First enemy attack completed, no vital damage our force...

Nimitz radioed back, "Congratulations on your glorious accomplishments," but this message had hardly been handed to Fletcher when, at 12:45 p.m. the LEXINGTON suffered a tremendous explosion and a little more than two hours later, had to be abandoned. Friendly torpedoes from the U.S. destroyer PHELPS sent her to the bottom of the Coral Sea.

175

Fletcher now faced a tactical defeat, but Admiral Hara, although ordered to pursue the enemy, did not do it, and Admiral Shigeyoshi Inouye blamed Hara's retreat for his decision to recall the invasion force which the Japanese had intended to land at Port Moresby. So, the U.S. could claim a strategic victory because Japanese troops never landed at Port Moresby and turned back to their staging base at Truk.

Nimitz was devastated by the loss of LEXINGTON, but quickly rebounded and told his staff, "Remember this. We don't know how badly he's hurt. You can bet your boots he's hurt, too! Remember this—the enemy has got to be hurt. His situation is not all a bed of roses."

Without radio intelligence and ship's radar, Fletcher would have been steaming blind every mile of the way in the Coral Sea battle. Because he ignored much of the intelligence data which had been passed on to him, he lost the initiative when the two opposing fleets came within range to strike each other. In spite of the excuses he made for not using the radio intelligence at his disposal more effectively, he made no objection to a secret wartime navy department appraisal of the Coral Sea action:

"It takes nothing from the achievement of the fleets of the U.S. Navy at Coral Sea to say that they had been brought to the right spot at exactly the right time by the work of radio intelligence."

It was no tactical victory for the U.S. to trade the sinking of the LEXINGTON for the sinking of the light enemy carrier, SHOHO. The Japanese carrier force still outnumbered the U.S. carrier force in the Pacific by nine to three, but for the first time in the Pacific war, an attempted Japanese landing, backed up by carriers, had been repulsed.

For Station Hypo on Oahu, the Coral Sea was an important victory because it convinced Nimitz to trust Rochefort over and above the conflicting intelligence which had come out of Station NEGAT in Washington, D.C. Rochefort had remarkable ability to fish out what the Japanese were up to now, and his sixth sense indicated that another and bigger Japanese offensive was building up even before the shooting started in the Coral Sea. Based on a shift in radio traffic, Rochefort believed that the main enemy objective would be in the central Pacific, even though there was data showing that the Japanese planned to invade the Aleutian Islands at the same time. Rochefort was right. On May 1 in Hashirajima Bay, Yamamoto was drawing up with his staff in his massive wardroom of the world's biggest battleship, his flagship YAMATO, plans for a massive attack on Midway with a diversionary assault on the Aleutians. Operation MI, the task force code name for Midway was the most ambitious operation ever mounted by the Japanese navy. It included two battleships, eight aircraft carriers, 23 cruisers, 65 destroyers and 20 submarines.

Admiral Nagumo's Kido Butai was to support amphibious landings in the capture of Midway. Two other carriers and their support vessels would support the capture of Kiska and Attu in the western Aleutians. Submarines placed west of the Hawaiian Islands would radio warnings and launch underwater attacks when the U.S. fleet ventured out of Pearl Harbor to protect Midway.

Once the American carriers were committed in their attempt to counter the Midway operation, the northern force of the Japanese fleet would cut off any retreat of the Americans back to Pearl Harbor and Yamamoto would lead the main force of the Japanese fleet to destroy the American carriers. With that accomplished, Japan would invade Hawaii, occupy it, and force the U.S. to sue for peace.

Message by message, decrypt by decrypt, the ingenious Joe Rochefort discovered the extent and direction of Yamamoto's grand design, and Admiral Nimitz, with the carrier odds three to one against him, counted on his code breakers, the intelligence officers, to avoid Yamamoto's trap and to spring one of his own at Midway.

THE THIRTEENTH TALE

"IF WE LISTEN TO WASHINGTON, WE WILL END UP AS...

The Thirteenth Tale–"If We Listen To Washington, We Will End Up As Japanese POWs"–Station Hypo Staff Member

What was the top secret intelligence work at Station Hypo? What did they do? What materials did it take? What were the former band members of the USS CALIFORNIA doing there?

Station Hypo was consuming about three million manila 3"x7" punch cards per month. Each one had to be hand punched and sorted by former band members of the battleship, CALIFORNIA Each card had five-digit groups punched into IBM cards

Decrypts were being processed at the rate of 500 to 1,000 per day on the 3" x 7", 80 column IBM cards. The IBM machines chattered 24 hours per day, seven days per week—around the clock and around the calendar. Each card had to be scanned, *if* the chattering machines ever stopped, the silence made people look up and ask about the silence, "what's that?"

Keeping the huge supply of cards coming in was a security risk. Storage and files of used cards was a big problem. Printouts from which Japanese messages could be translated were piled high on desks, floors, any surface which could hold them, extending into every nook and cranny in Station Hypo.

"We didn't have time to cross-file or cross- index," said Rochefort, "and it was one reason why people thought we were crazy."

As Fleet Intelligence officer, Layton had security clearance to get by the armed Marine guard at the door, and once he got inside, he thought the place looked like a tornado had hit it.

The work proceeded without regard to any heirarchy of command. The man in charge, Captain Thomas Dyer, had under glass in his desk what was reputedly the best collection of pin-ups in the Pacific fleet and a sign which stated:

"You don't have to be crazy to work here, but it helps."

Yeomen didn't dare to clean up Dyers desk. It looked like bedlam, but Dyer knew where everything was and what it was, and he would roast anyone who dared tidy up his desk.

Other than the IBM punches, tabulators, and sorters; no hardware was involved. Dyer and Rochefort kept everything in their heads.

Rochefort received about 140-decrypted messages in Japanese per day. They always had blank spaces and Rochefort would fill in the blanks, sometimes diving back into the files for related information several days or even months back.

Donald M. Showers described the work which he did after he joined the Hypo team as an ensign in Feb., 1942. (Showers eventually became a rear admiral and chief of staff of the Defense Intelligence Agency).

"We typed the translated decrypts onto a 5"x8" card, the entire message: call signs, date-time groups, frequency of transmission when known, and then the text. We underlined everything that was meaningful."

Joe Rochefort was a workaholic and any visiting, spit-and-polish superior was in for a shock. Rochefort wore a battered smoking jacket and slippers (the air conditioning kept the place frigid). He went into Honolulu only twice in the first six months of the war, had a cot installed in his work area so that he could be on call at any time, night or day.

Everybody at Hypo put in long hours. Benzedrine pills were passed around like jelly beans, but the impossible work load for all hands notwithstanding, morale was sky high. Everybody knew that the stakes were: who was going to control the Hawaiian Islands, the Japanese or the U.S.; and that the approaching Midway battle was going to decide that, and that if Washington was allowed to dominate Hypo and to give Admiral Nimitz erroneous information (which they had been prone to do) Rochefort quoted one of his staff as saying:

"If we listen to Washington, we will all end up as Japanese POWs."

In the looming action between the Pacific fleets, we could not afford to swap carrier losses with Japan. We had to destroy theirs and save ours.

Rochefort knew that it wasn't enough for him to prove beyond any doubt that the Japanese were going to attack at Midway. He had to determine their N-day (the day of their attack), and of course Station Negat in Washington had a conclusion about that which they wanted to ram down Hypo's throat, and Rochefort would have no part of that. He knew that he had to determine the N-date with absolute accuracy just as he had proved that the Japanese code for Midway was "AF." He set out to show Negat that its N-date was wrong and to give Admiral Nimitz the exact date at which the Japanese fleet would hit Midway.

It was one of Rochefort's assistants who thought up the idea to send a fake message about a water shortage on Midway to trap the Japanese into confirming that their code name for the Island was AF. That was Lt. Commander Jasper Holmes. When Holmes was with the Engineering School at the University of Hawaii before the war, he had studied the Midway PanAmerican facility, and he knew that the island's entire fresh water supply came from an evaporator plant.

Rochefort liked Holmes' idea and took it to Layton. The fleet intelligence officer took it to Nimitz. The date was May 19.

Nimitz authorized that a submarine cable dispatch be sent to the Midway garrison commander, instructing him to radio a plain-English emergency request for fresh water. A detailed follow-up message, telling of an explosion in their water distillation system was to be made, using one of the strip-code systems which Layton knew the Japanese had capured at Wake Island.

Midways broadcast about the fake water shortage was picked up by the Japanese listening post at Kwajalein in the Marshall Islands and flashed to the Owada headquarters of the Special Duty Radio Intelligence Group on the same day. Within a few hours, the commander of the Japanese air unit designated to attack Midway was signalling his headquarters to provide his force with emergency water supplies, and that message was intercepted at Pearl Harbor.

Rochefort decided to be tactful about breaking the news to Washington. He asked the allied Australian Station Belconnen in Melbourne to inform Washington. Station Belconnen obliged him, sending this transmission to Washington the next day:

'THE AF AIR UNIT SENT FOLLOWING RADIO MESSAGE TO COMMANDANT 14TH NAVAL DISTRICT AK (PEARL HARBOR) OF 20TH. WITH REFERENCE TO THIS UNIT'S REPORT DATED 19TH. AT PRESENT TIME WE HAVE ONLY ENOUGH WATER FOR TWO WEEKS. PLEASE SUPPLY US IMMEDIATELY."

Continuing the deception, Pearl Harbor radioed the Midway garrison that barges of fresh water were on the way. A couple of days later, Rochefort sent this message to Washington:

"AS STATED PREVIOUSLY AF CONFIRMED HERE AS MIDWAY."

The fact that there were actually high rankers in Washington who really believed that Yamamoto's main target in the spring of 1942 was the U.S. West Coast, made Admiral Nimitz grateful to no longer have to wrestle with that particular delusion as he set about mustering every defense he could find to stop the Japanese fleet at Midway.

Nimitz had flown to Midway on May 2. In Washington, Admiral King was not one of those who thought that the Japanese would be attacking the Pacific Coast. He was wrong in another direction. He thought that the main Japanese target would be against U.S. bases in the South Pacific The result of that was that King instructed Nimitz that our carrier aircraft should be deployed to operate from land bases at New Caledonia and Fiji. That would put U.S. carrier air power in the wrong place at the wrong time, leaving Midway wide open to the Japanese attack there.

Nimitz now could breathe a sigh of relief at the confirmation by the Japanese air unit commander that the enemy was going to Midway.

In Washington, King was working to get more ships. and planes directed to the defense of our Pacific bases, but Roosevelt's chief military adviser, Army General George C. Marshall, told King that he would have to fight the Japanese with the ships and planes already assigned to the Pacific.

The sinking of the LEXINGTON really had been a personal blow to Admiral King. The LEXINGTON had once been his flagship, and he realized the situation that Nimitz had been placed in by the Washington priority to send virtually all arms to the European Theatre of Operations, leaving the Pacific forces to fend off the Japanese with whatever they had. That policy already had left many thousands of Americans and their allies stranded as POWs at Wake Island and in the Philippines.

That's why the Hypo staff officer had commented, "If we listen to Washington, we will all end up as Japanese POWs'

There was some truth to the statement. Dyed-in-the-wool American conservatives were much more concerned about protecting Washington, D.C., than they were Hawaii. The Japanese had considered that in their decision to attack Pearl Harbor. After all, some had advised the emperor, Hawaii is only a territory of the United States, not part of that nation. As for Midway, hardly anyone who lived exclusively in the eastern seaboard

183

of the United States knew where that was or the strategic importance it was about to assume in stopping the Japanese fleet.

That was why Rochefort and Layton would not hold still for the ideas of naval communications director Captain Joseph R. Redman or his younger brother, head of the restructured OP-20-G, even though those two high rankers had worked their way in to Admiral Turner's little power triumvirate who wanted to control all naval intelligence analysis and to deal with Layton and Rochefort only as subordinates.

Layton summarized his situation: "Joe and I had a difficult task. We had the confidence of Nimitz, but now we had to demonstrate beyond any doubt that the evaluations being made in Washington were wrong."

Even after Washington conceded that Station Hypo had identified the central Pacific target of the Japanese as Midway with the code designation of AT, they predicted that June 15 would be N-Day.

Rochefort had to disagree with that conclusion, also.

As the third week in May found the Japanese combined fleet on maneuvers south of Japan, their instructions for a pre-battle conference at Saipan were received at Station Hypo. Those instructions contained an important clue that the Japanese combined fleet was to depart for Midway on the 27th of May.

Rochefort calculated that since Saipan was 2,191 miles from Midway, it would take five days for the combined Japanese fleet to make the trip, travelling at 20 knots. That would put them off Midway on June 2 or 3 as N-Day, almost two weeks earlier than the Washington estimate.

It would take only three days to rush the ENTERPRISE, HORNET, and the damaged YORKTOWN at top speed from Pearl Harbor to Midway, and since Halsey's task force with the ENTERPRISE and the HORNET was due on the 26th of May at Pearl, that gave Nimitz no margin for error if we were going to concentrate our forces to resist the Japanese combined fleet on the earlier N-Day, June 2 or 3. The Japanese still thought, due to Admiral Hara's report from the Coral Sea that YORKTOWN had been sunk along with the LEXINGTON.

Again, Rochefort could and did prove that he was right and Negat was wrong, because that Japanese air unit request for a two-week water reserve on May 18 revealed that the Japanese planned for their Midway occupation to be completed 10 or 11 days before Washington's predicted date of June 15.

Nimitz called his staff together on May 26, the eve of Halsey's return to Pearl Harbor. Layton's best advise was that one Japanese attack force had left from Ominato in northern Japan for the Aleutian Islands on May 25 or on that same day of the Nimitz staff meeting, May 26, and that the larger Midway assault force would sail from Saipan a day later. That meant that U.S. forces would have to be in position off Alaska by June 1, and off Midway by June 3.

Washington intelligence analysts continued to cast doubt on Station Hypo's analysis and gave only grudging concessions that Midway probably was the Japanese main target. The Cominch intelligence summary of May 24 from Washington stated:

"While all available information indicates that attack and occupation of Midway is the objective of the force assembled at Saipan, attention is invited to the fact that from this base a force can move with almost equal facility southward in the direction of Australia."

Washington also got the Hawaiian Army Commander, General Delos C. Emmons, in on the act to question Nimitz mobilization of all available forces for the effort at Midway. Emmons was alarmed at losing control of his B-17 and B-24 long-range bombers that Nimitz was urging him to send to Midway.

Rochefort clinched the pivotal dates of the Midway operation with an intercept on May 26 of orders for two groups of Japanese destroyers which were to escort the invasion troops to Midway. They were to leave Saipan on May 28 and proceed at 11 knots for a June 1 rendezvous with the invasion transports; then "at 1900 (7:00 p.m.) arrive at AF." Unless that message was part of a very elaborate ruse, there could be no doubt N-Day was to be either June 4 or 5.

Nimitz asked Layton to name the dates and dispositions of the Japanese fleet at Midway. Layton started to reply with his usual caution about being positive and specific.

Nimitz said, "I want you to be specific. After all, this is the job I have given you—to be the admiral commanding the Japanese forces, and tell me what is going on."

185

Layton took a deep breath and replied that the carriers probably would attack on the morning of June 4 from the northwest on a bearing of *325* degrees, which meant that they could be sighted at about 175 miles from Midway at around 0700.

Admiral Nimitz accepted the conclusions and confidently passed them on to his staff on May 27.

Layton did not sleep for the next seven nights. He said:

"I knew very well the extent to which Nimitz had staked the fate of the Pacific Fleet on our estimates, and his own judgment, against those of Admiral King and his staff in Washington.

No sooner did Layton make those predictions than three different types of bad news had to be absorbed by Nimitz.

1. The YORKTOWN limped into Pearl Harbor, trailing a ten-mile oil slick from her leaking tanks. Nimitz put on waders and led an inspection party of shipwrights and engineers under YORKTOWN's hull in Dry Dock #1. He ordered minimum repairs to make her seaworthy, a giant steel patch to be welded to the hull where her plates had been sprung, and internal bulkheads to be shored up with timbers.

"We must have the ship back in three days,' he told the engineers. Fifteen-hundred workers went to work immediately, continuing under glaring lights at night in violation of blackouts, working around the clock.

2. During the night of May 27, the Japanese put a new version of their naval code system into action, negating 18 months of allied code-breaking and forcing the code breakers to begin all over again. Had the Japanese put their new code into effect a few days earlier, it would have been disastrous to the code breakers at Station Hypo.

3. A haggard and worn Admiral Halsey was ordered by Nimitz to a hospital bed upon his arrival at Pearl Harbor aboard his flagship ENTERPRISE. He had been suffering for weeks from a progressive skin irritation. His place was taken on the ENTERPRISE's flag bridge by his cruiser commander, Rear Admiral Raymond A. Spruance

As the HORNET and ENTERPRISE slipped out of Pearl Harbor on May 28, and Admiral Spruance set course for Point Luck about *350* miles northeast of Midway, Layton began a scheme of radio deception to make the Japanese decoders at the Owada Intelligence Center think that Halsey's two carriers were more than 1,000 miles away from Midway in the South Pacific. At Efate, 1,500 miles to the southwest in the New Hebrides, the seaplane tender, TANGIER, sent out radio signals, pretending to be an aircraft carrier flying routine air operations. In the Coral Sea, the heavy cruiser, SALT LAKE CITY was carrying on the same pretense.

On May 29, Japanese troops comprising the 5,000 strong Midway occupation force, convoyed by an armada of carriers, cruisers, battleships and destroyers, left Saipan for Midway.

THE FOURTEENTH TALE

COULD HAWAII STOP A JAPANESE INVASION?

The Fourteenth Tale–Could Hawaii Stop A Japanese Invasion?

In the first six months since Pearl Harbor, the soldier and marine population of Oahu had risen from 43,000 to 135,000. The 7th Army Air Corps had been beefed up to include several scores of long range bombers (B-17s and B-24s) and new fighter planes.

The Signal Corps, Aircraft warning radar system was operating around the clock on Oahu, Kauai, Maui, and the big island. Each island had its own filter center and fighter-intercept planes. Kauai, the western-most island, had tracked successfully the second attack force (those three four-engined "Emilies" March 5th) through its radar filter center at Lihue before the Emilies were picked up by the north shore radar station on Oahu at Kahuku Point (Opana) and passed on to the Oahu Radar Filter Center, "Little Robert," at Fort Shafter.

The WARDs (Women's Air Raid Defense) were on duty around the clock at all of the radar filter centers. On Oahu, they had moved out of the old filter center, "Little Robert" down by the Fort Shafter dump, and into a brand new, underground tunnel nicknamed "Lizard" with its own auxiliary power, lounges, snack bar, and security system.

General Emmons was quoted in the Honolulu ADVERTISER as warning the civilian population that Japanese assaults were expected against Hawaii.

At Lizard our most charismatic and high-ranking Osage warrior, Major General Clarence Tinker, Commander of the 7th Army Air Corps, called a special alert at the end of the third week in May. It would turn out to be within the last three weeks of Tinker's life.

He gathered two other high rankers about him to tell the WARDs assembled in the Recreation Room that they would be dependent upon their own resources during an air attack. The WARDs would be expected to stay at their posts and prepare fire-fighting equipment (ladders, buckets of sand and water, litters for the injured), etc.

After that, everyone at Radar Filter Center Lizard took the impending battle of Midway very strenuously. The WARDs knew as well as anybody in the Hawaiian Islands what kinds of distances, types of airplanes and ships, and sea and air routes between Hawaii and Midway would be involved; and they were under the same rules of punishment as the GI's if they deserted their posts or blabbed about their work.

One of the WARDs, Nancy West, got the news that all service wives dreaded most when the ENTERPRISE returned to Pearl Harbor on May 27. She was a widow. Her husband, Bill, had suffered a fatal crash in his SBD dive bomber on takeoff from the ENTERPRISE. She got the news from Bill's best friend and shipmate, Ens. Cleo J. Dobson.

Not that anyone needed tragic news to know that a war was going on. On Oahu, martial law had brought with it curfews from dusk till dawn, gas rationing, and censorship of all written materials.

Fresh military troops and more defense workers arrived in Honolulu almost daily. There was constant hustle and bustle; more than a million miles of barbed wire had been strung on Hawaiian beaches. Infantry was constantly on maneuvers, repulsing prospective invasion forces. Patrol planes roared off around the clock. Three marine divisions were training for invasion of south sea and central Pacific island beaches.

Yamamoto's top researcher, Capt. Sigenori Kami, had advised the admiral that Japan probably could capture Hawaii, but would find it difficult to supply troops there because of a shortage of ships.

Kami pointed out that Japan would have to send 30 shiploads of supplies every month to keep the occupation going, creating a constant drain on food and war supplies which already were in short supply in Japan. Losses of supply ships would be certain to occur under attacks from U.S. submarines and aircraft across 4,000 miles of the Pacific Ocean between Japan and Hawaii.

Two-million, 900-thousand tons of supplies had been shipped to Hawaii from American ports in 1941, Kami continued. Hawaii did not produce enough food for its civilian population. Pre-war Hawaii produced 84% of its fruit, but only 10% of its rice, 21% of its dairy products, 30% of its fish, 40% of its eggs, 41% of the needed meat, and 46% of the required vegetables.

Chances were that not just civilians and American POWs would go hungry, but that Japanese soldiers also would be on short rations. Furthermore, one out of three people in Hawaii's civilian population was doho. [Doho means of Japanese ancestry, no matter what the citizenship status is]. Hawaii had 160,000 dohos—120,000 of whom were Japanese-American citizens, and 40,000 still citizens of Japan.

What would the Hawaiian dohos do under Japanese occupation? Would they cooperate with the occupation troops or fight them?

Radio Tokyo buzzed with 'expert" opinions, including the following:

A.   Americans will not defend Hawaii with gyokusai (to the last man). After all, Hawaii is just a territory of the U.S., not one of its states.

B. Dohos would welcome Japanese liberation from hateful American rule. The haole-controlled big five corporations which dominate the Hawaiian economy (Castle & Cooke, Theo H. Davies, American Factors, C. Brewer & Co., and Alexander & Baldwin) are exploiters of an island nation which rightfully belongs to the Greater East-Asian Co-prosperity Sphere under Japan.

C. The entire Pacific Ocean, including the waters between the U.S. West Coast and Hawaii is already under the control of Japanese warships.

D.   The logical extension of recent Japanese victories is the Hawaiian Archipelago. The Hawaiian Archipelagos western end at Midway Island is closer to Japan than the eastern end is to the mainland of the U.S.

The military affairs reporter for the TOKYO SHINBUN newspaper, Hajemi Mochizuki, could not contain himself as he rhapsodized about the triumphant entry of the Imperial Japanese navy into New York Harbor.

"The rising sun flag flutters proudly over Rocky Mountain peaks . . . The stars and stripes vanish forever from the globe . . . . As the Imperial fleet enters New York Harbor, huge crowds throng to the shoreline waving Rising Sun flags and screaming 'Banzai'."

In spite of all such rosy predicitions in Japan about the call to the Rising Sun flag among Hawaiian dohos, the only person convicted of espionage in wartime Hawaii was Otto Kuehn, a German.

Ironically, the reasoning of the American military for not carrying out mass evacuation of dohos from Hawaii to the mainland (similar to the mass evacuations of Japanese-Americans which began in March, 1942, on the U.S. Pacific Coast under Executive Order #9066), had little to do with justice.

What discouraged it most effectively was the impossibility of providing transportation for somewhere between 40,000 and 160,000 people from Hawaii to the mainland U.S. at a time when there was not enough shipping and air transportation to get needed troops and skilled workers and vital supplies to locations throughout the vast Pacific Ocean.

As for the idea to concentrate Hawaii's dohos on one Hawaiian Island, such as Molokai, that would create impossible problems in housing, feeding, sewage and water systems, and supervision. After all, who was prepared to hold one-third of all Hawaiians captive? Further, to try such a thing might alienate dohos who were loyal to the U.S.

Caught in the middle, Japanese families turned in or threw away old heirlooms (samurai swords, kimonos, etc.); threw away pictures of the emperor; took down Buddhist and Shinto shrines, even threw away pictures of relatives in Japan — books, letters, family records were burned because they might cause suspicion of the owners if local troops should search homes.

And the US. Army Signal Corps did carry out house-to-house investigations, looking primarily for contraband goods, particularly cameras and ham radio sets.

Feeling ran very high against the Japanese in those eventful days of May, 1942. Chinese Hawaiians and Korean-Hawaiians already were outraged by war grievances against the Japanese military, and now Filipino-Hawaiians were aggrieved by the fall of the Philippines and the brutal treatment of captives which had started with the Bataan Death March.

The crippled American fleet moved out to stop the Japanese at Midway.on May 28, 1942. By the next two days (May 30) 145 Japanese warships were at sea and the sleepless Layton calculated that the 1,534 acres of coral sand which was Midway represented less dry land than the total deck area of the Japanese ships on their way to take over the place. To stop that massive armada, the U.S. fleet numbered a total of 35 surface ships. Just in sheer numbers of ships, the odds were 4 to 1 against us. Every night at midnight, Nimitz's staff could see those odds laid out on massive, color-coded overlays.

Layton's Cincpac operation plotting room was not impressive to look at. It consisted of a huge chart representing most of the Pacific Ocean, laid over plywood across a pair of sawhorses. On tracing paper, plotting officers indicated the movements of our ships in blue crayon and the movements of Japanese ships in orange crayon. Fresh overlays, incorporating the latest intelligence data and predictions, were laid out every midnight.

Midway was an unlikely place, one of the world's most remote islands, to become the pivotal battle site of the WWII naval struggle between Japan and the United States. It is a coral reef which encircles Sand, Eastern, and Spit islands, located 1,250 miles west-northwest of Honolulu. The reef is approximately five miles in diameter, showing 1,534 acres of sand and coral surface above the sea. Geologists figure it is 25,000,000 years old, give or take *5-million* years.

Before man ever got there, the birds claimed it. They came by the millions; albatrosses, frigates, boobies, terns, petrels, noddies and other migrating shorebirds. They shared the place with seals, sea turtles, dolphins and many varieties of fish.

Workers from the Commercial Pacific Cable Company laid cable there in 1903. In the 1930's, Pan-American World Airways built facilities for its Pan-American World Airways Flying Clipper seaplane service, which included a 45-room hotel with a swimming pool.

Then, in 1938, the U.S. Navy took over, dredged a channel through the reef, and built an air station and submarine bases on Sand and Eastern Islands.

Now, on the eve of the Midway battle, the 7th AAF had flown in all of the big, four-engined B-17 bombers which Midway could hold. Marine fighter planes and Navy PBYs carried out patrols.

Layton had arranged for one presence at Midway which never appeared on his plotting board or in any message out of Admiral Nimitz's headquarters at Pearl Harbor.

Hollywood director John Ford was detached to Pearl Harbor as a Lt. Commander in the navy. Layton called Ford in and without revealing details, asked if he was interested in a trip into the Pacific that could yield exclusive film action. Ford was interested. Layton told Nimitz of the film directors agreement and Nimitz, maintaining absolute secrecy with Ford, approved of sending him and a cameraman to Midway.

By 1500 (3:00 p.m.) that afternoon, Ford and his cameraman left Kaneohe air station on two PBYs bound for Midway. They did not know where they were going. Layton had told Ford only:

"Where you are going, you won't know till you get there, and you won't be able to send any messages."

Layton didn't mention to Ford that, if things went wrong, he and his cameraman would probably spend the rest of the war in a Japanese POW camp if they didn't get killed in the enemy assault, but Ford and his cameraman probably understood that. Compared to how far out on a limb Layton had gone with Nimitz in his Midway predictions, that was an incidental matter.

THE FIFTEENTH TALE

PRELUDE TO MIDWAY

The Fifteenth Tale–Prelude to Midway

Yamamoto and Nagumo really believed that the American carrier YORKTOWN was with the LEXINGTON at the bottom of the Coral Sea.

The Japanese pilots who returned back to the ZUIKAKU with the certainty that they had sunk her were not really lying. They were mistaken, but they had left her on fire and trailing an oil slick ten miles long. It did not seem possible to them or to many of the American crewmen on board the YORKTOWN that she could make it almost 4,000 miles back to Pearl Harbor. The pilots convinced their task force commander, Admiral Hara, that they had sunk two carriers, not just one.

From the American perspective, even if she did get back to Pearl Harbor, with her steel plates sprung and her bulwarks in no shape to re-enter combat, how could she possibly get back into combat condition to damage the Japanese fleet in the foreseeable future?

By the American estimate, she needed three months to complete her repairs. Nimitz allowed three days after YORKTOWN arrived, trailing her 10-mile oil slick, at Drydock #1 at Pearl Harbor.

For a true perspective on just how remote the American chances were for us to be able to carry out the extensive repairs needed to put the YORKTOWN back into action in three days, one has to look back at the state of mind of Admiral Nagumo on the afternoon of Dec. 7, 1941, when he turned his back on Commander Fuchida and his technical advisor and decided against another attack on the repair facilities at Pearl Harbor.

If Nagumo had let loose his 400 pilots and planes to destroy our fuel supplies, repair facilities including drydocks (all plainiy in view on that clear day of Dec. 7, 1941, at Pearl Harbor), the nearest place where repairs of that magnitude could have been done would have been Bremerton, Washington, or San Diego or Long Beach, California, providing we could have found the fuel to get the ship that far.

Clearly, what enabled the YORKTOWN to become seaworthy enough to go back into action at Midway was a failure by Admiral Nagumo to press his advantage at Pearl Harbor, and the incredible insistence of Admiral Nimitz to command that a three-month repair job be narrowed down to three days, and the incredible industry and ingenuity of 1,500 shipyard workers who flooded the night with lights in apparent violation of the admiral's own blackout orders and got the work done.

Without taking a lot of risks, YORKTOWN could not possibly have gotten into the fight at Midway—a fight she did not survive, but in which she and her planes played a vital part.

So, Yamamoto and Nagumo had every reason to believe that YORKTOWN was sunk and permanently out of action. Granted that, why didn't they check to make sure? Why didn't they send reconaissance aircraft over Pearl Harbor to find out for sure what ships were in drydock there? They might have learned, not only that the YORKTOWN was being repaired instead of lying sunken in the Coral Sea, but also that the HORNET and the ENTERPRISE were not in the south Pacific, that they were facing three American carriers moving in to oppose them at Midway instead of one.

They tried to do that. They moved a submarine fleet to French Frigate Shoals to arrange for a reconaissance flight over Pearl Harbor, using the same long-range "Emilies" to be refueled by submarines in order to complete the round-trip from their base at Wotje in the Marshall Islands to Pearl Harbor.

But Nimitz had foreseen that move and countered it by mining the harbor at French Frigate Shoals and sending U.S. warships there to patrol it. The Japanese had tipped their hand and alerted Nimitz as to their capabilities in the ineffectual raid over Pearl Harbor on March 5. Really, Admiral Hara also could have prevented YORKTOWN's resurrection if he had pressed his advantage and sent her to the bottom of the Coral Sea. Hara had failed to check his pilots' reports and confirm that YORKTOWN had gone down, and like Admiral Nagumo at Pearl Harbor five months earlier, had turned to go home one day too soon.

Both Nagumo and Hara had become so conservative that they acted as if they already had won the war and had no need of further risk-taking.

In this regard, their intelligence teamwork failed to match that incredible, risk-taking team of Admiral Nimitz, Edwin Layton and Joe Rochefort. The same home front, bureaucratic, power grubbing influences were at work in Washington as those which were at work in Tokyo. Both over-simplified and distorted with home-front provincialism the intelligence picture being assembled by the Japanese at Kwajalein and by

199

the Americans at Oahu, but Nimitz, Layton, and Rochefort were using every device at their command (including ship-and-shore radar, radio code breaking, and even lesser warships masquerading vis-a-vis radio communications as aircraft carriers in the South Pacific) in avoidance and sometimes defiance of Washington's insistence on telling them how to fight their war.

Nimitz was a master at keeping a clear mind on who he was fighting and who he was not fighting. He realized that, in MacArthur and FDR, he had two egomaniacs with a strong tendency to pose dramatically and take credit for anything that the navy could accomplish in the Pacific, but he did not let that send him into egotistical battle with them. He simply avoided confronting them and worked around them (no matter how bothersome they were) to preserve and make effective use of his Pacific fleet.

Layton, spurred on by Nimitz, was working with all of the skill and expertise at his command to give the admiral the Japanese mentality along with their battle plans and up-to-the-minute operations coming to focus on Midway.

Layton had missed one major part of the Japanese plan—the personal.presence of Yamamoto on his giant flagship, YAMATO, to entrap the American carriers with superior firepower from his massive battleships and destroy them, to lie in wait and finish off the enemy carriers after the Japanese carriers got through with them.

Joe Rochefort had pushed himself to the limit to plot his predictions of the Japanese in the Aleutians and at Midway.

You might say that Rochefort was (in infantry terms) the point man against the inaccuracies and arrogance of the intelligence bunglers in Washington. He did not reckon the cost to himself personally, in terms of not being advanced in rank and not getting credit for his work. He had become the spirit of American intelligence in the Pacific, and he worked with a sixth sense about what the enemy forces were going to do at Midway, where they were going to be, and when they were going to be there.

If the Japanese had commanded a Rochefort and a Layton to work for them, they still would not have had an Admiral Nimitz to give them the direction combined with the freedom that would have allowed them to work as creatively as they did. Rochefort was dedicated to his work beyond the reasonable, the profitable, and even in defiance of his own self interests. He didn't give a damn what happened to his navy career.

He did not blink at the risks involved to his own reputation.

"If we get ready for this attack on June 3 and it does not come off, we may look silly," Rochefort told Layton, "but there will be time for our ships to refuel and get back on station. If we are not prepared and the Japs strike, it will be a case of Pearl Harbor all over again—and the Navy will have no excuse."

Rochefort, driven by his mania to check and re-check his work, occasionally could do something absolutely stupid in the eyes of his superiors, even in the eyes of Nimitz, who knew how good at his decrypting Rochefort was. At such times, it was easy for Navy hard-liners to discount Rochefort as a product of the University of California instead of the Naval Academy at Annapolis. It was true that Rochefort had entered the navy from U C., Berkeley, not from Annapolis.

On May 27, Nimitz had invited Commander Rochefort to his staff meeting, which included a visitor from Washington, Atty. General Robert C. Richardson, who had been sent by the Army Chief of Staff, General Marshall. General Emmons also had been invited. Nimitz had invited him to reassure him that the Navy was on top of the situation at Midway. Nimitz wanted Rochefort to give this four-star assemblage perspective, the whole intelligence picture on the approaching battle.

Looking like an unmade bed, bleary eyed from lack of sleep, Rochefort showed up 30 minutes late and got an ice-cold reception for his brief apology. Then, he gave a timely and brilliant analysis of the situation at Midway.

In the rigidly disciplined Japanese navy, an officer like Rochefort would not have been tolerated.

Richness in diversity and willingness to take risks, spurred on by being the underdog to the point of desperation, had brought these three together at exactly the right time in the right place, and Nimitz understood who he was fighting, and who (in spite of the dramatic posturing and arrogance going on to discredit him by people who were trying to establish their own intelligence power base in Washington) he was not fighting, and he stayed focused on the approaching battle at Midway.

He also realized that the dramatic posturing of MacArthur struck a common chord with the dramatic posturing of FDR, and he let it all pass him by, like an irrelevant parade, in the wake of the American Pacific fleet which he, alone, commanded in its desperate need for a victory at Midway.

THE SIXTEENTH TALE

THE AMBUSH AT MIDWAY

The Sixteenth Tale–The Ambush at Midway

Away back in 1281, a huge armada of Korean and Chinese ships carrying an army of 150,000 men to invade Japan was destroyed by a typhoon (kamikaze). Ever since then, Japanese leaders had believed and taught their people that their sacred homeland could not be reached by an invader because Japan was protected by divine winds.

With more than a 4 to 1 advantage in surface ships (145 to 35), the Japanese had every reason to expect another great victory at Midway— perhaps the total destruction of the American fleet, and the consolation of Japanese gains against the allied nations in the Pacific inside a circumference far removed from the Japanese homeland.

How could the Japanese hope to destroy the American Pacific fleet at Midway? They could because Nimitz was throwing everything he had into the Midway battle.

The only advantage the Americans had was the element of surprise. Our code-breaking gave us advance knowledge of the enemy's plan of action. We had become proficient in our uses of radar by this time, both on board our warships and in the army Signal Corps coastal installations, and the Japanese still were not using radar effectively. By maintaining radio silence until we were sighted, our carriers might achieve an ambush of the enemy carriers.

The first rule of battle when an admiral faces a major engagement is to concentrate his forces. Yamamoto knew that as well as any naval commander in history. Yet, he divided his powerful forces between Attu and Kiska in the Aleutian Islands and Midway, 1,500 miles away on the eve of battle.

Why?

Because his intelligence sources told him that no American carriers were *in* position to oppose him at Midway. Layton's intelligence predictions for Nimitz proved accurate, and the Japanese task force, Kido Butai, including four carriers, appeared exactly where and when he had plotted them on the map. The date was June 3. Layton was in Nimitz's office at Pearl Harbor when the dispatch came in.

Nimitz face broke into a big smile as he waved the message in the air and handed it to Layton, exclaiming: "Have you seen this?"

A PBY based on Midway had sighted the main Japanese force. The message read:

"Main body... bearing 262, distance 700 miles. .. eleven ships, course 090, speed 19 knots."

That "main body" was not the strike force which would support the troop landings at Midway, and to avoid any chance of confusion among his top commanders, Nimitz sent urgent dispatches to Admirals Spruance and Fletcher: [Fletcher had learned his lesson about the uses of intelligence in the Coral Sea. When he had sat down in Nimitz's office to give an oral report about why he had passed up opportunities to attack the Japanese carriers in the Coral Sea, Nimitz had informed him that Admiral King wanted a detailed, written report; and Fletcher since then was paying close attention to Nimitz's orders, which were based upon Layton's predictions about the enemy's fleet movements off of Midway.

"Main body. .. that is not, repeat not, the enemy strike force."

The Japanese strike force was attacked that afternoon of June 3 by 19 B- 17s of the 7th Army Air Force, and later that evening by Navy PBYs based at Midway, but they failed to halt the approach of Japanese troop ships.

By dawn of June 4, Nagumo's carriers were off to the northwest of Midway. Our carriers were 400 miles away from them to the northeast of Midway. The difference was that we knew where their carriers were, and Nagumo and Yamamoto had no idea that we had three carriers only 400 miles away and closing. it would be the ENTERPRISE, the HORNET and the patched-up YORKTOWN against the AKAGI, KAGA, HIRYU and SORYU.

Admiral Spruance's ENTERPRISE and HORNET were accompanied by five heavy cruisers, one light cruiser and nine destroyers. Admiral Fletcher's YORKTOWN task force included two heavy cruisers and six destroyers.

The four Japanese carriers in the strike force under Admiral Nagumo were accompanied by two battleships, four heavy cruisers and 12 destroyers. Their back-up force included one carrier, two battleships, four heavy cruisers, two light cruisers and ten destroyers. On patrol off of Midway were 14 Japanese submarines.

The two U.S. task forces commanded by Spruance and Fletcher had slipped by the Japanese picket fleet of submarines undetected.

At dawn on June 4, the four Japanese carriers, steaming 300 miles ahead of Yamamotos main force proceeded unaware that three American carriers soon would be within striking distance of them. As the Japanese pilots of 76 bombers and 36 escorting fighters of Kido Butai prepared to take off to hit Midway, they were read a Tokyo intelligence radio message by their briefing officer:carriers which were about 240 miles northeast of Midway, heading south at 20 knots. Obviously, Nimitz calculated, Nagumo was still unaware that U.S. carriers were in the area. Otherwise, he would be holding his planes, armed and ready to launch, when he came within range of the American carriers

It was nervous time in the Nimitz headquarters at Pearl Harbor. The Spruance and Fletcher task forces had been ordered to maintain radio silence until such time as they were sighted by the Japanese. The garrison commander at Midway confirmed that he was under attack at 0625 with a three-word message:

"AIR RAID MIDWAY."

From then on, the minutes dragged by like hours. Each minute that passed in silence was really good news for Nimitz and Layton because it meant that our carriers were maintaining radio silence and that meant that they had not been spotted, but that didn't make the silence any less nerve-wracking. Nimitz went into his office and Layton retired to his office where he could use a private telephone line to keep in touch with with Joe Rochefort at Station Hypo.

The idea of course was to strike the first blow and catch the enemy aircraft returning to their carriers with empty fuel tanks, empty bomb racks and empty guns. Under those conditions, an aircraft carrier is a floating ammunition and fuel dump with its wings clipped.

All of the land-based aircraft at Midway had been scrambled and were either getting into position to beat off the Japanese raid or heading for the Japanese carners.

Shortly after eight o'clock, Rochefort called Layton with the news that a Japanese plane had spotted an American task force and signaled:

"Enemy is accompanied by what appears to be a carrier
    bringing up the rear."

Layton plotted the enemy pilots position and decided that it was the YORKTOWN which had been spotted, but that the Japanese did not yet know about the presence of the ENTERPRISE and the HORNET.

The same news on board his flagship, AKAGI, put Nagumo into a dilemma. Did he have time to wait for his planes to return from the Midway strike before attacking the lone American carrier which his scout plane had sighted?

At the same time, Admiral Spruance on the still undetected ENTERPRISE and the accompanying HORNET saw his chance to catch Nagumo's carriers with their flight decks jammed with refueling aircraft. To do that, he would have to launch his slow-moving torpedo planes (which had a combat radius of only 175 miles) at the limit of their range, but if they didn't have enough gas to get back to the American carriers, Midway gave them an alternative landing site.

Spruance launched 27 torpedo bombers and 67 dive bombers, and held back 36 fighters to counter any enemy attack. Sixteen miles astern, YORKTOWN launched 17 dive bombers, 16 Devastators, and 6 Wildcats. Fletcher retained half of his planes to counter any enemy strike. The total number of American carrier planes on their way to attack the Japanese carriers was 155.

Meanwhile, Nagumo's fleet had to dodge and weave, not only to avoid the bombs of the land-based B- 17s from Midway, but also the torpedoes of the U.S. submarine, NAUTILUS. On the AKAGI's hangar deck, a second strike against Midway had been prepared, and crews were starting to arrange planes with high-explosive, impact-fused bombs. Still under the impression that he was facing attacking planes from only one American carrier, Nagumo decided to delay the arming of planes for the second strike so that he could land and refuel the planes returning from the first strike on Midway.

So, the decks of the Japanese carriers were covered with planes, interwoven with gasoline hoses, and trolley loads of bombs and ammunition. Below decks, rows of torpedoes and high-explosive bombs which were being loaded on planes for the second strike at Midway, had not been returned to their racks in the protected magazines.

Into that frenzied picture came a Zeros scouting report to Nagumo:
'TEN ENEMY TORPEDO PLANES HEADING TOWARD YOU.

The slow Devastators of the HORNET's Torpedo Squadron 8 were cut down to the last plane with only one survivor afloat in the water. That was Ensign George Gay, who described the low-level attack led by Lt. Commander John C. Waldron:

"He went straight for the Japanese fleet as if he had a string tied to them."

Next to attack were 14 Devastators from the ENTERPRISE. Nine of the 14 were shot down without scoring a single hit on the enemy carriers. Then, ten of 12 torpedo bombers from YORKTOWN fell under a curtain of anti-aircraft fire. Still, the enemy carriers were not hit.

Back at Pearl Harbor, none of this slaughter of his carrier planes was yet reported to Nimitz, and he was frantic to know what was happening. Not until shortly after 1000 did Pacific Fleet Headquarters at Pearl Harbor report hearing the ENTERPRISE air officer yell:

"ATTACK! ATTACK! IMMEDIATELY!"

Flight leader, Lt. Commander Clarence W. McClusky radioed back to the ENTERPRISE:

"WILCO, AS SOON AS I CAN FIND THE BASTARDS!" The Japanese carriers had changed to a northerly course to recover their returning planes from the first strike at Midway. Thirty-five dive bombers from the HORNET searched for an hour without success, and had to land at Midway to refuel. But McClusky discovered a Japanese destroyer, followed it back as it rejoined Nagumo's carriers, and led ENTERPRISE'S 67 dive bombers over the enemy carriers, catching the intercepting Zeroes as they flew at deck level to chase off torpedo planes.

The Devastators went into a 70-degree dive and hurtled down on the AKAGI and KAGA.

The scene from below decks on the AKAGI was described by the same man who had led the first flight of Japanese attackers at Pearl Harbor. That was then commander, now Captain Mitsuo Fuchida. He had risen from his berth in sick bay after undergoing an operation for a ruptured appendix. He had heard first the screams of the dive bomber followed by a direct bomb hit.

"I was horrified at the destruction that had been wrought in a matter of seconds. There was a huge hole in the flight deck just abaft the midship elevator. The elevator itself twisted like molten glass, was drooping into

208

the hangar. Deck plates reeled upward in grotesque configurations. Planes stood tail up belching livid flames and jet-black smoke."

Nagumo's flagship AKAGI was mortally damaged, and he had to abandon ship. Then, off the flagship's starboard quarter, four direct bomb hits blasted the KAGA. Then, YORKTOWN's dive bombers arrived and concentrated their bombs on SORYU Their explosions blew the elevator against the bridge, torched the parked planes, and blew apart the hangar. Later that afternoon, two torpedoes from the submarine NAUTILUS sank the SORYU.

At a cost of 47 U.S. carrier planes, three of the *four* Japanese carriers attacking Midway had been destroyed.

All of YORKTOWN's dive bombers survived the raid and headed back to their carrier, but HIRYU's pilots found YORKTOWN around noon as she was recovering her dive bombers. The HIRYU raiders scored three direct hits. One bomb detonated in YORKTOWN's smokestack and put five of the carrier's six boilers out of commission. An hour later, Hiryu's planes struck again and sent two torpedoes into YORKTOWN's port side, jamming the rudder and ripping open her patched-up hull.

Meanwhile, the crippled YORKTOWN's Dauntless scouts located the HIRYU 110 miles northwest of Midway, and Spruance at 1530 launched another strike of 24 dive bombers, including ten from the stricken YORKTOWN. Their bombs tore into the deck, elevator and hangars of the doomed HIRYU Admiral Tamon Yamaguchi's flagship became a flaming torch which burned through the night and carried him to the bottom with it the next morning.

For a day and a half, the captain and crew of the YORKTOWN struggled to save their ship. After having abandoned ship, they reboarded the stricken carrier and brought her under tow with a destroyer alongside, supplying power for the pumps that kept her afloat. But on the afternoon of June 6, a Japanese submarine fired a salvo of torpedoes which split the destroyer HAMMANN in two and opened up another gash in YORKTOWN's hull. The carrier capsized and plunged to the bottom 150 miles off Midway in pre-dawn darkness on June 7.

The battle of Midway was over. We had lost 347 men, a carrier, a destroyer, and 147 aircraft. In its first defeat suffered by the Japanese navy in 350 years, Japan had lost four carriers, one cruiser, 2,500 men and 322 aircraft. Those 2,500 fatalities included the best navy pilots Japan had in the Pacific.

At the radar filter center, Lizard at Fort Shafter, we had lost the 7th Army Air Corps General Tinker, whose B-17 failed to return to its base. We thought that he had been killed in the naval battle, but it turned out that his B-17 had fallen out of formation during a raid on Wake Island.

Radio Tokyo tried to trumpet the occupation of Attu and Kiska in the Aleutian Islands by Japanese troops as a major victory, but Nimitz recalled Spruance's task force from chasing after the enemy up that far north and ordered him back to Pearl Harbor. He was unwilling to risk his surviving carriers in the zone of icy northern storms where they might be subject to ambush by enemy battleships and submarines.

Back in Hawaii, Army General Emmons graciously arrived at Pacific Fleet headquarters on Sunday morning with a jeroboam of champagne, done up in blue and gold ribbons, navy style. Admiral Nimitz sent his own car to bring Commander Joe Rochefort over to share the champagne. Rochefort arrived after all of the champagne was gone, but Nimitz declared to his assembled staff

"This officer deserves a major share of the credit for the victory at Midway."

It was clear to Nimitz that, without his intelligence team in the Pacific, there would have been no American victory at Midway. It was also clear to him that if he had listened to the power brokers who were running the navy's intelligence show in Washington, he would have been caught flat-footed with his carriers out of range of the Japanese invasion fleet at Midway.

THE SEVENTEENTH TALE

THE FINAL OUTCOME

The Seventeenth Tale–The Final Outcome

It would be wonderful to report that the Koa (the warriors) who did the fighting and the code breakers who led them to the right place at the right time got the credit, the plaudits and the promotions for their victory at Midway, but that is not what happened.

Unknown to Admiral Nimitz, the two chief intelligence power brokers in Washington, the Redman brothers, had used their ready access to senior members of the naval staff to claim credit for the Midway victory and to lie expansively that it was their cryptographers who had established June 3 as the N-day instead of their actual prediction that the Japanese attack would occur in mid-June. Furthermore, they crowed, if it weren't for their cryptanalists in Washington, both Midway and the Hawaiian Islands would have been captured by the Japanese.

Inside the naval establishment in Washington, their lies worked Within two months the elder brother was promoted to rear admiral, and the younger brother was promoted to captain.

Furthermore, Rear Admiral Joseph R. Redman in his second tour of duty as director of Naval Communications was awarded the Distinguished Service Medal, whereupon he remarked that "Pearl Harbor had missed the boat at the battle of Midway but the Navy Department had saved the day."

Is it any wonder that combatants are rendered speechless by what happens back in the homeland while they are fighting a war in foreign waters?

Didn't the truth about what had happened at Midway ever get to Washington?

Yes, it did, but it was kept under lock and key for 40 years.

One of Rochefort's traffic analysts, Commander John S. Holtwick, had played a key part in providing the intelligence that proved Washington's OP-20-G station wrong about Midway. When he found that Redman had re-written history to give himself credit for the Midway victory, Holtwick got boiling mad and ultimately got another ranking officer in the intelligence community to write a monograph, headlined "THE INSIDE STORY OF MIDWAY AND THE OUSTING OF COMMANDER ROCHEFORT." The author wisely remained anonymous, considering what was happening to Rochefort.

212

The monograph remained locked in the safes of Washington's naval intelligence establishment for 40 years. After all, the monograph contained a classified listing of sequential changes in the Japanese naval codes. That made it top secret. It was the same sort of gag that had been placed on Kimmel and Short when the blame for the Pearl Harbor disaster had been placed on them by the Washington brass. They were not allowed access to secret files. Only this time, the Washington crowd was claiming credit for a great victory instead of denying their part in the responsibility for a great disaster.

It wasn't until late 1984, after Rear Admiral Edwin Layton's death (all of the senior combatants in the World War II Pacific, such as Kimmel, Short, Nimitz, Halsey, MacArthur, etc., were gone by that time) that the monograph was "officially" declassified and released for publication after a navy security review had determined that it contained "no currently declassified information."

Having conspired to cover up the truth about Joe Rochefort's part in the victory at Midway, the Redman brothers carried out a vendetta against Rochefort to get him cast out of Station Hypo and insofar as possible out of the navy establishment. Working through Vice Admiral Frederick J. Home, Admiral King's chief of naval operations, the Redman's charged that Station Hypo on Oahu "has been, by virtue of seniority, in the hands of an ex-Japanese language student not technically trained in naval communications," and that the navy's war effort against the Japanese was "suffering because the importance and possibilities of the phases of Radio Intelligence are not realized."

This is the type of lie and trash writing in official-sounding rhetoric which would never get by anyone looking for facts. What the hell did he mean in saying that "the importance and possibilities of the phases of Radio Intelligence are not realized?"

Rochefort had not only been in on the birth of modern radio intelligence in the World War II Pacific when it counted the most in our fortunes of war, he had been its most expert practioneer.

The younger Redman's memorandum went on to accuse Rochefort of insubordination with the ridiculous conclusion "that units in combat areas cannot be relied upon to accomplish more than the business of merely reading enemy messages and performing routine work necessary to keep abreast of minor changes in the cryptographic systems involved."

Only the non-combatants in Washington, it seemed according to the Redmans, could be trusted to keep a clear head about wartime activities in the Pacific. None of this trash writing in high circles had ever been forwarded to the combat zone at Pearl Harbor through Admiral Nimitz's office. The conspiracy by the Redman brothers was used only to convince other naval bureaucrats in Washington. It worked there because it enabled the bureaucrats to keep control of naval intelligence under administration of the Chief of Naval Operations Along with that control went the promotions and the medals.

Rochefort's desk at Hypo had a note on it which read:

"WE CAN ACCOMPLISH ANYTHING PROVIDING NO ONE CARES WHO GETS THE CREDIT."

That was the attitude which actually won the battle of Midway.

Vice Admiral George C. Dyer, another of Rochefort's colleagues at Station Hypo at the time of the Midway battle, wrote shortly before his death in 1985:

"I have given a great deal of thought to the Rochefort affair, and I have been unwillingly forced to the conclusion that Rochefort committed the one unforgivable sin."

"To certain individuals of small mind and overweening ambition, there is no greater insult than to be proved wrong. I have rather a bitter personal memory of having been threatened with reprisal for being right when Washington was wrong."

For his unforgivable sin of proving Washington wrong, Rochefort was ordered to Washington on a 10-day detachment, ostensibly to be used there as an intelligence "expert." Nimitz suspected that the temporary assignment was to get Rochefort back in Washington where he would be vulnerable to those who were carrying out a vendetta against him, and Nimitz protested that Rochefort was needed at Station Hypo, right where he was.

But Rochefort realized that when Nimitz could not get the order reversed by Admiral King for his temporary detachment to Washington, he was not going to be allowed to return to Nimitz's command. As he

214

turned over his keys to his desk at Station Hypo to Layton, he told his friend:

"When I leave Pearl, I'm not coming back."

Stressing that Rochefort had been instrumental in effecting the Midway victory, Admiral Nimitz protested to Admiral King, who cabled back to Nimitz in a personal message, "I will do all that I can."

But two weeks later, the Hypo team was introduced to "your new boss," Captain William B. Goggins, whose arrival from Washington had not been announced either to Nimitz or the 14th Naval District at Pearl Harbor.

About ten days later, Nimitz sent for Layton and showed him a paragraph from a personal letter which he had received from Admiral King. The paragraph, written on Kings personal stationery, read: "Now that I have taken care of Rochefort, I will leave it up to you to take care of Layton."

Layton was dumbfounded because he did not know about the machinations of the Redman clique in Washington. Ruefully, Layton suggested that the admiral might find a destroyer for him to command.

Nimitz pulled from his desk a portrait of himself, which he signed:

"To Commander Edwin T. Layton. As my intelligence officer you are more valuable to me than any division of cruisers." Layton stayed on as Nimitz's fleet intelligence officer right up through the signing of the Japanese surrender ceremonies on the deck of the USS. Missouri.

Unfortunately, it was too late for Nimitz to intercede for Rochefort. And Rochefort refused to be assigned in Washington where some brass wanted to put him in as commander of OP-20-G. He was assigned to command a floating drydock at San Francisco. It was not until April, 1944, that he was returned to Washington to work on plans for the invasion of Japan.

Unlike the Redman brothers, Nimitz would not elevate any personal feud above fighting the Japanese. He felt keenly the injustice that had been done to Rochefort and he suspected the fraudulent conspiracy of the Redman brothers in Washington, but he reminded Layton:

"I've got enough to do to fight this war right now."

The removal of Rochefort as commanding officer from Intelligence station Hypo at Oahu damaged morale, caused eventual fleet losses at

Guadalcanal in the summer of 1942, and undoubtedly lengthened the naval war in the Pacific.

But in September, 1943, after Rochefort had been gone from Station Hypo almost a year, Nimitz was named Commander-in-Chief Pacific Ocean Area, and he put into operation Rochefort's plans for Station Hypo on Oahu. Hypo's code breaking and traffic analysis function was placed directly under Nimitz's command as the Fleet Radio Unit Pacific Fleet (FRUPAC). Members of the army, navy, air force, marines and coast guard made it one of the most effective intelligence organizations in military history. Intelligence teams became combat units. They went ashore with the first wave of each landing, looking for documents that would aid the assault teams.

In spite of the chicanery in Washington, Nimitz succeeded in moving naval intelligence and communications from rear echelon offices to combat units. The combat intelligence teams used every source of intelligence from radio intercepts to prisoner of war interrogations.

In the Pacific area, the Hypo team on Oahu with a direct line to Layton's office at Nimitz's headquarters at Pearl Harbor became even more important. The men who had been inspired by Rochefort (Thomas H. Dyer, Wesley A. "Ham" Wright, Joseph Finnegan, and others) continued their work at Hypo, and there never was a long period of time during the war, in spite of code changes, when they could not read commnications in the principal Japanese operational system (JN-25).
During the entire war, the enemy's radio traffic was read in detail and in great volume. Even General MacArthur conceded that it "saved us many thousands of lives and shortened the war by no less than two years.

On the personal level, it involved great poignancy for Ed Layton when a radio intercept from Hypo enabled him to plot the death of his favorite Japanese host back in 1937. That was Admiral Yamamoto, designer of the Pearl Harbor attack and Commander in Chief of the Japanese fleet.

Admiral Yamamoto had arrived in Rabaul in April, 1943, to direct a naval air offensive against our troops in Guadalcanal in the Solomons, and in New Guinea. When he decided to make a personal tour of the Japanese bases in the northern Solomon Islands, the information was sent by army and navy codes which we had broken. Army Major Alva B. Lasswell had the duty at Hypo that day and broke the code on the vital message. It gave the date and details of Yamamoto's tour.

The date cited was April 18, 1943, and the places were Ballale and Bum on the southern tip of Bougainville. Yamamoto would be in a medium attack plane escorted by six fighters. Since the message was addressed to the garrison commander on Ballale island, it was clear that the first part of the trip would bring Yamamoto's plane within range of our P-38 fighters from Guadalcanal. Layton took the message in to Nimitz, who studied it and checked his wall chart to confirm that Yamamoto's route would bring him within range of our fighters. Satisfied on that point, Nimitz sent the information to Halsey, and Halsey responded by confirming that the army air commander on Guadalcanal could arrange for the shootdown by long-range P-38 fighters, providing that the action did not alert the Japanese that we were breaking their codes.

Layton already had prepared for Nimitz a directive to all personnel involved (particularly the pilots of the P-38s who might become prisoners of the Japanese) that the information came from Australian coastwatcher's near Rabaul. Nimitz got FDR's approval via the secretary of the navy, and the intercept plan went forward.

"There were some qualms of conscience on my part," Layton reflected. "I was signing the death warrant of a man whom I knew personally. . . It was not as though we were involved in the shooting of somebody whom I had never met."

Planning the deaths of enemies in wartime is commonplace. But it never is commonplace to plan the death of someone that you know, who (in peacetime circumstances on his home turf) treated you with kindness and respect.

The intercept plan succeeded. P-38s led by Major John W. Mitchell, shot down two light bombers escorted by Zeroes over the Bum area April 18. Four Zeroes also were shot down One P-38 failed to return to its base at Guadalcanal. On May 21, Radio Tokyo announced that Yamamoto's ashes had been returned to Japan after he was killed in aerial combat in April while directing strategy in the front line.

It was a severe blow to Japanese morale. As Layton said, it was just as though they had shot Nimitz down. There was no one in the Japanese navy with the stature to replace Yamamoto. The nearest man to

Yamamoto was Admiral Yamaguchi, who had gone down on the carrier HIRYU at the battle of Midway.

The man chosen to replace Yamamoto. Admiral Mineichi Koga, lacked his flair and vision as well as his prestige.

If the timing of a warriors death may be seen as merciful, then that would be true of Yamamoto. A month later in May, 1943, we recaptured Attu in the Aleutian Islands and the Japanese abandoned Kiska. Within the year, we had captured Tarawa in the Gilbert Islands, and in February, 1944, the army took Kwajalein in the Marshall Islands. Clearly, we were on the way to Tokyo across the central Pacific. Yamamoto did not have to watch the deterioration of his fleet and the inexorable capture of each base closer to the Japanese homeland.

Admiral Koga ordered all of his warships west to the Palau Islands after we took Kwajalein, but the support vessels were left behind at Truk, where they were caught in a two-day raid by our carrier planes in February, 1944. The destruction of the enemy's oilers, submarine tenders and supply ships proved just as effective in curtailing their combined fleet operations as it would have been if we had caught their capital ships at Truk

After the war, Layton interviewed Japanese admirals who referred to the raid on Truk as the one which "broke their back." They had endured the loss of carriers and their invaluable air crews at Midway with hopes of continuing offensive operations, but those hopes died at Truk, where all of those submarine and supply bases built up in secret through the 1930s and 1940s were left to die on the vine.

On Feb. 17 and 18, 1944, Admiral Marc Mitscher's carriers destroyed 275 Japanese planes and a quarter of a million tons of Japanese auxiliary shipping.

Nimitz, a submariner, knew that the fastest way to destroy the Japanese supply lines to their far-flung outposts in the Pacific was via unrestricted submarine warfare. But his first problem was to get rid of those faulty torpedoes which usually failed to explode when they hit their targets.

The Bureau of Ordnance, which supplied the torpedoes, at first refused to admit that they were faulty.

Nimitz found the evidence that he was looking for to convince the Ordnance Bureau that something had to be done about its torpedoes in the log of the U.S. submarine, TUNNY. Operating at close range to an enemy task force south of Truk on April 10, 1943, TUNNY fired 10 torpedoes and recorded that two out of three Japanese carriers had been hit. But within a few hours, Truk's port director reported the safe arrival of the entire task force.

A string of torpedo failures followed on June 11, 1943, reported by U.S. submarines in Tokyo Bay, including the sub, TRIGGER, which reported a string of explosions following hits after a full salvo of torpedoes had been fired at the Japanese carrier, HIRYU. Layton then received a radio intelligence report in which HIRYU had signalled that she was only slightly damaged.

Nimitz called in his submarine force commander, Rear Admiral Charles Lockwood, and they concluded that the magnetic detonators on our torpedoes were probably defective. Nimitz promptly ordered that the magnetic detonators used in all U.S ships and airplanes be deactivated.

The correction of the faulty torpedoes correlated the breaking of the Maru code system through which the Japanese scheduled the time and routes of its supply ships. Every day at 0900 Commander Jasper Holmes met with the operations officer of the Pacific Fleet submarine force at Pearl Harbor to update their plot of Japanese convoys and allocate targets to submarine patrols.

By the end of 1943, the annual sinking rate of enemy merchantmen had zoomed to a million and a half tons. Japanese troops were being left unsupplied with food and ammunition and unreinforced throughout the Pacific. By 1945, eight and a half million tons of Japanese shipping had been sunk.

This insurmountable destruction rate of Japanese supply ships by U.S. submarines led Admiral Nimitz to by-pass many of the Pacific islands held by the Japanese and, as he put it, "just let them wither on the vine." By 1944, our intelligence sources were so well informed about the distribution of Japanese troops in the Marshall Islands that Nimitz decided to by-pass all of outer islands except Majuro and to by-pass the Carolines (including the abandoned enemy naval base at Truk) entirely.

Exceptions were Tarawa in the Gilberts, Kwajalein in the Marshalls and Saipan in the Marianas Islands, where fierce resistance had to be overcome by Marines and Army infantry.

Nimitz saw a short road to Tokyo which could be opened by routing through the Marianas to the north, the Palaus to the west, and Formosa as the springboard for the invasion of Japan. Admiral King agreed with him. But MacArthur's grand design was built around a picture of himself in command of a navy fleet as well as land forces routing through the Philippines.

MacArthur, of course, could not make any large amphibious assault in the Philippines without the Pacific Fleet. The general launched a bitter campaign in Washington in the spring and summer of 1944 via the President and the Joint Chiefs of staff to plan the entire strategy of the advance on the Japanese homeland around his return to the Philippines with him in command of the naval as well as the landing forces. He wanted to proceed first through Rabaul.

In March, the joint chiefs in Washington postponed a final decision on the route to Tokyo. MacArthur bombarded Nimitz's headquarters at Pearl Harbor with inflammatory rhetoric about how right he was and how wrong the navy was in their proposed passages to Tokyo. By the time MacArthur's staff arrived at Pearl, tension ran high between the two staffs. MacArthur eventually told Nimitz that his chief of staff had issued those inflammatory dispatches without his knowledge. That, of course, was a lie. MacArthur's chief of staff would not have lasted through the day if he ever had issued any such dispatches without MacArthur's knowledge and approval.

Meanwhile, on July 26, 1944 (a Wednesday) FDR kicked off his bid for reelection to a fourth term with a journey to Pearl Harbor. With Saipan having been captured in June, the army and navy staffs still were divided on whether we should by-pass or assault the Philippines on the road to Tokyo. MacArthur was campaigning furiously for the assault. King was opposed to it. Nimitz was somewhere in the middle, but it fell to Nimitz to oppose MacArthur when the big three in the Pacific (Roosevelt's being the deciding vote as commander-in-chief) met at Pearl Harbor.

In the "Turkey Shoot" at Saipan, the U.S. virtually had wiped out the Japanese air force except for the kamikaze planes. At the battle of the

Philippines Sea, the combined Japanese fleet had lost three carriers and all but 36 of its aircraft, along with a large part of its land-based air power. After the fall of Saipan, Guam and Tinian fell within three weeks of our landings there.

Saipan and Tinian were just 1,500 miles from Tokyo and half way between them, 750 miles from Tokyo, was our obvious target, Iwo Jima. That was the direct route of our combined naval and land-based air power to be unleashed on the Japanese homeland.

For the big meeting, Roosevelt arrived at dockside, Pearl Harbor, aboard the heavy cruiser BALTIMORE. Nimitz was there to meet him. MacArthur had arrived by air on Oahu on time, but contrived to be an hour late when he rolled up in a presidential-style motorcade like a conquering hero.

Layton had prepared a battery of charts to support Nimitz's contention that it was necessary only to neutralize the Japanese air bases in the Philippines before invading Formosa as the final launching pad to Japan. MacArthur orated profusely, without charts or notes, and warned the president dramatically that any by-passing of the Philippines would be politically disastrous in FDR's bid for a fourth term as president.

"American public opinion will condemn you, and it should" said he, posturing very much as he later would for the press in the "1 have returned" photographs taken on a Philippines beach.

FDR approved MacArthur's strategy for a land assault in the Philippines, led by MacArthur. Nimitz had warned unsuccessfully that it was not necessary to risk American lives in land forces to capture Morotai (off northeastern New Guinea) or Peleliu in the Palaus with the enemy now possessing only 7 battleships, 4 aircraft carriers, 20 cruisers and 29 destroyers against the U.S. Pacific fleet's 32 carriers, 12 battleships, 23 cruisers, 100 destroyers and 1,400 planes in the Third Fleet alone.

The assault on the Philippines went forward with 430 troop transports covered by the navy's 7th fleet on a scale that rivaled the D-Day landings of the Allied Armies in Normandy.

At the close of 1944, the Pacific Fleet still had nine months of hard fighting against the deadly kamikazes, first off Iwo Jima in February of 1945, and in the four-month campaign at Okinawa which began in April, 1945

In the same month, on April 12, 1945, President Roosevelt died.

Admiral Nimitz never said a word of criticism about the political nature of the president's decision to go along with MacArthur in the Pacific in the face of the realities of that war. Nimitz knew well how frustrating it could be to have other commanders second-guessing his own command decisions. So, he never second-guessed anyone else's, not in public at any rate.

He didn't mention the vainglorious MacArthur, either, as that general virtually replaced Emperor Hirohito in occupied Japan after running the surrender ceremonies on the USS MISSOURI on Sept. 2, 1945. Nimitz and his fleet intelligence officer, Layton, were there along with Admirals Halsey, Spruance, Marc Mitscher, Arleigh Burke—all standing by as MacArthur took the spotlight and the lion's share, by implication, of the credit for the Allied victory.

And that's how it ended, all by the signing of a pen by a stove-piped hat clad, elderly Japanese in a morning coat. No one seemed to know who this aged diplomat was, but it didn't matter, it was over. He was accompanied by three other Japanese military clad officers, swords and all; who signed the surrender documents one after another in grim silence.

The American, British and Australian officers in sharp contrast to the formally clad Japanese, were dressed in khaki, completely informal, even so far as to omit any ties or jackets. And that was that; there was a short speech by MacArthur and nothing by Nimitz, Halsey or Spruance who had far more to do with actually winning the war than the posturing MacArthur.

As the Japanese silently filed off the Missouri, to board the battered, rusty looking destroyer, by some pre-arranged signal, a massive fly-by of thousands of Halsey's Third Fleet planes roared over at masthead height.

Without any more ceremony the entourage of Admirals and Generals dissipated and World War II was over. Mankind's greatest tragedy of the century ended and the carnage involving the death of millions world-wide would end. How did this all start? Could anything this tragic happen again?

REMEMBER PEARL HARBOR

EPILOGUE
EVEN HITLER KNEW

Epilogue–Even Hitler Knew

The fact that this book is being produced so many years after Pearl Harbor, gives credence to the charge that a massive coverup has been in place for over half a century.

In the words of one of Admiral Kimmel's counsel, "Pearl Harbor never dies, and no living person has seen the end of it."

For years it has been the habit of many to brand anyone who doubts the guilt of Admiral Kimmel and General Short as a "Revisionist" and is dismissed summarily.

However, the recent flood of uncovered evidence with it's astonishing revelations has changed all that, and the word "Revisionist" is losing its meaning. Perhaps the most damning evidence of the duplicity of Roosevelt, is the release of the transcripts of a telephone conversation between Churchill and FDR, eleven days before Pearl Harbor. These transcripts prove that Roosevelt knew the attack was about to happen, but interestingly, he did not inform Churchill that he already knew; in fact he discussed ways to conceal the warning, and absent himself from Washington until after the attack took place.

The original intent of this book was to reveal the code breaking scandal in Washington, and the efforts to conceal the devastating events that were about to happen, but as time went on it was decided to include the multitude of evidence that was piling up against Roosevelt, and his personal guilt. The original title "Six Months and Forever" was changed to "Deceit at Pearl Harbor-From Pearl Harbor to Midway", and included new evidence that never existed in the years before this book was to be published.

It is quite possible that this work is the first and only written by two aging survivors of Pearl Harbor, who for over half a century have struggled with the knowledge that Kimmel and Short were scapegoats, and to this day most of the country is not concerned and probably never will be.

The appalling disclosure of Churchill's warning by "scrambler" telephone to Roosevelt that "the Japs were coming" on November 26, 1941, just eleven days before Pearl Harbor, and the fact that Hitler's Gestapo, had decoded the scrambler (unscrambled), is the most historically significant event in this book, and shows that "Even Hitler Knew!"

APPENDIX A

ROOSEVELT'S DAY OF INFAMY: NOV. 26, 1941

Appendix A–Roosevelt's Day of Infamy: Nov. 26, 1941

Ever since December 7, 1941, there has been heated debate and finger pointing to determine the true culprit for the debacle at Pearl Harbor. The Roosevelt administration immediately pounced on the hapless commanders at Pearl Harbor, Adm. Kimmel and Gen. Short and commenced a rigged investigation to fix the blame and squelch further inquiries under the guise of "National Security".

This deception worked for over fifty years, when five separate congressional investigations covered up the blame by delays, obfuscations, and invoking National Security issues until the Freedom of Information Act was passed. The picture then changed dramatically as a tidal wave of evidence was released and is now being made public by researchers and historians, such as the authors of this book.

The historical role played by Roosevelt as the guilty party who engineered the "Causus Belli," has been thoroughly uncovered by the release of the telephone warning by Churchill on November 26, 1941. This warning proves that FDR was fully aware of the impending attack and is perhaps the most damning piece of evidence to be revealed in this greatest of American military tragedies.

Starting with the revelation of FDR's madcap scheme to unleash the forces of war by sacrificing the Tethered Goats, to the spectacle of his ignoring the warning by Churchill, this book endeavors to unravel the greatest mystery of the century—Who was to blame for WW II?

~~~~~~~~~~~

This is an excerpt of a telephone call from Winston Churchill to Franklin Delano Roosevelt on November 26, 1941, just eleven days before the fully known attack on the U.S. Fleet at Pearl Harbor. The Democratic party, in full control of the government since 1933, intentionally let thousands of sailors be slaughtered in what appeared to be a sneak attack but was not. Millions of innocent civilians were also slaughtered in an unnecessary war in the Philippines, Malaya, Singapore, Hong Kong, Guam, Wake and hundreds of Pacific Islands.

Heinrich Muller's Gestapo Chiefs files contain a large number of historically interesting documents among which are a selection of transcripts of German intercepts of personal telephone conversation held during the war between US President Franklin D. Roosevelt and Prime Minister Winston Churchill. On March 6, 1941, German Minister of Post, Dr. Wilhelm Ohnesorge, sent the following letter to Adolph Hitler. To it was attached a sample manuscript of intercepted conversation:

The Reichspost Minister Berlin
Geheime Reichssache (Secret State Matter)
Decoding of the American-England telephone system
Mein Fuhrer!
The research section (Forschungsanstalt) of the German Reichspost has, as the latest of its efforts completed a unit designed to intercept the telephone message traffic between the United States and England which had been rendered unintelligible by their use of current communications technology. Because of the significant work of its technicians, the Reichspost is the sole agency in Germany that is now able to make immediate interception and decoding of these hitherto unintelligible conversations. I will present these results to the Reichsfuhrer SS Pg Himmler who will forward them on the 22nd of March. It is my intention, pending your approval to strictly limit the circulation of these communications in order that no news of our success reaches the English. This might seriously jeopardize future interceptions.

Heil mein Fuhrer!

Dr. Wilhelm Ohnesorge

In 1937, the American Telephone and Telegraph Company put into use a telephone scrambling device called the A-3. This device, which permitted telephone communications to be scrambled at one end and descrambled at the other, effectively prevented interception of the conversations en route. The German Reichspost (state post system responsible for the telephone and telegraph systems in Germany) had purchased the A-3 system from AT&T before the war for use on lines in service between Germany and the

United States. However, each set of scrambling devices was different and in practice, the possessors of one set could not intercept the transmission of another. The A-3 system in use between Roosevelt and Churchill was housed, in America, in a secure area of the AT&T offices at 47 Walker Street in New York and the British A-3 counterpart was located in London. Roosevelt's calls to Churchill were routed through this New York office where technicians constantly supervised the conversations to be certain that the transmitted speech was unintelligible after passing through the scrambling devices.

In September of 1939, the A-3 system was in use by the White House and on the first day of that month, Roosevelt heard from his personal friend and Ambassador to France, William Bullitt, that the Germans had invaded Poland. The Germans were well aware that Roosevelt used this device through an indiscreet article in the New York Times of October 8, 1939 entitled "Roosevelt Protected in Talk to Envoys by Radio scrambling to Foil Spies Abroad." The spies abroad found this indiscretion stimulating and Dr. Ohnesorge determined to find a way to unscramble the President's messages. He assigned a specialist in the field, Kurt Vetterlein, to work on the project using the A-3 equipment then in the hands of the Reichspost as a basis. By late 1940, Vetterlein and his team of specialists had effectively broken Roosevelt's secure system. Vetterlein then built a device that was able to descramble each conversation as it progressed without the loss of a single word and Ohnesorge ordered an intercept station to be established in the occupied Dutch coastal town of Noorwijkaan Zee, just north of den Haag. Here, in a former youth hostel, Vetterlein set up all the equipment he needed to begin a full-scale 24 hour program of interception and transcription of the trans-Atlantic radio telephone traffic. The first intercept was made a 7:45PM on September 7, 1941. The daily number of intercepted calls, on a 24 hour basis, ranged from a high of sixty to a low of thirty and were screened by experts for their intelligence value. Important material was transcribed in the original English and sent by courier either to Hitler's military headquarters or to Heinrich Himmler in Berlin.

Himmler, in turn, had copies made and distributed them within his organization. General Gottlob Berger, head of Himmler's main office, was one of the recipients and the head of the Overseas Intelligence branch of the Sicherheitsdienst, or SD, received others. In his capacity as chief of the government's counter-espionage section, Muller received occasional intercepts. It was no doubt Muller's interest in Soviet intelligence sphere that resulted in his being given an original intercept between Roosevelt and Churchill of a highly secret, and in retrospect, explosive, conversation of November 26, 1941. Ever since the Japanese attack on Pearl Harbor on December 7, 1941 and the subsequent entry of United States into what then became World War II, there has been a heated and protracted debate about the historical role played by Roosevelt. His detractors have claimed that the President was fully aware of the impending Japanese attack and allowed it to proceed because it supplied him a causus belli that would permit him to actively engage his real enemy, Hitler. Much is made of the interception and decoding of Japanese messages, which in hindsight would appear to point clearly to a Japanese attack. Certainly, the decoding of Japanese Foreign Office diplomatic traffic would indicate the possibility of the kind of an attack if the Japanese and American governments were unable to resolve their problems in the Pacific. None of the diplomatic messages, however, were specific about such an attack and all that can be gained from them is that the Japanese did not want war with the United States and were desperately seeking some kind of a peaceful solution. On November 26, 1941, the German intercept station in Holland recorded the following conversation between Roosevelt and Churchill concerning the situation in the Pacific. It is of such historical importance that it is reproduced in full.

Secret State Matter No. 321/41 Time: 26.11.41 Hour: 03.15

Conversation Participants

A=Franklin Roosevelt, Washington

B=Winston Churchill, London

In this conversation, Winston Churchill explains to Franklin Roosevelt about the Japanese planned action against America. The conversation is as follows:

B: I am frightfully sorry to disturb you at this hour, Franklin, but matters of a most vital import have transpired and I felt that I must convey them to you immediately.

A. That's perfectly all right, Winston. I'm sure you wouldn't trouble me at this hour for trivial concerns.

B: Let me preface my information with an explanation addressing the reason I have not alluded to these facts earlier. In the first place, until today, the information was not firm. On matters of such gravity, I do not like to indulge in idle chatter. Now, I have in my hands, reports from our agents in Japan as well as the most specific intelligence in the form of the highest level Japanese naval coded messages (conversation broken) for some time now.

A: I felt that this is what you were about. How serious is it?

B: It could not be worse. A powerful Japanese task force comprising (composed of) six of their carriers, two battleships and number of other units to include (including) tankers and cruisers, has sailed yesterday from a secret base in the northern Japanese islands (2)

A: We both knew they were coming. There are also reports in my hands about a force of some size making up in China and obviously intended to go (move) South. (3)

B: Yes, we have all of that. (Interruption)...are far more advance than you in our reading of the Jap naval operations codes. (4) But even without that, their moves are evident. And they will indeed move South but the force I spoke of is not headed South, Franklin, it is headed East....

A: Surely you must be. ..will you repeat that please?

B: I said to the East. This force is sailing to the East.. .towards you.

A: Perhaps they set an easterly course to fool any observers and then plan to swing South to support the landings in the southern areas. I have...

B: No, at this moment, their forces are moving across the northern Pacific and I can assure you that their goal is the (conversation broken) fleet in Hawaii. At Pearl Harbor.

A: This is monstrous. Can you tell me....indicate...the nature of your intelligence? (conversation broken) reliable? Without compromising your sources

B: Yes, I will have to be careful. Our agents in Japan have been reporting on the gradual (conversation broken) units. And these have disappeared

232

from Japanese home waters. (5) We also have highly reliable sources in the Japanese foreign service and even in the military

A: How reliable?

B: One of the sources is the individual who supplied us the material on the diplomatic codes that (conversation broken) (6) and a Naval officer (sic) whom our service has compromised. You must trust me, Franklin, I can not be more specific.

A: I accept this.

B: We cannot compromise our code breaking. You understand this. Only myself and a few (conversation broken) not even Hopkins.(7) It will go straight to Moscow and I am not sure we want that.

A: 1 am still attempting to..the obvious implication is that the Japs are going to do a Port Arthur on us at Pearl Harbor. (8) Do you concur?

B: I do indeed. Unless they add an attack on the Panama Canal to this vile business. I can hardly envision the canal as a primary goal, especially with your fleet lying athwart their lines of communications with Japan. No, if they do strike the canal, they will have to first neutralize (destroy) your fleet (conversation broken).

A: The worst form of treachery. We can prepare our defenses on the islands and give them a warm welcome when they come. It certainly would put some iron up Congress' ass (asshole).

B: On the other hand, if they did launch a bombing raid, given that the aircraft would only be of the carrier-borne types, how much actual damage could they inflict? And on what targets?

A: I think torpedoes would be ruled out at the outset. Pearl is far too shallow to permit a successful torpedo attack. (9) Probably they would drop medium bombs on the ships and then shoot (conversation broken) damage a number of ships and no doubt the Japs would attack our airfields. I could see some damage there but I don't think either an airfield or a battleship could sink very far. What do your people give you as the actual date of the attack?

B: The actual date give is the eighth of December. That's a Monday. (10)

A. The fleet is in harbor over the weekend. They often sortie during the week..

B: The Japs are asking (conversation broken) exact dispositions of your ships on a regular basis.

A: But Monday seems odd. Are you certain?

B: It is in the calendar, Monday is the eighth (conversation broken)

A:Then I will have to consider the entire problem. A Japanese attack on us, which would result in war between us and certainly you as well..would certainly fulfill two of the most important requirements of our policy. Harry has told me repeatedly.. .and I have more faith in him than I do in the Soviet ambassador that Stalin is desperate at this point. The Nazis are at the gates of Moscow, his armies are melting away.. .the government has evacuated and although Harry and Marshall feel that Stalin can hang on and eventually defeat Hitler, there is no saying what could transpire (happen) if the Japs suddenly fell on Stalin's rear. In spite of all the agreements between them and the Japs dropping Matsuoka, there is still strong anti-Russian sentiment in high Japanese military circles. I think we have to decide what is more important, keeping Russia in the war to bleed the Nazis dry to their own eventual destruction (conversation broken) supply Stalin with weapons but do not forget, in fact he is your ally, not mine. There are strong isolationist feelings here and there are quite a number of anti-Communists...

B: Fascists...

A: Certainly, but they would do all they could to block any attempt on my part to more than give some monetary assistance to Stalin.

B: But we too have our major dispersions, Franklin. Our shipping upon which our nation depends, is being sunk by the huns faster than we could ever replace (conversation broken) the Japs attack both of us in the Pacific? We could lose Malaya which is our primary source of rubber and tin. And if the Japs get Java and oil, they could press South to Australia and I have told you repeatedly, we cannot hold (conversation broken) (11) them much but in truth I cannot deliver. We need every man and every ship to fight Hitler in Europe..India too. If Japs get into Malaya, they can press on virtually unopposed into Burma and then India. Need I tell you of the resultant destruction of our Empire? We cannot survive on this small island, Franklin, (conversation broken) allow the nips to attack, you can get your war declaration through your Congress after all. (Conversation broken).

A: Not as capable as you are at translating their messages and the army and navy are very jealous of each other. There is so much coming in that

234

everyone is confused. We have no agents in place in Japan and every day dozens of messages are (conversation broken) that contradict each other or are not well translated. I have seen three translations of the same message with three entirely different meanings (conversation broken) address your concern about British holdings in the Pacific... if the Japanese do attack both of us, eventually we will be able to crush them and regain all of the lost territories. As for myself, I will be damned glad to be rid of the Philippines. (sic)...

B: I see this as a gamble (conversation broken) what would your decision be? We cannot procrastinate over this for too long. Eleven or twelve days are all we have. Can we not agree in principle now? I should mention the several advisors have counseled (advised) against informing you of this and allowing it to happen. You see by my notifying you where my loyalty lies. Certainly to one who is heart and soul with us against Hitler.

A: I do appreciate your loyalty, Winston. What on the other hand, will happen here if one of our intelligence people is able to intercept, decipher and deliver to me the same information you just gave me? I cannot ignore it...all of intelligence people will know about it then. I could not ignore this.

B: But if it were just a vague message then?

A: No, a specific message. I could not just sweep it under the rug like that (conversation broken)

B: Of course not. I think we should let matters develop as they will.

A: I think that perhaps I can find a reason to absent (leave) myself from Washington while this crisis develops. What I don't know can't hurt me and I too can misunderstand messages, especially at a distance (conversation broken)

B: Completely. My best to you all there.

A: Thank you for your call.

2) Hittokappu Bay in the Kuriles.
3) There was such force destined for Malaya.
4) The Americas had broken the Japanese Naval Operations codes, called by the US Navy *JN-25*, but were not as advanced in translating them as were the British.

5) The Pearl Harbor Strike Force was sent by different routes to their assembly point, leaving behind their radio operators who kept up a regular traffic to mislead eavesdroppers.

6) It has long been thought that the breaking of the so-called Japanese Purple diplomatic code was due to treasonable activities on the part of a Japanese diplomatic official and not to the efforts of US code breakers.

7) Harry Hopkins was Roosevelt's confidant whom the British strongly suspected was selling highly secret material to the Soviets on his visits to Stalin.

8) In 1904, the Japanese Navy launched a surprise attack against the Russian fleet stationed in Port Arthur, inflicting considerable damage on the unsuspecting Russians and beginning the Russo-Japanese War.

9) This was a common error in US thinking. The Japanese had developed special fins for their aerial torpedoes that would permit them to be used in shallow waters. Normally, torpedoes dropped from an aircraft would sink to a considerable depths before beginning their run in shallow anchorages like Pearl Harbor, in effect these torpedoes would embed themselves in the mud at the bottom of the harbor.

10) The date quoted by Churchill accurately reflects the one given in Japanese Naval intercepts. Unfortunately, neither Churchill nor British intelligence realized that the eighth was Tokyo time, one day ahead of the time at Pearl Harbor. The International Date Line lies between Hawaii and Japan.

11) The missing words here obviously were "I have promised" which in fact he did. Delivery consister of two battleships the Repulse and the Prince of Wales which he sent to Singapore and which were promptly sunk by Japanese bombers off Kuantun on December 10, 1941.

12) On Friday, Noverber 28, Roosevelt left Washington in his special armored train for what he called a "belated Thanksgiving" at Warm Spring, Georgia. Although Roosevelt did not like to travel on a Friday, he did so on this occasion. The trip took twenty-three hours and he was in Warm Springs long enough to deliver a speech and carve the Thanksgiving turkey. He was recalled by frantic messages from Henry Stimson, Secretary of War, and Cordell Hull his Secretary of State. Roosevelt arrived back in Washington on December 1 to deal with the mounting crisis.

APPENDIX B

CHURCHILL'S WARNING REVISITED

Appendix B–Churchill's Warning Revisited

Looking at this astonishing revelation of Churchill's telephone warning and Roosevelt's feigning of ignorance of the approaching armada on Pearl Harbor, one must marvel at the duplicity of FDR and his determination to accept the first blow - no matter what the consequences.

It is also amazing to discover that the British were far advanced in the business of decoding Japanese messages. For years, Washington felt secure in the knowledge that they were decoding any and all Japanese codes with the Purple Machine.

Another interesting, discovery in Churchill's conversation is the fact that some of his advisors were against warning the US and preferred letting events develop as they may.

Roosevelt's disclosure that he did not completely trust Harry Hopkins, his closest advisor, and feared he would disclose too much to Stalin, was something the British strongly suspected. The British had warned that Hopkins had been selling secret material to the Soviets. This is something FDR must have known, but somehow ignored.

The last part of the telephone conversation is perhaps the must unbelievable of all Roosevelt ended the call by stating that *"I think I can find a reason to absent myself from Washington while this crisis develops—What I don't know can't hurt me and I too can misunderstand messages, especially at a distance"*.

With eleven days warning, the possibilities of orchestrating an ambush, as at Midway, and saving the lives of thousands of sailors, plus other strategic traps on the unsuspecting Japanese fleet, boggles the mind and brings forth a host of "What ifs".

Instead of a prolonged and bloody four year war it is quite possible that there would have been a much shorter and different conflict especially in the Pacific. But of course, we will never know.

The above disclosures on Churchill's telephone call to Roosevelt is taken from excerpts of the May 1997 Issue of The Shield, published by the National Intelligence and Counter intelligence Association.

APPENDIX C

DID PRESIDENT ROOSEVELT AND HIS TOP AIDES KNOW OF
THE COMING ATTACK ON
PEARL HARBOR AND WAS THERE A COVER UP?

Sept. 3, 1939   Britain and Germany go to war and by early 1941 Britain feared an invasion, plus their resources could not substain them for very much longer. The war was costing Britain $500,000,000 per day plus the loss of many lives and property. Six countries had already fallen to Hitler's Nazi-ism.

Oct. 30, 1940   Roosevelt's deceit to the American people had begun as he very well knew a lot of the people in the US did not want to get mixed up in Europe's problems. The extention of the Conscription Act of October 16, 1940 requiring the registration of all American males between twenty-one and thirty-five for peacetime was renewed by just one vote. When Roosevelt was in Boston with third term asperations he addressed the nation pledging parents, "I have said this before, but I shall say it again and again and again: Your sons are not going to be sent into any foreign wars."

Apr. 2, 1940   U.S. fleet sails from west coast ports for maneuvers in Hawaii area, arriving at Lahaina Roads on April 2.

May 7, 1940   Roosevelt, using his "Commander in Chief" powers, made the decision for the Navy to keep the fleet in Hawaii waters, against the judgement of Admiral Richardson whom he later fired because of Richardson's outspoken objection to keeping the fleet some 2000 miles from its supplies and repair facilities. Churchill made the same political judgement and mistake later, proven by keeping the HMS Battleship Prince of Wales in dangerous waters far from base off Malaya. Both the Prince of Wales and the HMS Battlecruiser Repulse were sunk December 10, 1941.

240

May 20, 1940   Roosevelt tells Churchill that in case of England's defeat, the British fleet should find shelter in American ports.

July 1940   Wm. Freidman, a United States civilian employee of Army Signal Corp., with the aid of Army and Navy personnel, breaks the new Japanese "Purple" cipher code.

Aug. 28, 1940   Roosevelt musters National Guard into Federal Service.

Sep. 16, 1940   Roosevelt signs first peacetime conscription bill in American history, whereby 42 million men were enrolled October 16th for military service.

Nov. 11, 1940   At Taranto, Italy the nights of November 11th and 12th should be remembered forever as having shown once and for all that in the Fleet Air Arm the Navy has its most devastating weapon. In a total flying time of about six and a half hours—carrier to carrier—twenty aircraft inflicted disastrous damage upon the Italian fleet. The Japanese made detailed studies of this raid and used this information December 7, 1941.

Jan. 1941   Admiral Richardson went to Washington to see Roosevelt and Secretary Knox in hopes of getting approval to return the fleet back to its home port on the west coast. Pearl Harbor was accessible only through a single entrance channel for ships to enter and exit. It was 2000 miles from its main supplies and repairs. Shortly after their meeting Richardson was relieved of Command and replaced by Admiral Kimmell on February 11th. Kimmel was promoted over thirty-two Admirals. In June, six months later, Kimmel stated he saw Pearl Harbor as "a damned mouse trap" and told Roosevelt so, and "if they sink one ship in the entrance of the harbor they have the whole Fleet bottled up and it can't get out.""

Jan. 9, 1941   Because of the passing of Bill #1776 a Lend-Lease Plan house bill which Roosevelt had sought became law. This gave Roosevelt such power as no American had ever had, granting unlimited aid to both Britain and China. More than 49 billion dollars in aid was granted.

Jan. 27, 1941   U.S. Ambassador Joseph Grew in Tokyo reported on several occasions that if trouble between the United States and Japan starts, the Japanese intend to make a surprise attack against Pearl Harbor. In Hawaii the Japanese consultate was on Nuuanu Avenue. The official diplomatic list showed only five assistant consuls. However, it was home base for more than two hundred subconsular spy agents scattered throughout the territory of Hawaii. Messages decoded in Washington from Tokyo to Hawaii spies revealed they wanted information for their pilots which would be needed for their bombing and torpedo attack training, such as: ship locations in port, movement of those in and out of port, if there were balloons up, or nets around the ships, and much more information asked for and received, yet none of this decoded information was forwarded to Hawaii Commanders.

July 1941   From July until December 7th, through the use of the "Purple" machine in Washington, up to 130 intercepts a day were rushed in locked briefcases by special messengers to Roosevelt and his chief advisers who scanned them without taking notes while the messenger stood by. All copies but one were then burned. These secret coded intercepts went to only nine persons, according to General Miles. They were—President Roosevelt, Secretary of War Stimson, Secretary of the Navy Knox, Secretary of State Hull, Chief of Staff Marshall, Chief of Naval Operations Stark, General Gerow, Col. Bratton and General Miles.

242

<u>With this secret information available</u>, not one word of all the Japanese requests for information about Pearl Harbor was ever given to the Army and Navy field commanders in Hawaii!! Why?? For one reason there was bitter feuding within the Naval Intelligence organization and the service high command, as quoted from the Richmond Times Dispatch and New Pearl Harbor Attack Theory, presented in the July 1986 GRAM, page 3.

<u>These men were all intelligent</u> people and must have grasped the significance of the reports going back and forth from Tokyo to her spies in Hawaii. Kimmel and Short certainly would have, and would have started preparing for the coming attack. Perhaps that was what Washington did not want. They wanted the United States in a war! – and so bad, that in November 1941 Admiral Hart, Commander in Chief of the Asiatic Fleet received a dispatch directing him to send out three picket ships to the Indochina coast, and if he did not have suitable craft available, he could commandeer small craft and fit them out for the purpose which was to have one Naval Officer with a small crew and one mounted machine gun. They were to patrol in an area known to be where the Japanese Navy may be. This was an odd order because the United States already had Catalina planes doing this now at much less risk.

<u>The conclusion by Admiral Hart and</u> others was that if these small boats were fired on, or sunk by the Japanese Navy, that would have been reason for the United States to declare war. Admiral Hart stated that to get these boats ready and equipped took time and that he was only able to get one craft started, the USS Isabel, and it was on the way to the Indochina coast when Pearl Harbor happened.

<u>July 1941</u>   Admiral Thomas C. Hart, Commander in Chief of the Asiatic Fleet said that – Roosevelt's freezing of Japanese

243

financial credits by Executive Order, caused much more strain on United States and Japanese relations.

In 1940 Japan had stockpiled enough oil to last two years, but with cut-off from the United States and other nations, they became desperate. Roosevelt had struck the Japanese a body-blow. Japan could supply only 10% of her own oil, with a further 10% from the Dutch East Indies; the remaining 80% had always come from the United States, and now, the Dutch East Indies, emboldened by Roosevelt, had reneged on their contract. If Japan was to go to war at this later date of 1941, their Navy alone had only one year oil supply at best. The Navy used 400 tons per hour. To switch to synthetic oil would involve a three-year conversion program, costing two billion yen.

In 1941 Japan had superiority in the air over the United States plus larger battle ships, larger and faster fleet of ships, which accounted for a large use of oil.

August 9, 1941 Churchill on the HMS Battleship Prince of Wales and Roosevelt on the USS Augusta, a cruiser, meet at Placentea Bay, Newfoundland, for three historical days, proclaiming the Atlantic Charter. It was at this meeting that Roosevelt stated, "I shall never declare war. I shall make War!"

He also made secret promises to Churchill without the United States Congress knowledge or approval, and thereby inviting hostilities.

As a result of this secret meeting and commitment by Roosevelt, without US Congress knowledge or approval, a dispatch on December 5, 1941 was received by Admiral Hart, in command of the Asiatic Fleet, from Captain John M. Creighton, American Naval Observer, then stationed at Singapore under the direct orders of the Navy Department,

244

stating from London that in certain eventualities the British had been assured of American support.

Oct. 5, 1941   On board the Japanese aircraft carrier the Akagi, in Shibushi Bay, 100 Japanese pilots were assembled and told by Admiral Yamamoto that Japan was being forced by the United States to war because of United States continued aid to China, and the United States oil embargo. He told them the United States fleet was their strongest enemy and they hoped to strike it unexpectedly at Hawaii. The decision to go to war was made in Tokyo at an Imperial Conference on December 1, and the attack forces received the next day a coded message "Climb Mount Nitaka" – meaning the attack for December 7 was firmly set after Nomura and Kurusu in Washington on November 30 had rejected United States proposals to settle the crisis. Tokyo, from their many spies in Hawaii, was able to give the attacking ships details and updated plans of where the United States hips were. Earlier in October they had sent the Japanese merchant ship Taiyo Maru across the Pacific on their proposed route to check ship traffic, winds, and sea conditions, and reported there were no ships operating in that area.

Oct. 1941   Dr. Richard Sorge, head of a Russian spy ring in Japan before World War II, informed the Kremlin that the Japanese intended to attack Pearl Harbor within 60 days. Stalin and company were trading secret information at that time with the United States and must have passed this information to the United States government, in turn for information about impending attack by Germany on Russia. Sorge was captured by the Japanese and before he was executed, in 1942, he made such a confession in a 32,000 word statement to the Japanese. This information was surrendered by the Japanese to General MacArthur in September 1945 but portions of the Sorge confession have been deleted from the Pentagon file copy, preserving still another secret of Pearl Harbor.

Nov. 3, 1941 Joseph Grew, U.S. Ambassador in Tokyo again warned Roosevelt administration that "Japan's resort to war may come with dramatic and dangerous suddenness."

The President and his War Cabinet meet and discuss war, not prospects of peace, and they dealt with the question of how war might start. This was later stated by Secretary Stimson, who had kept a diary of some of the cabinet meetings with Roosevelt, and later gave testimony at Congressional Committee hearings of secret decisions and operations during the days preceding Pearl Harbor, which he described as maneuvering the Japanese into a position of firing the first shot. On December 7th he also made the following entry in his diary that when the news first came that Japan had attacked us "my first feeling was of relief that the indecision was over and that a crisis had come in a way which would unite all our people." Secretary of Labor, Frances Perkins, observed at the cabinet meeting in the evening of December 7th a much calmer air. Roosevelt's terrible moral delemma had been resolved by the event. Postmaster General Frank Walker was quoted as saying, "I think the Boss really feels more relief than he has had for weeks."

Nov. 27, 1941 Chief of Naval Operations Admiral Stark sent "war warning" message to Commanders of Pacific and Asiatic Fleets. The Army had likewise sent this notice to General Short. These messages were confusing; for, if the Washington superiors of the two Commanders had written clear and precise instructions in their messages, it would have been unnecessary for General Short and Admiral Kimmel to consult and confer with each other at length for the purpose of finding out what the language of the messages meant. They were not to alarm the civil population. Short assumed they were concerned about the sabotage, and proceeded to bunch up his aircraft, and so informed Washington. Kimmel's message warned against amphibious expedition against either the Philippines, Thai, or Kra Peninsula, or possibly Borneo, but no mention of facts about Hawaii already known in Washington. If Kimmel had known, he would not have had his three aircraft carriers away at that time with no air protection of his battle-fleet, and General Short certainly would not have bunched up his aircraft to prevent sabotage, but whereby did make them most vulnerable to bombing which did happen.

Nov. 28, 1941 Admiral Kimmel sent the aircraft carrier U.S.S. Enterprise from Pearl Harbor, flying the flag of Vice Admiral Halsey, to deliver fighter planes to Wake Island. The planes were delivered December 5th and on December 7th they were on their way back to Pearl Harbor. On December 5th Admiral Kimmel sent the aircraft carrier U.S. Lexington under Real Admiral Newton to deliver planes to Midway Island. The third aircraft carrier, U.S.S. Saratoga had left Pearl Harbor for repairs in San Diego. At the height of the Japanese attack on December 7, 1941 at 9:10 AM., eighteen torpedo bombers and fighters from the U.S.S. Enterprise flew into Pearl Harbor to land at Ford Island Naval Air Station. The pilots were unaware the Japanese were attacking and six American aircraft were shot down by Japanese pilots, and anti-aircraft fire got two of our own planes.

The question arises, would Admiral Kimmel have dispersed all his carriers and air protection from Pearl Harbor if he had in any way been warned of an oncoming attack? One reason the fleet was tied up in Pearl Harbor was the fact they would have had no air protection if at sea. All the west coast assigned battleships were in Pearl Harbor December 7th, except for

247

the U.S.S. Colorado which was undergoing overhaul in Bremerton.

Dec. 2, 1941   Seaman First Class Robert D. Ogg, working for the United States Naval Intelligence office on Market Street in San Francisco had a background knowledge of electronics, radio, and navigation. He was assigned an unusual job by Lt. Ellsworth Hosmer, which was to monitor and collect radio reports from ships in the Pacific. He noted radio signals coming from the northern Pacific and plotted them. Unknown to U.S. Naval Intelligence, the 31-ship Japanese attack force sailed out from the Kurile Islands on November 26th bound for Hawaii. Ogg's information was first given on December 2nd to Captain McCullough, Commander of 12th Naval District, who was a close personal friend of Roosevelt. These signals were heard and traced again on the 3rd, 4th, 5th, and again on the 6th, where they were then estimated to be about 500 miles north of Hawaii.

On each of these days that the signals were recorded, they were reported to Washington. (For more detailed information, please see Pearl Harbor Survivors' Magazine, the "GRAM" July 1987).

The SS Lurline just out of Honolulu picked up similar signals coming from the North of Hawaii. When the ship tied up to a Honolulu pier an official came on-board, took the recordings presumably to Washington, and all without the Hawaiian Command's knowledge.

United States intercepted Japanese coded message directing all diplomatic and consular posts to destroy codes and ciphers, burn confidential and secret material. This important information was not given to the Hawaiian Command by Washington.

248

<u>Decoded messages revealed</u> that on December 2nd, spies in Hawaii were informed by Tokyo "that in view of the present situation, the presence in part of warships, airplane carriers, and cruisers, is of the utmost importance. Hereafter, to the utmost of your ability, let us know day-by-day. Wire in each case whether or not there are any observation balloons above Pearl Harbor, or if there are any indications that any will be sent up. Also, advise us whether or not the warships are provided with anti-mine nets."

<u>The irony of Kimmel's predicament</u> was that the information which the Roosevelt administration denied the Commander in Chief of the United States Fleet, was being freely given to the British all through 1941.

<u>Dec. 4, 1941</u> Naval Intelligence Officer Arthur H. McCollum had information that had been decoded regarding Pearl Harbor. He wanted to send a war warning to Hawaii, but Admiral Stark declined to do so. Many other messages were decoded between December 4th and 7th, which suggested an attack on Pearl Harbor. President Roosevelt, after reading one, stated "This means War!" <u>Yet, Hawaii was never notified!</u>

<u>Dec. 6, 1941</u> At 6:30 P.M., with the Japanese fleet nearby, the Japanese spies had become brave enough with the desire for up-to-date information, they used the open telephone lines which were monitored by the FBI. They requested up-to-date information from their spies in Honolulu about plans, search lights, ships, the weather, and a coded message about flowers in bloom. This information was given to General Short well before the attack on the following day, yet nothing was done about it.

Admiral Kimmel, uninformed of all this known information which was
withheld from him by Washington, tells war correspondent
Joseph C. Harsch, "There is not going to be a war out
there." His theory that Germany was going into winter
quarters in front of Moscow, meaning Moscow will not fall
that winter, and Japan would not want a two-front war.
This statement by Kimmel at this late date shows again that
he had no idea of what was being withheld from him by the
Roosevelt administration.

Secretary of State Cordell Hull confides with a friend. Joe Lieb meets the
Secretary in Lafayette Park near the Capitol and is told by
Secretary of State Cordell Hull that Pearl Harbor would be
attacked on December 7th. That he wanted his close friend
Joe Lieb to know that if anything should happen to him he
wanted a witness. He then took out of his pocket a dispatch
so stating. This statement was later so documented and is
on tape in a 1989 documentary titled "Sacrifice at Pearl
Harbor". It first aired on TV Arts & Entertainment
network December 7, 1989.

Dec. 7, 1941   0915 time, Washington, D.C.
Captain Wilkinson, Chief of Naval Intelligence, brought
into Admiral Stark's office, Tokyo's Part 14 of their
message to Washington, which broke off diplomatic
relations. Wilkinson suggested to Admiral Stark that he
call Admiral Kimmel via phone and inform him of this
latest development, but Admiral Stark again refused. He
had previously asked Rear Admiral Turner, the Head of
War Plans on two different times prior to December 7th, to
warn Hawaii because of decoded information they had, but
the Admiral turned him down. Admiral Turner took a dim
view of anyone suggesting to him how to perform.

General Marshall and Admiral Stark, as heads of the Army and Navy,
knew the last Japanese decoded messages meant war, and

250

definitely established that Pearl Harbor would be the scene of the attack. They had plenty of time at that time to send a message, thereby preventing the attack that followed.

Dec. 7, 1941   After being incommunicado, and after stalling as long as they could, a message was finally sent via Western Union. In San Francisco the message was then sent by RCA Commercial Radio to Honolulu. It reached General Short six hours after the Japanese attack, and Admiral Kimmel had it two hours later. They appeared not to want to warn the Hawaiian Command before the attack because with all chance of surprise gone, the spies in Hawaii would have notified the oncoming Japanese ships and Tokyo.

General Marshall stayed out of touch that vital Sunday morning by going horseback riding where he could not be contacted, and Stark spent the evening of the 6th at a theater where he also could not be reached.

The night of December 6th, and the morning of the 7th, was the most important in the lives of the President and the men who were charged with the defense of the United States. It is most unbelievable that they could have forgotten what happened, but General Marshall and Admiral Stark later repeatedly testified under oath they could not remember.

Dec. 7, 1941   0740 – Japanese Air Group Commander, Commander Nitsud Fuchida, radioed To-To-To (attack-attack-attack), and before 0800 he radioed again the signal of triumph Tora-Tora-Tora (Tiger-Tiger-Tiger). Their six attacking carriers carried 360 aircraft of all types in the two-wave attacks. Twenty-nine of these planes were shot down. There were also 75 submarines involved in the attack, but they proved to be a complete failure.

Dec. 7, 1941   0840 – The second wave of Japanese planes attack, and by 1000 it was all over.

Dec. 7, 1941   Six B17's get a surprise.   Scheduled to go to the Philippines, they arrived over the Oahu area from stateside about 0900 on December 7th. Carrying no ammunition to lighten the load for the long flight, they landed as soon as possible. On aircraft was shot at and burned while landing at Hickam Field, one crew member died of wounds. Another B17 crashed while landing at Bellows Field, several members of the crew were wounded.   The remainder of the flight landed safely at Hickam Field and sustained only slight damage.

Dec. 8, 1941   United States declares war on Japan!

Dec. 11, 1941 Roosevelt had requested that the United States declare war on Germany and Italy, but they did not until on December 11th. Germany and Italy declared war on the United States, so in the resolutions of Congress, on December 11, 1941, it was said that a state-of-war had been thrust upon the United States by Germany and Italy, and that this state-of-war is hereby formally declared.

Upon Secretary of Navy Frank Knox' arrival at Pearl Harbor shortly after the attack, when he was sent to insepct the damage, one of his first questions to Admiral Kimmel was "Didn't you receive the war warning I had sent Saturday night, December 6th?" Kimmel replied he received no such message. One can only speculate that it must have been stopped by someone higher up than Secretary Frank Knox.

On April 5, 1945, the Democratic controlled Senate passed a bill introduced by Senator E. Thomas of Utah to prevent the disclosure of any coded matter on Pearl Harbor except by permission of the head of Government. This would have closed the door forever to any further investigation of Pearl Harbor. Admiral Kimmel had not known of this bill

252

until he read it in a newspaper. He immediately went to work making events public to the press and to Congressmen so when it did come up before the House of Representatives it was not passed. This was due largely to Admiral Kimmel's efforts.

In 1989 a documentary titled, "Sacrifice at Pearl Harbor" which was made by a British firm was aired on TV Arts and Entertainment network December 7, 1989. This documentary gave in detail information that indicts President Franklin Delano Roosevelt in a no surprise attack on Pearl Harbor. The British documentary relying on recollections of participants, re-examined documents to piece together how American, British and Dutch intelligence seemed to know what was happening in late 1941, even if military commanders in the Pacific did not. Coded Naval broadcasts and communications between Japanese government leaders in Tokyo and Washington were monitored relentlessly, but not reported publicly. This documentary states that they believed FDR did have known knowledge of events leading to the Japanese Government attack on Pearl Harbor.

Captain Oliver Lyttalton, a British Minister who was in Churchill's cabinet stated before the American Chamber of Commerce in London, that "America provoked Japan to such an extent that Japanese were forced to attack Pearl Harbor, and it is a travesty on history even to say that America was forced into war." They were receiving 80% of their oil from US sources before Roosevelt turned off the tap.

Brits knew of Jap Attack Plans! So stated a 90-year old former British code-breaker. He said Britain knew of Japanese plans to attack Pearl Harbor in 1941, because they routinely broke Japanese codes. In an unpublished book, Eric Nave says he was stunned by the attack. He believed Winston Churchill had told President Roosevelt. If Britain had shared the wealth of intelligence from the decoded messages, Nave says, "The attack on Pearl Harbor would never have occurred....and Yamamoto's task force would have been decimated in a well-laid trap." A British newspaper obtained portions of the book, written jointly with a former British Intelligence Officer and Nave, a wartime code-breaker who

253

later headed Australia counter-intelligence. The book remains unpublished because of Britain's Official Secrets Act. UPI quoted the newspaper article March 9, 1989 (From Vol. 11-4 Edition May 1989, Chapters 25 & 28.)

George Bender, a Congressman from Ohio said FBI Director Hoover had said they had warnings before Pearl Harbor of a possible attack. Hoover told Roosevelt of these warnings and was told not to mention it, that he (Roosevelt) would take care of it. Washington didn't wish to warn Pearl Harbor because they were breaking Japan's code and did not want Japan to find out. From John Toland's book "The Rising Sun Secrets and Mysteries" questions about Japan's attack on Pearl Harbor.

The Japanese returned to Pearl Harbor six times after the Pearl Harbor raid. Five of these visits were by small seaplanes launched by Japanese submarines in the area and they took photographs of Pearl Harbor and the airfields. The sixth visit was in March 1942, when two giant six engine seaplanes flew over Honolulu and Pearl Harbor at a height of 32,000 feet and took photos and dropped several bombs. One bomb landed in an open area near Punahou Valley and the others fell into the sea. Because of a communications mixup, the Navy and Air Force failed to send up fighters and no anti-aircraft guns were used. The giant flying boats came from Truk Island and refueled from a Japanese submarine at French Frigate Shoals (600 miles from Midway) on both directions. None of this was publicized at the time because of embarrassment by the military authorities.

Clara Boothe Luce a Congresswoman at that time and later an Ambassador to Italy, stated that Roosevelt tricked and lied us into war with Germany through the back door. Hamilton Fish, a Congressman at the time spoke of Roosevelt's lust for power.

Who in Washington let the gallant men at Pearl Harbor and our Nation down? It wasn't Kimmel and Short, but they were blamed for it. It is unbelievable that with the many known facts at their finger tips, information that could have been passed on to the Hawaiian Command in time and would have saved many lives that President Roosevelt, General Marshall, Admiral Stark and other high ranking officials, both civilian and military who had this information before Pearl Harbor was attacked, yet they went on to be re-elected, promoted, some even to receive five-stars with their Pearl Harbor secrets kept until recently. One exception being Admiral Stark who was later cashiered by Secretary Forrestal and publicly discredited by the official declaration that henceforward he should hold no office calling for "superior judgement."

Never in all known recorded history that I am aware of has a President, Premier, King, Czar, Dictator, or any other world leader who had vital information that there was a strong possibility of a coming attack on his troops, yet did nothing to inform his Field Commanders about it ahead of time.

Had the dawn of government deceit and cover-up arrived and were those at Pearl Harbor December 7, 1941 "Sacrificial Lambs?"

A Pearl Harbor Survivor,

LAWRENCE LESTER McNABB

APPENDIX D

BACK TO ETERNITY
BY REX GUNN

Appendix D–Back to Eternity
By Rex Gunn

Two buddies … ragamuffin kings of the street in the capitol city of a land-locked state, where both might have spent their lives if it had not been for war. War was the matrix. War changed everything. It placed us in exotic machines with exotic weapons and scattered us like leaves in a cosmic wind. Ed Herron was the cleverest. His grandfather Banks was a skilled carpenter, neat and organized. Before he was 17, Ed could take the family's 1936 Ford or a camera apart, repair it, and put it back together again; and triple-tongue the trumpet; but he was killed in the air above Europe, shot from the sky at the controls of his B-17, dead before his 24th birthday. He was among the doomed.

I went to the other side of the world. I was transported to an ocean paradise, from there to Micronesian Islands, wracked by explosive battles which subsided into eternal quiet broken only by the sounds of surf and the cries of seabirds. I was lucky … so lucky that only a prisoner of war or a disabled war veteran could tell you how lucky. Although I was a mechanical idiot, the engines of the B-24s in which I flew over Truk and Iwo Jima on bombing missions never missed a beat. Flak hit one of the planes but it didn't hit a vital spot.

War changed my thinking about death. I count anyone lucky now if he or she dies of natural causes among friends. Grief among relatives and friends is balm for the dying. Oh sure, men act tough, but it is comforting to think that somebody cares. In prisoner of war camps and in combat, killers either exult or become calloused. Sometimes, the killing becomes grotesque, i.e.: the cannibalistic commanders of Japanese troops on Chi Chi Jima in the Bonin Islands, who ate the bodies of downed airmen at banquets. President George Bush was shot down in his Navy plane off of Chi Chi Jima. He was thrown a life raft by his airborne squadron mates and (after floating around for 12 hours) was rescued by a U.S. submarine.

Some of the war horrors have come to light only as recently as 1994. Marshall Islands Senator Kejjo Bien gave an eye-witness account of mass executions of Marshallese Islanders on Mili (we used to spell it "Mille" in our magazine, Brief—it was one of our by-passed targets which bomber crews called a "milk run" until Brief correspondent Lt. Frank A. Tinker was lost on one of those "milk runs" over Mille).

There were 17,000 Japanese soldiers on Mili in 1944 as food became scarce. American victories at Kwajalein and Entiwetok had enabled our ships and planes to block transport of any food into by-passed Marshallese islands such as Mili.

As starvation loomed on Mili in 1944, Bien said, people were ordered by Japanese soldiers "to stand in a ditch to wait for their New Year's eve surprise ..." Japanese soldiers then jumped down on the unsuspecting Marshallese, stabbing and beheading men, women and children with their bayonets. More than 70 were killed."

Bien told of the 1944 incident at an international symposium on war atrocities held in Tokyo in 1994. At the same symposium, Korean "comfort women" who were forced into sexual servitude by the Japanese military also spoke. The Japanese government has announced it is going to spend $1-billion on direct compensation over the next decade, with plans to appropriate the first funds in fiscal 1995.

Such horrors in the Pacific were different than the ones in Europe, where mass killing became institutionalized as state policy. The Nazis were bent on wiping out whole ethnic strains. Under that policy, the Nazi government destroyed millions of people.

In the Pacific, the killings seemed to happen almost at random— sometimes to individuals (the public beheading of five pilots downed in the Doolittle raid); to prisoners in unaccountable groups because of some random characteristic (Caucasian men with red hair captured on Wake Island); and to prisoners in the thousands (the Filipinos and Americans in the Bataan Death March). The Australians and the Americans, once they had experienced combat with Japanese soldiers who had rather die than be captured, often initiated their own policy, unit by unit but never en masse, of "take no prisoners." Psychologically, for us, the imminent beheading of one American with head bowed, hands bound behind him, forced to his knees, under the upraised sword of a Japanese executioner, may prove more graphic and traumatic than the deaths of untold millions in gas ovens in Europe. We can see the horror of the beheading. The muted disappearance of hordes of people into gas ovens boggles the mind, but presents no clear picture.

In Korea and Viet Nam, whole villages were wiped out because the combatants couldn't distinguish friends or innocents from enemies. If one waited to make sure that the villagers were unarmed, he might find out the hard way. Was it changes brought on by those Asian wars which have reduced our global village to a violent place where kids who used to shoot beebee guns at each other now turn assault rifles on homes, offices, classrooms and subways filled with relatives or strangers? Life seems cheaper and we wonder how succeeding generations will deal with it.

The youngest of the survivors of Pearl Harbor, both Japanese and American, are in their seventies. A universal sense of wonder binds us together now. Many of us want to see the Arizona Memorial and the places where we were stationed on that Sunday so long ago, and perhaps the old battlegrounds where we went afterward. Here is a typical tour, announced by the Sunsetter's Gazette, newsletter of the 7th Fighter Command Association:

A RETURN TO IWO JIMA

"Should anyone have a desire to return to Iwo Jima, such a tour is being planned for March 10-16, 1995, by Military Historical Tours, 1500 King St., Suite 200, Alexandria, VA 22314. Phone: 703-739-8900."

On March 14, 1995, 800 American veterans and their families went to Iwo Jima for a 50th anniversary memorial. A handful of Japanese survivors, along with 100 or so relatives of soldiers who fought on Iwo Jima (Including the widow of the island's Japanese Commander, Tadamichi Kuribayashi) also attended the ceremony.

Today, the island's only full-time inhabitants are a few hundred Japanese soldiers who operate an airfield.

The fighting raged from Feb. 19 to March 16, 1945, and took the lives of 6,821 Americans and 95% of the 21,000 Japanese defenders.

Why do the survivors, Japanese and American, go back to the old battlegrounds: Guadalcanal, Tarawa, Saipan, Kwajalein, Iwo Jima? They go because the people aside from one's own comrades who know most about the battle and the ground that it was fought on are the enemy

260

survivors. They have common ties which no one else can share. I recently made by own pilgrimage back to the Central Pacific Islands.

Some remarkable changes have taken place.

The equator and the international dateline meet very close to Tarawa, but you won't find Tarawa located in the Gilbert Islands in the last three decades. Tarawa is the capitol of Kiribati now. And what is Kiribati? That's the preferred transliteration for the Gilberts. Tarawa is the largest of the 33 low-lying coral islands spread across nearly 1,500 miles of water. The whole country totals only 313 square miles of land, spread like tiny stepping stones across that 1,500 miles of water.

Robert Louis Stevenson wrote that the Gilberts "enjoy a superb ocean climate, days of blinding sun and bracing wind, nights of heavenly brightness."

Sir Arthur Gamble more recently wrote in his book, A Pattern of Islands:

"The tropic stars did flame for us, just as the travel books had promised. The nights were amethyst clear and cool. Eddies of war air, loaded with earth scents and jungle dreams from islands beyond sight enmeshed us and were gone again."

When I was first there in 1944, I got carried away myself by another of the Gilbert or Kiribati Islands, Apemama, and waxed rhapsodic about Stevenson's associations with the legendary Tembinok, the King of Apemama. The same magic still pervades that island for me.

Kiribati claims an "Exclusive Economic Zone" of 1.4 million square miles, giving it the largest sea-to-land ratio of any nation in the world: 1.4 million miles of sea to 313 square miles of land. It wasn't until my most recent trip to the Pacific, 1994, that I realized those 313 miles of Kiribati are divided between 33 islands. I had been on only three of them in 1944: Tarawa, Apemama and Makin.

I took with me, in addition to current maps, Stevenson's book, In the South Seas, first copyrighted in 1891. It contained a three-fold map, done in red for the islands and light green for the ocean. That map lists 17 groups of islands and the nationality to which each group belongs; and not once is there any mention of the United States or Japan. All are under British, French or German rule except the "Sandwich Islands," Samoa and Tonga (the Friendly Islands)—all three listed as independent.

Since 1944, things have changed.

The Federated States of Micronesia and the Republic of the Marshall Islands now sit as members of the United Nations.

American Samoa is represented in the U.S. House of Representatives by a delegate who may vote in committee and party caucuses but not on the House floor. In the post-war period till 1951, the U.S. Navy governed American Samoa, but President Harry Truman transferred administration of American Samoa from the secretary of the Navy to the Secretary of Interior.

Now Samoa is ruled by a popularly elected governor, has a bicameral legislature and a constitution. Samoans now are U.S. Nationals, with most of the rights and responsibilities of U.S. citizens.

Guam does not have constitution, but residents of Guam are U.S. citizens; and like American Samoa, are represented in the U.S. House of Representatives by a delegate who may vote in committee and party caucuses but not on the House floor

Closest to Japan is the Northern Mariana Islands, a Commonwealth now. Until 1990, it was one of the districts of the Trust Territory of the

262

Pacific Islands under the administrative authority of the U.S., so appointed by the Security Council of the United Nations.

The Northern Marianas include the old WWII battlegrounds of Saipan, Tinian, and Rota along with ten other islands.

But possibly the most changed of all the Pacific Island nations is the Republic of the Marshall Islands. It includes 29 atolls and 1,225 islands— 70 square miles of land in 750,000 square miles of ocean. The population in 1990 was approximately 45,000. A sovereign government made it a Republic in 1979, and in 1986, the Compact of Free Association was formed, giving independent national status to the Republic.

Where the fiercest fighting in the Marshalls took place in 1944 at Kwajalein, the U.S. maintains a missile testing base. American nuclear testing on Bikini and on the old B-24 staging base for missions over Truk, Eniwetok (now spelled on the maps Enewetok) is regarded by the Republic as a history lesson which they do not intend to repeat.

The capitol island is Majuro, where the Air Marshall Islands jet service to Honolulu bases its lone DC-8. The AMI ended four and a half years of red ink and earned a profit in October, 1994.

"This is the first time for us to have a winning month for the DC-8," said David Tejada, Air Marshall Island's commercial manager. "It's very promising."

But if you are planning a trip to the Marshalls on the DC-8, make room for the tuna. The major factor in the turnaround was the heavy loads of sashimi-grade tuna being exported from Majuro to Honolulu. Tejada said cargo, primarily tuna, is accounting for 54 per cent of AMI's total revenue.

The airline has three regularly scheduled flights per week to Honolulu and back; and has replaced the canceled Air Nauru service by operating weekend charters between Honolulu and Christmas Island in Kiribati (the Gilbert Islands).

Majuro has modern accommodations: small and large hotels, guest cottages, rental cars, taxis and buses, restaurants, pubs, discos, and of course, diving and fishing charter boats. It also has the longest paved road in Micronesia—30 miles from Rita at one end of Majuro to Laura at the other end. Rita and Laura were named by J.S. Gis during WWII.

Tourism is burgeoning at Truk (called Chuuk now) because of the Ghost Fleet, which can be safely explored by scuba divers. The crystal clear waters of Truk Lagoon contain the world's greatest concentration of underwater wrecks, relieved by brilliant tropical fish and coral growth. Officially, it's called the "Truk Lagoon State Monument."

The state of Truk is one of the Federated States of Micronesia. On Aug. 14, 1971, the Truk Legislature enacted a law, which reads in part:

> "All ships, other vessels and aircraft, any and all parts thereof, which formerly belonged to or were part of the armed forces of Japan and were sunk or otherwise deposited on the bottom of Truk Lagoon prior to Dec. 31, 1945, shall be and hereby are set apart as state monuments, which shall be collectively called 'Truk Lagoon State Monument.'"

The old wrecks are undergoing Shakespeare's "Sea Change" into fantastic and sometimes beautiful coral forms.

Getting back to the Marshall Islands, not all is harmony between the U.S. and the new Republic. The Marshall Islands government is dickering with three Asian countries for disposal of those countries nuclear wastes on an uninhabited island in the Marshalls. The three Asian countries are Japan, South Korea and Taiwan. The U.S. has refused to participate in the study, but says the Marshall's ambassador to the U.S., Wilfred Kendall, the refusal by the U.S. is "no problem to us." Kendall sees to conflict between the pursuance of nuclear waste with the Asian nations on the one hand and the search for additional funds from the U.S. for a cleanup of islands which have been contested on another.

Kendall didn't specify which islands were being considered for waste sites, but he said it would not necessarily be Bikini.

> "A project of this magnitude will involve 3,000 to 4,000 workers on site," he said. "We may have to use a (different) uninhabited island."

Meanwhile, a new cellular phone system has arrived in Majuro. A pair of 200-foot towers at opposite ends of Majuro allow for the use of cellular phones within a 30-mile radius. The cost is $50.00 per month and 15 cents per minute for "air time" in addition to long distance charges.

Rabaul, which survived severe bombing in WWII was virtually buried by two volcanic eruptions, which put the port city under 30-inch-deep blankets of ash in Sept., 1994. The whole city of 51,000 people was displaced. Papua New Guinea Prime Minister Julius Chan flew over the area and reported,

"You cannot see Rabaul. You cannot see the landscape. You can only see smoke and ash."

U.S. Air Force planes flew in supplies from Okinawa. They had to land at Tokua because the Rabaul airstrip was not even visible.

Rabaul lies ringed in by six volcanoes, three of which have erupted in this century. Eruptions from Vulcan and Matupit killed 507 people in Rabaul and closed the town in 1937. They rebuilt it. Then, came the bombing raids in WWII. They rebuilt. Then, came an earthquake and a tidal wave in 1971. Once again, Rabaul was rebuilt. Now, the future of Rabaul (they call it the "garden city of the Pacific") is uncertain. There's talk of moving it 31 miles away to Kokopu.

Saipan once again has become a rest and recreation center for Japan— not officially of course, but the 11-month total of visitors through August, 1994, was 533,009; most of them from Japan and South Korea. In August alone, reported the Marianas Visitors Bureau, 59,124 visitors came to the Northern Marianas (Guam not included—Guam is the southernmost of the Marianas Islands).

In Western Samoa near Apia, residents marked the 100th anniversary of Robert Louis Stevenson's death on Dec. 3, 1994, by restoring the author's home to a splendor it never had during his lifetime. It was the only real estate RLS ever owned. He named it Vallma. It included one well-preserved wall in his favorite color: bright peacock blue.

Some things remain the same or, at least, recognizable.

The U.S.S. Arizona lies where she settled in Pearl Harbor with her steel decks removed and a forward gun turret still receiving the ashes of

265

survivors who want to be cremated and buried with their shipmates. As of the new year, 1995, nine men who were aboard the Arizona on Pearl Harbor day have willed their ashes back to the Arizona.

Of the 1,777 men who died aboard the Arizona or in the waters immediately adjacent, most are entombed in the ship—officially buried at sea. Others, blown into the water, are in Punchbowl National Cemetery;, where 26,000 other veterans have been buried since 1949. Only two civilians are buried there: World War II correspondent Ernie Pyle who was killed on Okinawa by a sniper's bullet after becoming famous for his reporting on GIs in European campaigns; and astronaut Ellison Onizuka, a civilian of Japanese descent, born in Hawaii, killed in the explosion of the space craft, <u>Challenger</u>.

The bullet holes fired into the barracks and into the mess hall at Hickam Field on that morning of Dec. 7, 1941, have been left intact, eroded only by time. Sixty men died in the mess hall. The old runway being used at the time of the attack is shaggy with plant growth, showing through the cracked pavement, but the runway is still intact, and is renowned as "Freedom Road." The first American troops on the way home from Viet Nam landed there.

At Fort Shafter where Lt. Gen. Walter C. Short, commanding the Army's Hawaiian Department was having a peaceful breakfast when the attack started, the two-story house in which he was living on Royal Palm Drive is virtually unchanged except for additional coats of paint. The stairway is flanked by command flags just as it was on that morning in 1941.

The first Radar Information Center at Fort Shafter, "Little Robert," is long gone, but the old Lizard Tunnel still stands. It has been converted into offices, but I was surprised to find that the old snack bar which I had supervised in 1942, close to the tunnel entrance, is still there it was and is still in use as a snack bar.

At Schofield Barracks, the six infantry quadrangles known as Quads A through F are still in use, looking much like they did when I pulled boot camp with the Signal Corps, Aircraft Warning Company, Special, at the foot of Kole Kole Pass. My boot camp lasted from mid-December, 1940, to the end of January, 1941.

For the next six months in 1941, I was a track man with the Staff Regiment, a jock (short of jock strap) who was except from KP because of his athletic activities. The non-commissioned officers who hazed Robert E. Lee Prewitt (Montgomery Clift) in the movie, "From Here to Eternity" were also jocks-members of an Infantry Regimental Boxing Team.

The movie won the oscar for the best picture of 1953. It was shot on location at Quad C, Schofield Barracks, and the parade grounds, ringed by the company structures, look so much the same as they did in 1941 that you expect to see Frank Sinatra as Maggio or Montgomery Clift as Prewitt or Burt Lancaster as First Sgt. Neil Warden stepping out of the Barracks along with the men who really were stationed there.

The author of the book, James Jones, did his soldiering in Quad D for the 27th Infantry Division, the "Wolfhounds." Present occupants (1995) are the 25th Infantry Division, "Tropic Lightning." Jones died in 1977, but a group of his fans dedicated a plaque to him on March 16, 1995, near Makapuu Point. That's close to the Blowhole in Halona and a secluded beach where Burt Lancaster and Deborah Kerr did their famous love scene for the movie in the surf. Kaylie Jones (the author's daughter, also an author) was one of 18 people who attended the dedication ceremony at Makapuu Point.

Where the old 7th Army Air Corps Fighter Base was at Wheeler Field, a Rapid Deployment force of helicopters is based now. One of the two fighter aces of Dec. 7, 1941, remained a test pilot and was killed in a crash in 1957. That was George Welch. Ken Taylor, the other first-day-of-the-war ace, still survived (April, 1995) and lives in Alaska.

The radar site where Joe Lockard and George Elliot caught the attacking Japanese planes approaching Oahu is marked by a memorial plaque at Opana, Kahuku Point.

Elsewhere around Oahu, Barber's Point is closed and the Marine Corps base at Ewa will close in 1996.

Former Marine Master Sgt. Don Jones, who was almost crushed by the first Japanese plane downed at Pearl Harbor, gave me a 1941 menu from the Black Cat Café in downtown Honolulu. Due to gas rationing, the Black Cat was a favorite meeting place, located next to the Pearl Harbor bus stop.

Nostalgic tape recordings often played by tour guides as they journey to and from Pearl Harbor feature Dinah Shore singing "Sentimental Journey," Kate Smith singing "God Bless America," Artie Shaw playing "Sunrise Serenade" and "Begin the Beguine;" Spike Jones "Cocktails for Two," and various artists playing the popular adaptation of Tchaikowsky's Piano Concerto Number One in B-Flat Minor, "Tonight We Love."

Here are the top ten on the Lucky Strike Hit Parade on Saturday night, Dec. 6, 1941:

1.   Tonight We Love.

2.   Elmer's Tune.

3.   Chattanooga Choo-Choo

4.   A Shepherd's Serenade.

5.   I don't Want to Set the World on Fire.

6.   This Love of Mine.

7.   You and I.

8.   Jim.

9.   A Sinner Kissed an Angel.

10.   Everything I Love.

One of the most popular restaurants in Honolulu was Wo Fat on Hotel Street, dating clear back to 1882. It lasted up until the end of 1994, and I tasted the beef tomato at Wo Fat before it was taken over in its last year by a Thai Restaurant Chain. Of course, I had to write a poem for the old restaurant, which completed 112 years under the same management (different generations of the family, of course).

BACK TO ETERNITY

By REX GUNN

Back to Eternity
By Rex Gunn

For me and Mary, from here to eternity is a short trip
Just down Hotel Street past the lost world of Mamie Stover
Where the drab hotels have new names (i.e., Top Gun)
But not new faces;
Then, on to the good beef tomato of Wo Fat.
Was it yesterday or 20,000 nights ago when first we tasted
The good beef tomato of Wo Fat (Wo Fat goes back to '82—
That's eighteen eighty two),
And saw the shuttered doors of the dingy hotels
With the young/old faces peering out of the unwashed doors?
Was it yesterday or 20,000 nights ago when down the street,
'Round the corner,
We finished the meal with a walk to Blaisdell's—
In the lotus blossom, garden room of Blaisdell's Bar and Grill,
Where one could lie back and drink the drink
And float effortlessly on wings of song back to the days
Of Forty-One,
Back to the days before we thought about eternity;
Back to the days before soldiers wrote about eternity?
Back to the good beef tomato of Wo Fat,
Back to the days of Forty-One.

Selected Bibliography

COHEN, STAN. EAST WIND RAIN. 1941

COSTELLO, JOHN. THE PACIFIC WAR. 1981

CLARKE, THURSTON. PEARL HARBOR GHOSTS. 1991

FLYNN, JOHN T. THE ROOSEVELT MYTH. 1948

GUNN, REX. SIX MONTHS AND FOREVER. 1999

GUNN, REX. SUDDENLY ON TA SUNDAY MORNING. 1996

KIMMEL, HUSBAND E. ADMIRAL KIMMEL'S STORY. 1955

LAYTON, EDWIN. AND I WAS THERE. 1985

PRANGE, GORDON. AT DAWN WE SLEPT. 1981.

SHEEHAN, ED. DAYS OF '41. 1976

SMITH, S.E. THE U.S. NAVY IN WORLD WAR II. 1966

TOLAND, JOHN. INFAMY. 1982

TOLLEY, KEMP. CRUISE OF THE LANIKAI. 1994

WINSLOW, W. G. THE FLEET THE GODS FORGOT. 1982

ZACHARIAS, ELLIS. SECRET MISSIONS. 1942